SIGNS

Complete Poetry and Language Skills
for Leaving Certificate Ordinary Level

GILL & MACMILLAN

and onwards   For Examination in 2007 and onwards   For Examinatic

KEEP
THIS
COUPON

JOHN McCARTHY and ANNE CLANCY

988049

Gill & Macmillan Ltd
Hume Avenue
Park West
Dublin 12
with associated companies throughout the world
www.gillmacmillan.ie

© John McCarthy and Anne Clancy 2005
0 7171 3900 X
Design and print origination in Ireland by Graham Thew Design

The paper used in this book is made from the wood pulp of managed forests. For every tree felled, at least one tree is planted, thereby renewing natural resources.

Photo Credits

For permission to reproduce photographs and other material, the author and publisher gratefully acknowledge the following:

pp.3, 9, 49, 93, 119, 127 Camera Press Ireland; **pp.5, 109** Associated Press; **pp.7, 79T, 123, 253B, 254B** Rex Features; **p.11T** Mark Gerson; **pp.11B, 21, 52, 67, 71B, 107B, 122** Alamy Images; **p.14** Elizabeth Bishop – Special Collections, Vassar College Libraries, Ploughkeepsie, New York; **p.16** © 2004, Digital Image, The Museum of Modern Art, New York/SCALA Florence; **pp.19, 23, 35, 95, 101, 111** The Irish Times; **p.25** Paddy Bushe; **pp.29, 38, 61, 99, 139** National Portrait Gallery, London; **pp.33, 71T** Topfoto/UPPA; **p.141** Topfoto; **p.157** Topfoto/WDS; **p.41** Corbis; **p.45** Kenny's Galway; **p.47** Kate Newmann & The Gallery Press; **p.51** Carcanet Press; **p.55** John Skelton/Patrick Kavanagh Rural and Literary Resource Centre, Inniskeen; **p.65** Corbis/Freelance Consulting Services Pty Ltd; **p.68** Photocall Ireland; **pp.69, 249R, 249TL, 250T, 250C, 254T** Irish Image Collection; **p.77** Corbis/Christopher Felver; **p.79B** educationphotos.co.uk; **p.81** Pacemaker Press International; **p.87** Derek Mahon; **p.107T** Edwin Morgan; **pp.113, 153, 161** Corbis/Bettmann; **p.114** Lonely Planet Images/Gareth McCormack; **p.117** Random House (Chatto & Windus); **p.133** Lebrecht Music and Arts; **pp.135, 245TL** Hulton/Getty Images; **pp.137, 143** Mary Evans Picture Library; **p.138** Corbis/Reza; Webistan; **p.142** Lonely Planet Images/David Else; **p.147** Getty Images; **p.155** Time Life Pictures/Getty Images; **p.156** Corbis/Christie's Images; **p.159** Coward of Canberra/Carcanet Press; **p.163** Corbis/Keren Su; **p.244** Regimental Museum of the Border Regiment and the King's own Border Regiment; photo David Orr; **p.245TR** Public Relations Section, Defence Forces, Ireland; **p.245B** National Library of Ireland; **p.249BL** Irish Picture Library; **p.250B** courtesy of the Head of the Department of Irish Folklore, University College, Dublin; **p.253T** Opera Theatre Company; Photo Tom Lawlor; **p.254C** RTÉ Music; **pp.258TL, 258BR** Inpho; **pp.258TR, 258CR, 258BL** Sportsfile.

COURSE OVERVIEW

Poems Prescribed for Ordinary Level
June 2007 Examination

Note: Ordinary level candidates sitting the exam in June 2007 may choose *either* the poems in the left-hand column or the poems in the right-hand column

Poems Prescribed for Ordinary Level
June 2008 Examination

Note: Ordinary level candidates sitting the exam in June 2008 may choose *either* the poems in the left-hand column or the poems in the right-hand column

Poems Prescribed for Ordinary Level
June 2009 Examination

Bishop	The Fish (p.12) The Filling Station (p.15)
Keats	On First Looking into Chapman's Homer (p.60) La Belle Dame Sans Merci (p.62)
Larkin	At Grass (p.70) An Arundel Tomb (p.72) The Explosion (p.74)
Longley	Last Requests (p.82) An Amish Rug (p.84)
Mahon	Grandfather (p. 86) After the *Titanic* (p.88) Antarctica (p.90)
Montague	The Locket (p.100) Like dolmens round my childhood... (p. 102) The Cage (p.104)
Rich	Aunt Jennifer's Tigers (p.126) Power (p.128) Storm Warnings (p.130)
Walcott	To Norline (p.146) Summer Elegies (p.148)

Angelou	Phenomenal Woman (p.4)
Boland	Naming My Daughter (p.22)
Bushe	Midwife (p.24)
Grennan	Taking My Son to School (p.44)
Hardie	May (p.46)
Heaney	Postscript (p.48)
Lochhead	Kidspoem/Bairnsang (p.78)
Meehan	Buying Winkles (p.94)
O'Callaghan	The Great Blasket Island (p.114)
O'Donoghue	Gunpowder (p.116)
Olds	Looking at Them Asleep (p.118)
Sassoon	On Passing the New Menin Gate (p.134)
Shakespeare	Fear No More the Heat O' the Sun (p.136)
Thomas	The Hunchback in the Park (p.140)
Wright	Request to a Year (p.158)
Wordsworth	Composed upon Westminster Bridge (p.156)

Note: Ordinary level candidates sitting the exam in June 2009 may choose *either* the poems in the left-hand column or the poems in the right-hand column

Poems Prescribed for Ordinary Level
June 2010 Examination

Boland	Child of Our Time (p.18) This Moment (p.20)	**Adcock**	For Heidi with Blue Hair (p.2)
Eliot	Preludes (p.36) Aunt Helen (p.39)	**Boland**	Naming My Daughter (p.22)
Kavanagh	Shancoduff (p.54) A Christmas Childhood (p.56) On Raglan Road (p.58)	**Grennan**	Taking My Son to School (p.44)
		Jennings	One Flesh (p.50)
Keats	On First Looking into Chapman's Homer (p.60) La Belle Dame Sans Merci (p.62)	**Kennelly**	Night Drive (p.66)
		Lochhead	Kidspoem/Bairnsang (p.78)
Longley	Wounds (p.80) Last Requests (p.82) An Amish Rug (p.84)	**McGough**	Bearhugs (p.92)
		Meehan	My Father Perceived as a Vision of St Francis (p.96)
Rich	Aunt Jennifer's Tigers (p.126) Storm Warnings (p.130)	**Milton**	When I Consider (p.98)
Walcott	To Norline (p.146) Summer Elegies (p.148) The Young Wife (p.150)	**Nemerov**	Wolves in the Zoo (p.112)
		O'Callaghan	The Great Blasket Island (p.114)
		O'Donoghue	Gunpowder (p.116)
Yeats	The Lake Isle of Innisfree (p.160) The Wild Swans at Coole (p.162) An Irish Airman Foresees His Death (p.164)	**Thomas**	The Hunchback in the Park (p.140)
		Vaughan	Peace (p.144)
		Williams	The Red Wheelbarrow (p.154)
		Wright	Request to a Year (p.158)

Note: Ordinary level candidates sitting the exam in June 2010 may choose *either* the poems in the left-hand column or the poems in the right-hand column

CONTENTS

POETRY
Poems, Biographies, Explorations

LANGUAGE SKILLS

Acknowledgments

We would like to thank the following for their support to the authors in this project:
Fiona and Tadhg, Mark and Kate, Jack and Rose, Mike and Maureen, Eric, Donal, Toni, Rose and Sheila, Mary, Niall and Molly, Michael and Siobhan, Mick, Paul, Julieanne, Aoife, Brian, Danny, Adam and David, Mark, Peggy, Shane, Mary and Elaine, Martin Collins, Sean Scully, Peter Tumelty, Kevin Morrison, Coleman and Nanette, the staff of Coláiste Dún Iascaigh, Cahir and finally the supportive staff of St Oliver's Community College, Drogheda.

POETRY

KEEP
THIS
COUPON

988046

988046

For Heidi with Blue Hair

FLEUR ADCOCK

Prescribed for the Ordinary Level exams in 2007 and 2010

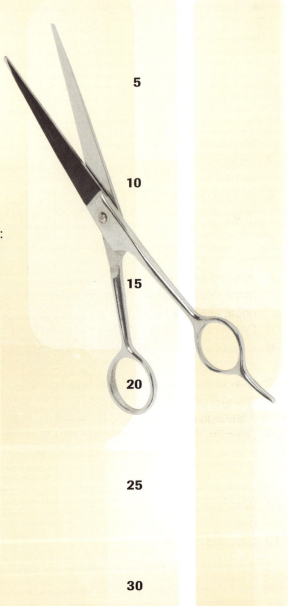

When you dyed your hair blue
(or, at least, ultramarine
for the clipped sides, with a crest
of jet-black spikes on top)
you were sent home from school   5

because, as the headmistress put it,
although dyed hair was not
specifically forbidden, yours
was, apart from anything else,
not done in the school colours.   10

Tears in the kitchen, telephone-calls
to school from your freedom-loving father:
'She's not a punk in her behaviour;
it's just a style.' (You wiped your eyes,
also not in a school colour.)   15

'She discussed it with me first –
we checked the rules.' 'And anyway, Dad,
it cost twenty-five dollars.
Tell them it won't wash out –
not even if I wanted to try.'   20

It would have been unfair to mention
your mother's death, but that
shimmered behind the arguments.
The school had nothing else against you;
the teachers twittered and gave in.   25

Next day your black friend had hers done
in grey, white and flaxen yellow –
the school colours precisely:
an act of solidarity, a witty
tease. The battle was already won.   30

GLOSSARY

Ultramarine: Deep bright blue
Clipped: Cut short
Punk: Follower of rebellious, outrageous rock music
(sometimes violent and aggressive)

Shimmered: Shone in a soft quivering light
Twittered: Made silly bird-like sounds of laughter
Flaxen: Pale yellow
Solidarity: Act of unity

FLEUR **ADCOCK**

• Born 1934 in New Zealand   • Left New Zealand. Spent much of her life in England   • Feminist poet   • This poem is from *The Incident Room*, which is dedicated to her godchild, Heidi Jackson   • Collections: *The Eye of the Hurricane*, 1964; *Tigers*, 1967; *High Tide in the Garden*, 1971; *The Inner Harbour*, 1979; *The Incident Room*, 1986; *Time Zones*, 1991

Pre-reading

1 When you read the title what kind of person do you expect Heidi to be?
2 Describe what you think of when you hear someone has blue hair.
3 What do you think is the relationship between the poet and Heidi?

First reading

4 Why did the headmistress send Heidi home from school if having dyed hair was not against the rules?
5 Describe Heidi's hairstyle.
6 Describe the scene in Heidi's house when she arrives home.
7 How does Heidi react? Does her reaction change? Is it what you would expect from a teenage girl?
8 Describe the headmistress and the teachers. Write down every sentence in which they are mentioned and then describe the image that is portrayed.
9 Why does Heidi's friend get her hair dyed?
10 Describe her hairstyle.

Second reading

11 Describe Heidi's father. Is he strict, supportive, typical, modern, old-fashioned?
12 Describe the relationship between Heidi and her father. Where do you see this?

Third reading

13 Discuss the tone each character would use when speaking – headmistress, teachers, father, Heidi, Heidi's friend.
14 Explain why the poet uses the word 'shimmered' when discussing Heidi's mother's death.
15 Why is Heidi's mother's death even mentioned?
16 Why do you think Heidi dyed her hair in the first place? Is she a typical teenager? Describe a typical teenager. (Stereotyping is when you generalise or standardise a character or idea.)
17 What is the theme of this poem? Is there more than one?
18 What do you think the poet means in the last line when she says 'The battle was already won'?

Link to language

19 Write a letter to the headmistress from Heidi's father outlining what he sees as the main problem.
20 Imagine you are Heidi. Write a letter to your aunt, Fleur Adcock, telling her about your new hair colour and your suspension from school.

Phenomenal Woman

MAYA ANGELOU

Prescribed for the Ordinary Level exams in 2008 and 2009

Pretty women wonder where my secret
   lies.
I'm not cute or built to suit a fashion
   model's size
But when I start to tell them,
They think I'm telling lies.
I say,   **5**
It's in the reach of my arms
The span of my hips
The stride of my step,
The curl of my lips.
I'm a woman   **10**
Phenomenally.
Phenomenal woman,
That's me.

I walk into a room
Just as cool as you please,   **15**
And to a man,
The fellows stand or
Fall down on their knees.
Then they swarm around me,
A hive of honey bees.   **20**
I say,
It's the fire in my eyes,
And the flash of my teeth,
The swing in my waist,
And the joy in my feet.   **25**
I'm a woman
Phenomenally.
Phenomenal woman,
That's me.

Men themselves have wondered   **30**
What they see in me.
They try so much
But they can't touch
My inner mystery.
When I try to show them   **35**
They say they still can't see.
I say,
It's in the arch of my back,
The sun of my smile,
The ride of my breasts,   **40**
The grace of my style.
I'm a woman
Phenomenally.
Phenomenal woman,
That's me.   **45**

Now you understand
Just why my head's not bowed.
I don't shout or jump about
Or have to talk real loud.
When you see me passing   **50**
It ought to make you proud.
I say,
It's in the click of my heels,
The bend of my hair,
The palm of my hand,   **55**
The need of my care,
'Cause I'm a woman
Phenomenally.
Phenomenal woman,
That's me.   **60**

MAYA **ANGELOU**

- Born 1928 in St Louis, Missouri, USA • Reared in segregated rural Arkansas • Raped at the age of eight and became mute for a time • Worked as a poet, educator, historian, actress, dancer, playwright, civil rights activist, producer and director • Was also a political co-ordinator for Martin Luther King • Autobiography: *I Know Why the Caged Bird Sings*, 1969 • Wrote President Clinton's inauguration poem • Writes for 'the black voice and for any ear which can hear it'

Pre-reading

1 Use the dictionary or thesaurus to find out the meaning of the word 'phenomenal'.
2 Describe the image that the title 'Phenomenal Woman' suggests to you.

First reading

3 Having read the poem through, what is your impression of the speaker? Do you like her? Describe her in five or six words.
4 In the poem the speaker is constantly promoting herself and presenting herself in a positive light. What words or phrases stand out to support this statement?
5 What reaction does the speaker get from the 'pretty women'?
6 What reaction does the speaker get from the men?
7 How does the speaker behave around men and women she comes into contact with?

Second reading

8 Why do you think the poet repeats the lines 'I'm a woman / Phenomenally. / Phenomenal woman.'?
9 What, in the poet's view, does she possess to make her a 'phenomenal woman'?

10 It has been said that the poetry of Maya Angelou 'reminds us of where we are as women at the dawn of a new century'. Do you agree that this poem is a true representation of women in the twenty-first century?
11 Maya Angelou is celebrating her womanhood in this poem. Where in particular do we see this? Go through the poem verse by verse and pick out the words and phrases in which she delights in womanhood.
12 Are we seeing the real person or is this all an act or show of pride and courage? Is it realistic? Do you know anyone like this?

Link to language

13 Maya Angelou has appeared on many chat shows in America, most notably *The Oprah Winfrey Show*. Write out the answer you imagine she may give to the question 'What does being a woman mean to you?'.

It Ain't What You Do, It's What It Does to You

SIMON ARMITAGE

Prescribed for the Ordinary Level exams in 2007 and 2008

I have not bummed across America
with only a dollar to spare, one pair
of busted Levi's and a bowie knife.
I have lived with thieves in Manchester.

I have not padded through the Taj Mahal,   5
barefoot, listening to the space between
each footfall picking up and putting down
its print against the marble floor. But I

skimmed flat stones across Black Moss on a day
so still I could hear each set of ripples   10
as they crossed. I felt each stone's inertia
spend itself against the water; then sink.

I have not toyed with a parachute cord
while perched on the lip of a light-aircraft;
but I held the wobbly head of a boy   15
at the day centre, and stroked his fat hands.

And I guess that the tightness in the throat
and the tiny cascading sensation
somewhere inside us are both part of that
sense of something else. That feeling, I mean.   20

GLOSSARY
Bowie knife: Long hunting knife
Padded: Walked softly or steadily
Taj Mahal: Famous monument in India – symbol of love

Black Moss: Lake between Lancashire and Yorkshire
Inertia: Losing power, slowing down
Cascading: Falling like a waterfall, overflowing

SIMON **ARMITAGE**

- Born 1963 in Huddersfield, England
- Worked as a social worker
- Collections: *Kid*, 1992; *Zoom!*, 1989

▬ Pre-reading

1 What usually comes after the line 'It ain't what you do'? Would it have the same effect?

• First reading

2 There are three things that the poet has not done and three things that he has. Compare them. Which is the more attractive to you?
3 What emotion does he get from living with thieves? How would this compare with the feeling that he would get if he was hiking across America?
4 How does he justify comparing a lake in Manchester with one of the seven wonders of the world?
5 How does helping a boy at the day care centre make the poet feel?
6 Describe how the boy might feel.

•• Second reading

7 Have you ever experienced the sensation that the poet describes in the final verse? When? Describe it.

••• Third reading

8 How does the poet use repetition in the poem? Why does he use repetition?

⠿ Fourth reading

9 Is the last sentence in the poem completely necessary?
10 What type of guy do you think the poet is?

Ⓛ Link to language

11 Write an essay based on the theme 'Live life to its fullest'.

Funeral Blues

W. H. AUDEN

Prescribed for the Ordinary Level exam in 2007

Stop all the clocks, cut off the telephone,
Prevent the dog from barking with a juicy bone,
Silence the pianos and with muffled drum
Bring out the coffin, let the mourners come.

Let aeroplanes circle moaning overhead   **5**
Scribbling on the sky the message He Is Dead,
Put the crêpe bows round the white necks of the public doves,
Let the traffic policemen wear black cotton gloves.

He was my North, my South, my East and West,
My working week and my Sunday rest,   **10**
My noon, my midnight, my talk, my song;
I thought that love would last for ever: I was wrong.

The stars are not wanted now: put out every one;
Pack up the moon and dismantle the sun;
Pour away the ocean and sweep up the wood.   **15**
For nothing now can ever come to any good.

W. H. **AUDEN**

• Wystan Hugh Auden, born 1907 in York, England   • Educated at Christ Church College, Oxford and Berlin   • Became an American citizen in 1946   • Also wrote prose and drama   • Professor of poetry at Oxford from 1956 to 1960   • Main themes of his poetry are political and social issues of his time. This made him one of the most important poets of the 1930s   • Prolific writer   • Died in 1973

Pre-reading

1 What do you think the poet means by 'Blues'?
2 Describe the usual procedure of mourning and the feelings of mourners at a funeral. Are there different types of mourners? Examine why people go to funerals. What images do you usually associate with a funeral?
3 List the feelings experienced at the death of a loved one.

First reading

4 How does the speaker feel?
5 What does the speaker want to do to mourn the death of his loved one?
6 As part of the poet's mourning he wants to stop the clocks, cut off the phone and stop the dog from barking. Examine these first three images put forward by the poet and say how each one affects him.
7 Is this a realistic reaction to the death of a loved one?
8 Which images dominate this poem?

Second reading

9 Why does the poet no longer need the stars, moon, sun, ocean and wood? What does he suggest be done with them?
10 The poet wants all sources of light to be cut off. What are these and why does he want them cut off?
11 What evidence is there to show that the poet and the deceased were very close?

12 In line 12 the poet says 'I thought that love would last forever: I was wrong.' Describe the poet's state of mind at this stage of the poem.
13 Is it realistic for the poet to ask for all of these various things to be done?
14 Explain what the poet means in the final line when he says 'For nothing now can ever come to any good.'

Third reading

15 How do you feel (i) about the poem, (ii) about the poet?
16 What do you think the future has in store for the poet?

Fourth reading

17 Is this a poem that you will remember? Why?
18 This poem can be seen as a deeply personal poem or a poem about universal mourning. Discuss.
19 Is this a love poem or a satirical attack on the self-importance of people in public life? How would you like to read it?
20 Do you think the poet is exaggerating his mourning or his love? Why would he do this? Is there a need for public displays of grief?
21 Describe the tone of the poem.
22 The poet wants everyone to know that this person, 'he', is dead. How does he suggest doing this?
23 What did the dead person mean to the poet? Where do you find evidence of this?

The Voice

PATRICIA BEER

Prescribed for the Ordinary Level exam in 2007

When God took my aunt's baby boy, a merciful neighbour
Gave her a parrot. She could not have afforded one
But now bought a new cage as brilliant as the bird,
And turned her back on the idea of other babies.

He looked unlikely. In her house his scarlet feathers   5
Stuck out like a jungle, though his blue ones blended
With the local pottery which carried messages
Like 'Du ee help yerself to crame, me handsome.'

He said nothing when he arrived, not a quotation
From pet-shop gossip or a sailor's oath, no sound   10
From someone's home: the telephone or car-door slamming,
And none from his: tom-tom, war-cry or wild beast roaring.

He came from silence but was ready to become noise.
My aunt taught him nursery rhymes morning after morning.
He learnt Miss Muffett, Jack and Jill, Little Jack Horner,   15
Including her jokes; she used to say turds and whey.

A genuine Devon accent is not easy. Actors
Cannot do it. He could though. In his court clothes
He sounded like a farmer, as her son might have.
He sounded like our family. He fitted in.   20

Years went by. We came and went. A day or two
Before he died, he got confused, and muddled up
His rhymes. Jack Horner ate his pail of water.
The spider said what a good boy he was. I wept.

He had never seemed puzzled by the bizarre events   25
He spoke of. But that last day he turned his head towards us
With the bewilderment of death upon him. Said
'Broke his crown' and 'Christmas pie'. And tumbled after.

My aunt died the next winter, widowed, childless, pitied
And patronised. I cannot summon up her voice at all.   30
She would not have expected it to be remembered
After so long. But I can still hear his.

PATRICIA **BEER**

- Born 1924 in Exmouth, Devon, England
- Educated at Exeter University and St Hugh's College, Oxford
- Lived in Italy from 1946 to 1953
- Taught at Goldsmiths College, London, 1962 to 1968
- Her favoured themes were mortality and religious faith
- Died in 1999

First reading

1 Why did the neighbour give the parrot to the aunt?
2 Did it have the effect that the neighbour wished?
3 Describe the parrot.
4 How did the aunt teach him to talk?
5 Why did she do it this way?
6 How successful was she?
7 What happened to him before he died?
8 Why can the poet still hear the parrot's voice?

Second reading

9 What is your favourite image in the poem?
10 What tone does the poet use in the poem?
11 How does she create this?

Third reading

12 Describe the parrot's character.
13 Do you see any hints of humour in the poem?
14 Describe the aunt's character.

Fourth reading

15 What did the poet think of her aunt?
16 How do you think the aunt felt in her last few years?
17 What do we learn about the poet from this poem?

The Fish

ELIZABETH BISHOP

Prescribed for the Ordinary Level exams in 2007 and 2009

I caught a tremendous fish
and held him beside the boat
half out of water, with my hook
fast in a corner of his mouth.
He didn't fight.   5
He hadn't fought at all.
He hung a grunting weight,
battered and venerable
and homely. Here and there
his brown skin hung in strips   10
like ancient wallpaper,
and its pattern of darker brown
was like wallpaper:
shapes like full-blown roses
stained and lost through age.   15
He was speckled with barnacles,
fine rosettes of lime,
and infested
with tiny white sea-lice,
and underneath two or three   20
rags of green weed hung down.
While his gills were breathing in
the terrible oxygen
 – the frightening gills,
fresh and crisp with blood,   25
that can cut so badly –
I thought of the coarse white flesh
packed in like feathers,
the big bones and the little bones,
the dramatic reds and blacks   30
of his shiny entrails,
and the pink swim-bladder
like a big peony.
I looked into his eyes
which were far larger than mine   35
but shallower, and yellowed,
the irises backed and packed
with tarnished tinfoil
seen through the lenses
of old scratched isinglass.   40

They shifted a little, but not
to return my stare.
  – It was more like the tipping
of an object toward the light.
I admired his sullen face,
the mechanism of his jaw,
and then I saw
that from his lower lip
  – if you could call it a lip –
grim, wet, and weaponlike,
hung five old pieces of fish-line,
or four and a wire leader
with the swivel still attached,
with all their five big hooks
grown firmly in his mouth.
A green line, frayed at the end
where he broke it, two heavier lines,
and a fine black thread
still crimped from the strain and snap
when it broke and he got away.
Like medals with their ribbons
frayed and wavering,
a five-haired beard of wisdom
trailing from his aching jaw.
I stared and stared
and victory filled up
the little rented boat,
from the pool of bilge
where oil had spread a rainbow
around the rusted engine
to the bailer rusted orange,
the sun-cracked thwarts,
the oarlocks on their strings,
the gunnels – until everything
was rainbow, rainbow, rainbow!

45

50

55

60

65

70

75

GLOSSARY

Fast: Fixed firmly
Venerable: Worthy of great respect, especially because of age
Barnacles: Shellfish which cling to rocks, boats etc.
Rosettes: Rose-shaped objects
Infested: Overrun in large numbers
Coarse: Rough
Entrails: Guts and internal parts
Peony: Big, red, floppy-petalled flower
Iris: Coloured part of the eyeball
Tarnished: Lost its shine, dull, discoloured

Isinglass: Semi-transparent, see-through whitish gelatine
Sullen: Showing annoyance or irritation
Frayed: Worn and torn into loose threads
Wavering: Unsteady, swaying
Bilge: Dirty, grimy water at the bottom of a boat
Thwarts: Seats for rowers
Gunnels: Rim around the top of the boat
Bailer: Bucket or jug used to scoop water out of a boat
Homely: Plain, not beautiful

ELIZABETH **BISHOP**

- Born 1911 in Worcester, Massachusetts, USA • Her father, a wealthy building contractor, died when she was eight months old • Her mother was a regular patient in mental hospitals and Elizabeth last saw her in 1916 when she was finally institutionalised • Reared by her grandparents in Nova Scotia in a small rural village • Graduated from an exclusive New York university, Vassar, in English Literature • Published poetry and prose since her college days • Travelled extensively through Europe, South America and North Africa • Won the Pulitzer prize in 1956 • Her poetry encourages the reader to look deeper at her subjects and delve beneath the façade • Died in 1979

Pre-reading

1 What would a fisherman consider a successful fishing trip?
2 Is fishing about sitting waiting for the 'bite' or about catching a fish?

First reading

3 Describe the fish.
4 How does the fish behave on being caught?
5 What kind of person is the fisher?

Second reading

6 The fish's skin is described as 'ancient wallpaper'. Why?
7 Describe the fish's appearance.
8 Describe how the poet imagines the fish internally.
9 The fish's gills are frightening. How does the poet create this feeling?

Third reading

10 There are two comparisons to flowers. What are they and why does the poet use them?
11 The poet looks into the fish's eyes. What does she see? Does the fish look back?

12 The five pieces of fishing line hanging from the fish's mouth were 'like medals'. Why does the poet compare them to medals?
13 Why does everything become 'a rainbow'?
14 Why does the poet let the fish go? Has the fish's history anything to do with his release?
15 What does the poet feel about the fish?
16 The poet has a moment of insight or epiphany. Discuss.
17 The poet was a painter as well as a poet. In what way is this poem like a painting? Describe the painting the poet might paint depicting this scene.

Link to language

18 Write Elizabeth Bishop's diary extract telling of her fishing experience. Remember that a diary is an outpouring of a person's innermost feelings. Outline how the poet felt on catching the fish, examining him and on releasing him.

The Filling Station

ELIZABETH BISHOP

Prescribed for the Ordinary Level exams in 2007 and 2009

Oh, but it is dirty!
 – this little filling station,
oil-soaked, oil-permeated
to a disturbing, over-all
black translucency.   5
Be careful with that match!

Father wears a dirty,
oil-soaked monkey suit
that cuts him under the arms,
and several quick and saucy   10
and greasy sons assist him
(it's a family filling station),
all quite thoroughly dirty.

Do they live in the station?
It has a cement porch   15
behind the pumps, and on it
a set of crushed and grease-
impregnated wickerwork;
on the wicker sofa
a dirty dog, quite comfy.   20

Some comic books provide
the only note of color –
of certain color. They lie
upon a big dim doily
draping a taboret   25
(part of the set), beside
a big hirsute begonia.

Why the extraneous plant?
Why the taboret?
Why, oh why, the doily?   30
(Embroidered in daisy stitch
with marguerites, I think,
and heavy with gray crochet.)

Somebody embroidered the doily.
Somebody waters the plant,   35

or oils it, maybe. Somebody
arranges the rows of cans
so that they softly say:
ESSO–SO–SO–SO
to high-strung automobiles.
Somebody loves us all.

40

Pre-reading

1 Jot down all the words that come to mind when you think of a petrol station.

First reading

2 What images of the filling station stand out after your first reading of the poem?
3 Is the poet a character in the poem?

4 Would living in this filling station appeal to you? Why?

5 'Oh, but it is dirty!' Describe, using quotations from the poem, just how dirty the filling station is.
6 Father and sons have a lot in common. Discuss.
7 Describe the filling station.
8 'Somebody' makes an effort to make the place pretty; what details has this person added?

Third reading

9 There are two exclamation marks in the first verse. Why? What do they add to the poem?
10 The tone changes as the poem progresses. Identify the different tones.
11 On the surface the filling station looks 'oil-soaked, oil-permeated' and 'grease-impregnated', but what lies beneath?
12 Discuss the musical qualities of this poem – alliteration, onomatopoeia, rhyme and assonance.
13 The poem ends with an unexpected 'Somebody loves us all.' Where does this idea originate in the poem?
14 Imagine this poem as a painting or series of paintings. What colours and images dominate?

Link to language

15 Write character sketches of (i) the father, (ii) the sons. Remember a good character should have a name, an appearance and a personality.

Child of Our Time

For Aengus

EAVAN BOLAND

Prescribed for the Ordinary Level exams in 2008 and 2010

Yesterday I knew no lullaby
But you have taught me overnight to order
This song, which takes from your final cry
Its tune, from your unreasoned end its reason;
Its rhythm from the discord of your murder   5
Its motive from the fact you cannot listen.

We who should have known how to instruct
With rhymes for your waking, rhythms for your sleep,
Names for the animals you took to bed,
Tales to distract, legends to protect   10
Later an idiom for you to keep
And living, learn, must learn from you dead,

To make our broken images, rebuild
Themselves around your limbs, your broken
Image, find for your sake whose life our idle   15
Talk has cost, a new language. Child
Of our time, our times have robbed your cradle.
Sleep in a world your final sleep has woken.

GLOSSARY
Idiom: Mode of expression

EAVAN **BOLAND**

- Born 1944 in Dublin
- Educated in London, where her father was the Irish Ambassador
- Later studied at Trinity College, Dublin
- Lectured for a while but gave up to become a full-time poet
- Writes about Irish history and the position of women in contemporary Irish society
- Collection: *Outside History*, 1990

First reading

1 What has happened to the child?
2 Why does the poet write this poem?
3 What type of poem does she want to write?
4 How can she 'learn from you dead'?

Second reading

5 How does the poet see the death of the child?
6 What does the poet mean by the phrase 'discord of your murder'?
7 What does the poet mean by the phrase 'our times have robbed your cradle'?

Third reading

8 Does the poet find any signs of hope from the death of this child?
9 What sounds help to create the mood of the poem?
10 Children have a purity that is only disturbed by interfering adults. From your reading of this poem do you think the poet might agree?

Link to language

11 Write a newspaper article about a bombing which has left a child dead.

This Moment

EAVAN BOLAND

Prescribed for the Ordinary Level exams in 2008 and 2010

A neighbourhood.
At dusk.

Things are getting ready
to happen
out of sight.

Stars and moths.
And rinds slanting around fruit.

But not yet.

One tree is black.
One window is yellow as butter.

A woman leans down to catch a child
who runs into her arms
this moment.

Stars rise.
Moths flutter.
Apples sweeten in the dark.

5

10

15

First reading

1 List the things that can be seen in this scene.
2 What different senses are used in the poem?
3 What does each sense do?
4 Describe the action in the poem.

Second reading

5 What happens 'out of sight'?
6 What do the images in the third and final verses suggest to you?
7 Which image is your favourite? Why?

Third reading

8 What effect do the short verses have on the overall poem?
9 Would you agree that there is a sense of mystery in this poem?
10 How is this created?

Link to Language

11 Write a short story beginning with the line 'Things were getting ready to happen'.

Naming My Daughter

ROSITA BOLAND

Prescribed for the Ordinary Level exams in 2009 and 2010

Beside my desk, I had pinned
A list of possible names for my unborn child,
Adding to it at intervals
As the months swelled slowly on.

She was born without colour   5
Among the yellow daffodils
And the greening trees of a wet March.

I chose none of those names for my daughter.
I gave her instead
The Caribbean name of *Rain*:   10
Wanting something soft, familiar and constant
To touch and touch again
Her thin coverlet of earth.

ROSITA **BOLAND**

- **Born 1965 in Co. Clare**
- **Has travelled widely**
- **Wrote a travel book: *Sea Legs*, 1995**
- **Lives in Dublin**
- **Works as a journalist for *The Irish Times***

◦ First reading

1 The speaker of the poem was preparing for the birth of her daughter. What kind of things does she tell us she did?
2 Why does the poet say, 'As the months swelled slowly on'?

◦◦ Second reading

3 What is the dominant feeling or mood of this poem? Does it change? Where?
4 'She was born without colour' is blunt and direct. What is meant here?
5 Why does the poet not choose a name from the ones she had gathered before the birth?
6 Why did the poet pick the name 'Rain' for the baby?
7 Why does the poet mention the 'yellow daffodils' and 'greening trees'?

◦◦◦ Third reading

8 How does this poem make you feel?
9 Is the poet looking for our sympathy? Why do you think she wrote this poem?

L Link to language

10 Write a story with the title 'Hopes raised and dashed'.

Midwife

For Ciairín

PADDY BUSHE

Prescribed for the Ordinary Level exam in 2009

Daughter, that time you fell
from the high bank, in slow
motion it seemed,
your two-year-old body turning
into the black and white   5
suddenly loud Caragh River,
and your wide eyes pleaded for breath
instead of that liquid burning :
that, indeed, was like a little death.

Daughter, after my stretched hand   10
had slipped – hair floating away –
and slipped again, grasped, pulled
you, gasping, from the heaving water,
you cried, you were not hurt,
and you were swaddled up   15
in someone's coat, while the whole earth
breathed again : o daughter,
that, indeed, was like another birth.

PADDY **BUSHE**

- Born 1948 in Dublin
- Lived in Australia
- Now lives in Waterville, Co. Kerry
- Runner-up in the Kavanagh Award in 1988
- Collection: *Digging towards the Light*, 1994

Pre reading

1 What does a midwife do?

First reading

2 Describe what happens to the daughter.
3 What is the father's reaction?

Second reading

4 Why does he describe the rescue as 'another birth'?
5 Outline the various senses that the poet tries to reflect in the poem.

Third reading

6 What do you think the father said to his daughter immediately after the incident?
7 Rewrite the poem from the child's point of view.

Fourth reading

8 Why is the poem called 'Midwife'?
9 There are a lot of 's' sounds in the poem. What effect do they have?
10 Make a list of other phrases which would also be used at the time of birth.

Link to language

11 Write the speaker's diary entry for the evening of the accident.

Jasmine

PADDY BUSHE

Prescribed for the Ordinary Level exam in 2007

What colour is jasmine? you asked
out of the blue from your wheelchair.
And suddenly the ward was filled
with the scent of possibility, hints
of journeys to strange parts.   **5**

The question floored us. But the gulf
was not the colours that we couldn't name
but that we couldn't recognise the road
your question had travelled, nor sound the extent
of the blue void to which it would return.   **10**

The ward remade itself in a hum
of conscientious care. Outside, the usual
traffic jams. We took the long way home.
Father, jasmine is a climbing plant
whose flowers are normally white or yellow.   **15**

And may the fragrance of its blossoms twine
around the broken trellises of your mind.

Pre-reading

1 What impression does the sound of the word 'Jasmine' give you?

First reading

2 Where is the poem set? What evidence is there to support your answer?
3 Who are the two main characters in the poem?
4 What is their relationship?
5 Do you think that there has been any recent change in their relationship?
6 Why does the question floor them?

Second reading

7 Why do they take the long way home? Suggest a possible reason.
8 Do you think this poem is too sentimental? Discuss this.
9 Explain how the Jasmine metaphor develops in the last two lines.

Third reading

10 How are the reader's senses challenged throughout the poem?
11 What is the atmosphere created in the poem? How is this done?
12 Write about the main idea in this poem.

Fourth reading

13 Compare this poem to 'The Present Moment' by Sharon Olds.
14 Do you think that this is a hopeful poem? Explain your answer.

The Flea

JOHN DONNE

Prescribed for the Ordinary Level exams in 2007 and 2008

Mark but this flea, and mark in this,
How little that which thou deny'st me is;
Me it sucked first, and now sucks thee,
And in this flea, our two bloods mingled be;
Confess it, this cannot be said   5
A sin, or shame, or loss of maidenhead,
Yet this enjoys before it woo,
And pampered swells with one blood made of two,
And this, alas, is more than we would do.

Oh stay, three lives in one flea spare,   10
Where we almost, nay more than married are.
This flea is you and I, and this
Our marriage bed, and marriage temple is;
Though parents grudge, and you, we are met,
And cloistered in these living walls of jet.   15
Though use make you apt to kill me,
Let not to this, self-murder added be,
And sacrilege, three sins in killing three.

Cruel and sudden, hast thou since
Purpled thy nail, in blood of innocence?   20
In what could this flea guilty be,
Except in that drop which it sucked from thee?
Yet thou triumph'st, and say'st that thou
Find'st not thyself, nor me the weaker now;
'Tis true, then learn how false, fears be;   25
Just so much honour, when thou yield'st to me,
Will waste, as this flea's death took life from thee.

JOHN **DONNE**

First reading

1 Who or what is the flea?
2 What happens to the flea in the first verse?
3 What is 'denied' to the poet?
4 In the second verse, what does the poet want the flea to do?
5 How does the poet's attitude change as the poem progresses?
6 What does the poet tell his lover in the second verse?

Second reading

7 How does the experience affect him? What language does he use?
8 What tone does the poet use in the poem?
9 How does the tone change in the poem?

Third reading

10 When you discovered that this poem was about sex, were you surprised?
11 Did you expect poems like this to be written back in 1633?

Song: Go, and Catch a Falling Star

JOHN DONNE

Prescribed for the Ordinary Level exams in 2007 and 2008

Go, and catch a falling star,
Get with child a mandrake root,
Tell me, where all past years are,
Or who cleft the Devil's foot,
Teach me to hear mermaids singing, 5
Or to keep off envy's stinging,
And find
What wind
Serves to advance an honest mind.

If thou be'est born to strange sights, 10
Things invisible to see,
Ride ten thousand days and nights,
Till age snow white hairs on thee,
Thou, when thou return'st, wilt tell me
All strange wonders that befell thee, 15
And swear
No where
Lives a woman true, and fair.

If thou find'st one, let me know,
Such a pilgrimage were sweet, 20
Yet do not, I would not go,
Though at next door we might meet,
Though she were true, when you met her,
And last, till you write your letter,
Yet she 25
Will be
False, ere I come, to two, or three.

GLOSSARY

Mandrake root: A poisonous plant believed to have human qualities

Cleft: Split
Befell: Happened to

First reading

1 What does the poet ask the reader to do in the first verse?
2 What does he say the reader will find?
3 What challenge does he lay down in the second verse from lines 10–15?
4 Does he think any of these challenges are attainable?
5 What does he say in the final three lines of the verse?
6 What does he suggest in the last verse?

Second reading

7 What is your favourite image in the poem?
8 What is the mood of the poem?
9 Does the mood change anywhere in the poem? How does it change?

Third reading

10 Do you think that the poet is very cynical?

Link to language

11 Write an updated version of 'Go, and Catch a Falling Star', using contemporary and modern images.

Valentine

CAROL ANN DUFFY

Prescribed for the Ordinary Level exams in 2007 and 2008

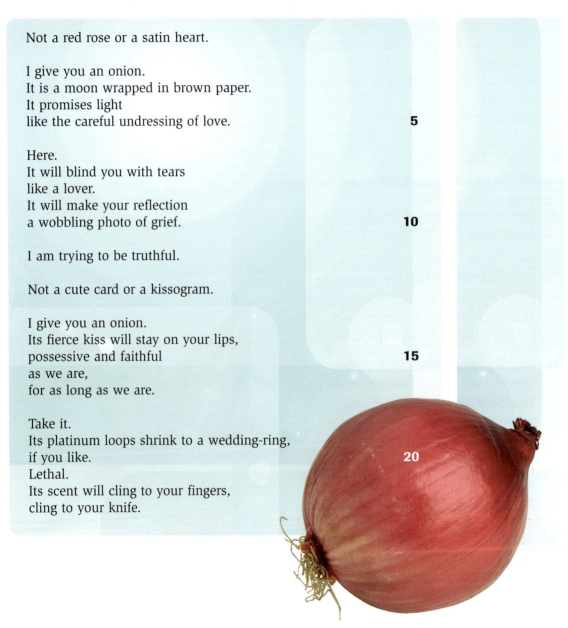

Not a red rose or a satin heart.

I give you an onion.
It is a moon wrapped in brown paper.
It promises light
like the careful undressing of love.   5

Here.
It will blind you with tears
like a lover.
It will make your reflection
a wobbling photo of grief.   10

I am trying to be truthful.

Not a cute card or a kissogram.

I give you an onion.
Its fierce kiss will stay on your lips,
possessive and faithful   15
as we are,
for as long as we are.

Take it.
Its platinum loops shrink to a wedding-ring,
if you like.
Lethal.
Its scent will cling to your fingers,   20
cling to your knife.

CAROL ANN **DUFFY**

- **Born 1955 in Glasgow, raised in Staffordshire, England**
- **Studied at University of Liverpool**
- **Also writes for children**
- **Collections: *Selling Manhattan*, 1987; *Mean Time*, 1993**

Pre-reading

1 What do you associate with Valentine's Day?

First reading

2 Are the effects that the onion has on the lover positive or negative?
3 How is the onion personified?
4 The onion is given four times. What does this indicate?

Second reading

5 How long will the taste of onion stay on the lover's lips? How long will the couple last?
6 What type of relationship does the couple have? Have they been in love for long?
7 How does the onion promise light?

Third reading

8 How would you feel if you were given an onion for Valentine's Day?
9 The poet uses very short lines regularly in the poem. What effect do these short lines have?
10 Describe each metaphor that the speaker uses to describe the onion.

Fourth reading

11 Read 'My Mistress's Eyes . . .' by William Shakespeare and compare it with this poem.
12 This poem manages to be 'cold and passionate'. How?
13 Do you think that this is a good love poem? What makes it good or bad?
14 Love is particular to individuals and can't be represented by love hearts and teddy bears. Does the poet agree? Do you?

Link to language

15 Write the lover's response to this unusual gift.

Going Home to Mayo, Winter, 1949

PAUL DURCAN

Prescribed for the Ordinary Level exams in 2007 and 2008

Leaving behind us the alien, foreign city of Dublin
My father drove through the night in an old Ford Anglia,
His five-year-old son in the seat beside him,
The rexine seat of red leatherette,
And a yellow moon peered in through the windscreen.   5
'Daddy, Daddy,' I cried, 'pass out the moon,'
But no matter how hard he drove he could not pass out the moon.
Each town we passed through was another milestone
And their names were magic passwords into eternity:
Kilcock, Kinnegad, Strokestown, Elphin,   10
Tarmonbarry, Tulsk, Ballaghaderreen, Ballavarry;
Now we were in Mayo and the next stop was Turlough,
The village of Turlough in the heartland of Mayo,
And my father's mother's house, all oil-lamps and women,
And my bedroom over the public bar below,   15
And in the morning cattle-cries and cock-crows:
Life's seemingly seamless garment gorgeously rent
By their screeches and bellowings. And in the evenings
I walked with my father in the high grass down by the river
Talking with him – an unheard-of thing in the city.   20

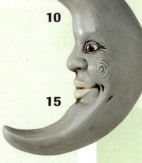

But home was not home and the moon could be no more outflanked
Than the daylight nightmare of Dublin City:
Back down along the canal we chugged into the city
And each lock-gate tolled our mutual doom;
And railings and palings and asphalt and traffic lights,   25
And blocks after blocks of so-called 'new' tenements –
Thousands of crosses of loneliness planted
In the narrowing grave of the life of the father;
In the wide, wide cemetery of the boy's childhood.

GLOSSARY

Alien: Unfamiliar, not part of what you know or understand
Rexine: Fake leather, plastic
Milestone: Stone showing distance to or from a certain place; an important stage reached
Seamless: No beginning, no end; no seams or joins
Rent: Torn apart
Outflanked: Outrun, got in front of

Chugged: Moved with dull, short, repeated sounds
Tolled: Stroke of a ringing bell (especially to mark death)
Mutual: Felt or done by both
Asphalt: Black tar and gravel road surface
Tenements: Large houses or buildings divided into apartments for those who cannot afford a full house

PAUL **DURCAN**

- Born 1944 in Dublin to country parents from Co. Mayo
- Spent his summer holidays with his relations in Mayo
- Educated at Gonzaga College and studied medieval history and archaeology at University College, Cork
- A regular guest on the Pat Kenny radio show
- A popular poet, much quoted and recognised in Irish society

Pre-reading

1 Where do you call home? Why do you call this place home? What makes a place a home?

First reading

2 How does the boy feel at the beginning of the poem?

3 What game do the father and son play on their journey westwards?

4 Describe the mood in the car on the journey to Mayo.

5 Mayo is attractive and homely to the poet. What images stand out to make it so?

6 The father and son go walking in the high grass. Why does this image stand out? Why is it important to the poet?

Second reading

7 Describe the journey to Mayo – images and mood.

8 Describe the stay in Mayo – images and mood.

9 Describe the journey back to Dublin – images and mood.

10 Durcan was five years old when he took this journey to Mayo. Was this his first journey to Mayo? What evidence is there to support your answer?

Third reading

11 Durcan's writing is very detailed. Why does he include so much detail?

12 Why is Dublin described as an 'alien, foreign city'?

13 This poem is divided between lines 1–20 and 21–29. Why is there a division? Why is the first section twice as long as the second? What are the main differences between the sections?

14 Is there a sense that Durcan is trying to resist reality and escape from real life in Dublin? Where do you see this?

15 Describe Durcan's relationship with his father as outlined in the poem. Are there any high points or low points in the relationship?

16 The last three lines present us with images of death. What are they? What do they mean in the context of the poem?

17 Is this a child's view of an event or an adult looking back on an event in his childhood? Support your answer with evidence from the poem.

Link to language

18 Paul Durcan is widely acclaimed as a popular modern Irish poet. Research his life, influences and works and prepare a report on his life and works.

Preludes

T. S. ELIOT

Prescribed for the Ordinary Level exams in 2007 and 2010

I
The winter evening settles down
With smell of steaks in passageways.
Six o'clock.
The burnt-out ends of smoky days.
And now a gusty shower wraps 5
The grimy scraps
Of withered leaves about your feet
And newspapers from vacant lots;
The showers beat
On broken blinds and chimney-pots, 10
And at the corner of the street
A lonely cab-horse steams and stamps.

And then the lighting of the lamps.

II
The morning comes to consciousness
Of faint stale smells of beer 15
From the sawdust-trampled street
With all its muddy feet that press
To early coffee-stands.

With the other masquerades
That time resumes, 20
One thinks of all the hands
That are raising dingy shades
In a thousand furnished rooms.

III
You tossed a blanket from the bed,
You lay upon your back, and waited; 25
You dozed, and watched the night revealing
The thousand sordid images
Of which your soul was constituted;
They flickered against the ceiling.
And when all the world came back 30
And the light crept up between the shutters,
And you heard the sparrows in the gutters,
You had such a vision of the street

As the street hardly understands;
Sitting along the bed's edge, where   35
You curled the papers from your hair,
Or clasped the yellow soles of feet
In the palms of both soiled hands.

    IV
His soul stretched tight across the skies
That fade behind a city block,   40
Or trampled by insistent feet
At four and five and six o'clock;
And short square fingers stuffing pipes,
And evening newspapers, and eyes
Assured of certain certainties,   45
The conscience of a blackened street
Impatient to assume the world.

I am moved by fancies that are curled
Around these images, and cling:
The notion of some infinitely gentle   50
Infinitely suffering thing.

Wipe your hand across your mouth, and laugh;
The worlds revolve like ancient women
Gathering fuel in vacant lots.

GLOSSARY

Withered: Shrivelled, shrunken
Consciousness: Alertness
Masquerade: False show, pretence
Dingy: Dirty, slimy

Sordid: Sleazy
Constituted: Made up of
Infinitely: Forever

T. S. **ELIOT**

- **Thomas Stearns Eliot, born 1888 in St Louis, Missouri, USA**
- **Educated at Harvard, the Sorbonne and Oxford**
- **Worked as a banker in London from 1917 to 1925**
- **He then joined Faber and Faber Publishers**
- **Took British citizenship in 1927**
- **Wrote 'The Waste Land' in 1921**
- **Died in 1965**

▬ Pre-reading

1 What does the word 'prelude' mean?

▪ First reading

2 What is the atmosphere in section I?
3 Which sense is affected most by this section?
4 In the second section which sense is affected?
5 What is the atmosphere in the 'thousand furnished rooms'?
6 What feeling does this image evoke in you?
7 What type of person is described in the third section?
8 How do you feel about this person?
9 What type of life do you think she has?
10 How does the man in the fourth section live?
11 How do you feel about him?

▪▪ Second reading

12 Which is your favourite image in the whole poem. Why?
13 What drives these characters from day to day?

▪▪▪ Third reading

14 In the second-last verse the poet tells us that he is 'moved by fancies that are curled / Around these images'. Why do you think they move him? He dismisses them in the last verse as something that will always be there. How does he reconcile this contradiction?
15 What do you think the poet's real feelings towards these people are?

Aunt Helen

T. S. ELIOT

Prescribed for the Ordinary Level exams in 2007 and 2010

Miss Helen Slingsby was my maiden aunt,
And lived in a small house near a fashionable square
Cared for by servants to the number of four.
Now when she died there was silence in heaven
And silence at her end of the street.   **5**
The shutters were drawn and the undertaker wiped his feet –
He was aware that this sort of thing had occurred before.
The dogs were handsomely provided for,
But shortly afterwards the parrot died too.
The Dresden clock continued ticking on the mantelpiece,   **10**
And the footman sat upon the dining-table
Holding the second housemaid on his knees –
Who had always been so careful while her mistress lived.

GLOSSARY
Dresden: A place in Germany associated with fine bone china

● First reading

1 In your own words, describe Aunt Helen.
2 Describe her house.
3 Do you think those who knew her respected her?
4 What was the undertaker's reaction to her death? Does this surprise you?

●● Second reading

5 How were her animals treated after her death? What does this tell us about Aunt Helen?
6 What were the footman and the second housemaid doing?
7 Why were they doing it now?

●●● Third reading

8 Is Eliot being fair to his aunt?
9 What tone does the poet use in the poem?
10 Why does he adopt this tone?
11 What is your favourite image in the poem? Why?

Out, Out-

ROBERT FROST

Prescribed for the Ordinary Level exams in 2007 and 2008

The buzz-saw snarled and rattled in the yard
And made dust and dropped stove-length sticks of wood,
Sweet-scented stuff when the breeze drew across it.
And from there those that lifted eyes could count
Five mountain ranges one behind the other   **5**
Under the sunset far into Vermont.
And the saw snarled and rattled, snarled and rattled,
As it ran light, or had to bear a load.
And nothing happened: day was all but done.
Call it a day, I wish they might have said   **10**
To please the boy by giving him the half hour
That a boy counts so much when saved from work.
His sister stood beside them in her apron
To tell them 'Supper'. At the word, the saw,
As if to prove saws knew what supper meant,   **15**
Leaped out at the boy's hand, or seemed to leap –
He must have given the hand. However it was,
Neither refused the meeting. But the hand!
The boy's first outcry was a rueful laugh,
As he swung toward them holding up the hand   **20**
Half in appeal, but half as if to keep
The life from spilling. Then the boy saw all –
Since he was old enough to know, big boy
Doing a man's work, though a child at heart –
He saw all spoiled. 'Don't let him cut my hand off –   **25**
The doctor, when he comes. Don't let him, sister!'
So. But the hand was gone already.
The doctor put him in the dark of ether.
He lay and puffed his lips out with his breath.
And then – the watcher at his pulse took fright.   **30**
No one believed. They listened at his heart.
Little – less – nothing! – and that ended it.
No more to build on there. And they, since they
Were not the one dead, turned to their affairs.

ROBERT **FROST**

- Born 1874 in San Francisco, USA
- Educated at Dartmouth and Harvard
- Worked as a farmer
- Lived in England
- Returned to America and taught at Amherst College
- Collections: *North of Boston*, 1914; *The Clearing*, 1962
- Died in 1963

First reading

1 Write a brief paragraph describing the action of the poem.
2 Describe the initial setting for the poem.
3 What impression do you have of the boy's life up until this day?
4 How does the setting change as the poem goes on?
5 What is the boy thinking to himself as the action of the poem develops?
6 How does the poet give life to inanimate objects in the poem?

Second reading

7 At what exact point does the poem change?
8 What happens to the pace of the poem?
9 Which sounds dominate the beginning of the poem? Read the poem out loud to make sure. Why do you think the poet included those sounds?
10 How do the sounds in the poem change? What sounds dominate later in the poem?

Third reading

11 Write about the importance of these phrases:
   'day was all but done.' (9)
   'Neither refused the meeting.' (18)
   'He saw all spoiled.' (25)
   'So.' (27)
   'Little-less-nothing!' (32)

12 What part is played by other people in the poem?

Fourth reading

13 How does the poet feel about the incident?
14 This poem is about the cruelty of life. Do you agree?

Link to language

15 Write the doctor's report after the boy died.

The Road Not Taken

ROBERT FROST

Prescribed for the Ordinary Level exams in 2007 and 2008

Two roads diverged in a yellow wood,
And sorry I could not travel both
And be one traveler, long I stood
And looked down one as far as I could
To where it bent in the undergrowth;   **5**

Then took the other, as just as fair,
And having perhaps the better claim,
Because it was grassy and wanted wear;
Though as for that the passing there
Had worn them really about the same,   **10**

And both that morning equally lay
In leaves no step had trodden black.
Oh, I kept the first for another day!
Yet knowing how way leads on to way,
I doubted if I should ever come back.   **15**

I shall be telling this with a sigh
Somewhere ages and ages hence:
Two roads diverged in a wood, and I –
I took the one less traveled by,
And that has made all the difference.   **20**

◘ Pre-reading

1 What do you think of the title of this poem?
2 What does the title suggest to you?

◘ First reading

3 What is the poet's dilemma?
4 What is his mood at the beginning?
5 Describe each of the roads.
6 Why does he choose to take the second road?
7 What would you have done?

◘ Second reading

8 Why do you think the poem is set in autumn?
9 What does the poet mean when he says that he will 'be telling this with a sigh'?

L Link to language

10 Write about an important choice you had to make. What were the important issues that helped you make that choice?

Acquainted with the Night

ROBERT FROST

Prescribed for the Ordinary Level exams in 2007 and 2008

I have been one acquainted with the night.
I have walked out in rain – and back in rain.
I have outwalked the furthest city light.

I have looked down the saddest city lane.
I have passed by the watchman on his beat   **5**
And dropped my eyes, unwilling to explain.

I have stood still and stopped the sound of feet
When far away an interrupted cry
Came over houses from another street,

But not to call me back or say good-bye;   **10**
And further still at an unearthly height,
One luminary clock against the sky

Proclaimed the time was neither wrong nor right.
I have been one acquainted with the night.

First reading

1   Describe the scene in the poem.
2   Describe the speaker.
3   How does the poet feel about being out
    at night?
4   What is the atmosphere outside?
5   What is the 'luminary clock'?

Second reading

6   What happens to time while he is outside?
7   Which sounds dominate the poem?
8   How does the poet create the atmosphere
    in the poem?
9   What does the poem tell us about the
    speaker?

Third reading

10 This poem is about being alone. Do you
    agree?

Taking My Son to School

EAMONN GRENNAN

Prescribed for the Ordinary Level exams in 2009 and 2010

His first day. Waiting, he plays
By himself in the garden.
I take a photo he clowns for,
Catching him, as it were, in flight.

All the way there in the car he chatters   5
and sings, giving me directions.
There are no maps for this journey:
It is the wilderness we enter.

Around their tall bespectacled teacher,
A gaggle of young ones in summer colours.   10
Silent, he stands on their border,
Clutching a bunch of purple dahlias.

Shyly he offers them up to her.
Distracted she holds them upside down.
He teeters on the rim of the circle,   15
Head drooping, a flower after rain.

I kiss him goodbye and leave him:
Stiff, he won't meet my eye.
I drive by him but he doesn't wave.
In my mind I rush to his rescue.   20

The distance bleeding between us,
I steal a last look back:
From a thicket of blondes, brunettes,
His red hair blazes.

It is done. I have handed him over.   25
I remember him wildly dancing
Naked and shining, shining
In the empty garden.

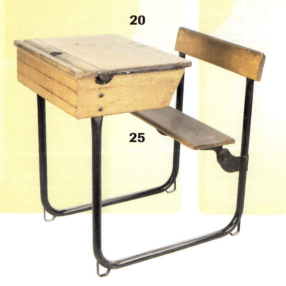

EAMONN **GRENNAN**

- **Born 1941 in Dublin**
- **Educated at University College, Dublin and received his PhD from Harvard**
- **Taught at City University, New York**
- **Presently professor of English at Vassar**
- **Influenced by the poetry of Patrick Kavanagh**
- **His poetry aims to tell of 'the miracle of the actual'**
- **Has also written criticism on contemporary Irish poetry, Shakespeare, Spenser and Chaucer**

First reading

1 Do you get an image of the son? What type of boy do you think he is?
2 What is the atmosphere in the car?
3 What happens when they get to the school?
4 How does the son feel initially?

Second reading

5 How does the father feel just as he's about to go?
6 How do you think the son gets on as the day progresses?
7 Does the father feel guilty at the end of the poem?
8 Do you think he is right to feel this way?

Third reading

9 Are there any particular sounds that dominate the poem?
10 What effect do they have?
11 What is your favourite image in the poem?

Link to language

12 Write about your own memories of your first day at either primary school or secondary school.

May

For Marian

KERRY HARDIE

Prescribed for the Ordinary Level exams in 2008 and 2009

The blessèd stretch and ease of it –
heart's ease. The hills blue. All the flowering weeds
bursting open. Balm in the air. The birdsong
bouncing back out of the sky. The cattle
lain down in the meadow, forgetting to feed.   **5**
The horses swishing their tails.
The yellow flare of furze on the near hill.
And the first cream splatters of blossom
high on the thorns where the day rests longest.

All hardship, hunger, treachery of winter forgotten.   **10**
This unfounded conviction: forgiveness, hope.

KERRY **HARDIE**

- Born 1951 in Singapore, grew up in Co. Down, Northern Ireland
- Worked for the BBC in Belfast
- Deeply affected by the troubles and violence in Northern Ireland
- Won the National Poetry Prize in 1996
- Joint winner of the Hennessy Award for Poetry
- Lives in Kilkenny with husband

▪ Pre-reading

1 What does the month of May mean to you? Freedom from school? Impending exams? Good weather? Summertime? Long evenings?

▫ First reading

2 What images of May dominate this poem? Imagine the picture the poet paints with her words and describe that picture.
3 What is the mood in this poem? How does May make the poet feel?
4 This poem describes a rural, country scene – find evidence of this in the poem.

▪▪ Second reading

5 In the first line 'The blessed stretch and ease of it', the poet could well be talking about the stretch in the evenings, the longer hours of sunlight that come with summertime. What do you think the poet means by adding the words 'heart's ease'?
6 This poem is full of movement and colour. Reread it and highlight the colours and movement. How do these add to the overall feel of the poem?
7 What does winter mean to the poet?

▪▪▪ Third reading

8 What is the effect of the alliteration in lines 3–4, line 5 and line 7, the sibilant 's' sounds and the repeated soft 'e' vowel sounds?
9 The final two lines sound different to the other nine lines; they are harsh and grim. What words in particular stand out? Why do you think this is so? What is their message?

L Link to language

10 This poem describes a summer's day in the countryside. Write a short passage describing a summer's day in the city.

Postscript

SEAMUS HEANEY

Prescribed for the Ordinary Level exams in 2008 and 2009

And some time make the time to drive out west
Into County Clare, along the Flaggy Shore,
In September or October, when the wind
And the light are working off each other
So that the ocean on the one side is wild   5
With foam and glitter, and inland among stones
The surface of a slate-grey lake is lit
By the earthed lightning of a flock of swans,
Their feathers roughed and ruffling, white on white,
Their fully grown headstrong-looking heads   10
Tucked or cresting or busy underwater.
Useless to think you'll park and capture it
More thoroughly. You are neither here nor there,
A hurry through which known and strange things pass
As big soft buffetings come at the car sideways   15
And catch the heart off guard and blow it open.

SEAMUS **HEANEY**

- **Born 1939 in Mossbawn, near Bellaghy, Co. Derry**
- **Son of a Catholic farmer**
- **Educated at St Columba's College in Derry and then at Queen's University, Belfast where he was awarded a first class degree in English Language and Literature**
- **Gained a teaching diploma in 1962 and became a lecturer in English at Queen's University, Belfast**
- **His first volume of poetry, *Death of a Naturalist,* is an outpouring of all he knew from his home life and local countryside**
- **A prolific writer – has published many collections of poetry, criticism and translations**
- **In 1988 he was elected professor of Poetry at Oxford**
- **In 1995 he won the much-acclaimed Nobel Prize for Literature**

◨ First reading

1 What suggestion does the poet make to the reader?
2 What does he say will be seen?
3 What does he mean when he says 'You are neither here nor there'?

◨ Second reading

4 Which is your favourite image in the poem?
5 Describe the swans.
6 Why is it 'useless to think you'll park and capture it / more thoroughly'?

◨ Third reading

7 What sounds dominate the poem?
8 What effect do they have?
9 Does the tone of the poem change as you read it? If so, how?

◨ Link to language

10 Write a description of your favourite place.

One Flesh

ELIZABETH JENNINGS

Prescribed for the Ordinary Level exam in 2010

Lying apart now, each in a separate bed,
He with a book, keeping the light on late,
She like a girl dreaming of childhood,
All men elsewhere – it is as if they wait
Some new event: the book he holds unread,   **5**
Her eyes fixed on the shadows overhead.

Tossed up like flotsam from a former passion,
How cool they lie. They hardly ever touch,
Or if they do it is like a confession
Of having little feeling – or too much.   **10**
Chastity faces them, a destination
For which their whole lives were a preparation.

Strangely apart, yet strangely close together,
Silence between them like a thread to hold
And not wind in. And time itself's a feather   **15**
Touching them gently. Do they know they're old,
These two who are my father and my mother
Whose fire from which I came, has now grown cold?

GLOSSARY
Flotsam: Debris from a shipwreck   **Chastity:** Lack of sexual contact

ELIZABETH **JENNINGS**

- Born 1926 in Boston, Lincolnshire, England
- Educated at Oxford
- Worked in advertising, libraries, publishing etc. before settling down to write full time
- Collection: *Collected Poems 1953-85*, 1985
- Died in 2001

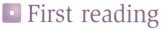 First reading

1 How can two older people seem so innocent?
2 Will there ever be a 'new event' for them?
3 How can they be 'strangely apart, yet strangely close together'?
4 Do they know that they are old?
5 How does the poet feel about her parents?

Second reading

6 If you had only read the first two verses, would you know that the poem was about the poet's parents? What effect did finding out this information have on you?
7 Explain the 'thread' simile.
8 Explain the last line.

Third reading

9 What rhyming scheme does the poet use? Why?
10 What effect do all the 'l' sounds in the first verse have?

Fourth reading

11 There is a sense in this poem that neither parent can be complete without the other. Do you agree? Where is this evident?

Link to language

12 Write the parents' conversation before they went to bed.

The Ladybird's Story

ELIZABETH JENNINGS

Prescribed for the Ordinary Level exam in 2008

It was a roadway to me.
So many meeting-places and directions.
It was smooth, polished, sometimes it shook a little
But I did not tumble off.
I heard you say, and it was like a siren,   5
'A ladybird. Good luck. Perhaps some money.'
I did not understand.
Suddenly I was frightened, fearful of falling
Because you lifted your hand.

And then I saw your eyes,   10
Glassy moons always changing shape,
Sometimes suns in eclipse.
I watched the beak, the peak of your huge nose
And the island of your lips.
I was afraid but you were not. I have   15
No sting. I do not wound.
I carry a brittle coat. It does not protect.
I thought you would blow me away but superstition
Saved me. You held your hand now in one position,
Gentled me over the veins and arteries.   20
But it was not I you cared about but money.
You see I have watched you with flies.

First reading

1 Who is talking in the poem?
2 What does she describe as a roadway?
3 What frightens her?
4 Why was she not blown away?
5 How does the person whom she is
  moving over treat her?
6 Why is she being treated like that?

Second reading

7 What is your favourite image that the ladybird uses to describe the person's face?
8 What is the overall mood of the poem?
9 Does the mood change as the poem
  progresses?

Third reading

10 What does this poem tell us about
   perspective?
11 What sounds dominate the poem? What
   effect do they have?

Link to language

12 Write a diary entry for a day in the life of a
   ladybird or some other insect.

Shancoduff

PATRICK KAVANAGH

Prescribed for the Ordinary Level exams in 2007 and 2010

My black hills have never seen the sun rising,
Eternally they look north towards Armagh.
Lot's wife would not be salt if she had been
Incurious as my black hills that are happy
When dawn whitens Glassdrummond chapel.   **5**

My hills hoard the bright shillings of March
While the sun searches in every pocket.
They are my Alps and I have climbed the Matterhorn
With a sheaf of hay for three perishing calves
In the field under the Big Forth of Rocksavage.   **10**

The sleety winds fondle the rushy beards of Shancoduff
While the cattle-drovers sheltering in the Featherna Bush
Look up and say: 'Who owns them hungry hills
That the water-hen and snipe must have forsaken?
A poet? Then by heavens he must be poor.'   **15**
I hear and is my heart not badly shaken?

GLOSSARY
Rocksavage, Shancoduff, Featherna Bush: Places in
County Monaghan near the poet's father's farm

PATRICK **KAVANAGH**

- Born 1904 in Inniskeen, Co. Monaghan
- Moved to Dublin in the 1930s
- Lung cancer in 1955; recovered
- Married Katherine Moloney in 1967
- Collection: *Ploughman*, 1936
- Novel: *Tarry Flynn*, 1948
- Died in 1967

First reading

1 The title of the poem is taken from the name of the place where Kavanagh's family had a farm. It is derived from two Irish words; *sean* and *dubh*. Do you know what these words mean? If not, find out. What sort of a place would you expect from such a name?

Second reading

2 How does Kavanagh describe this place? Draw a picture or find one that would represent what you would imagine this place to look like.
3 What is the cattle-drovers' attitude to the hills?
4 How does he feel about the cattle-drovers?

Third reading

5 The speaker personifies the place. How does he do this? What effect does it have?
6 The speaker names a lot of specific places in the poem, e.g. Glassdrummond, Featherna, Rocksavage. Why does he do this?
7 The speaker repeatedly uses the possessive 'my' when talking about the hills. Why does he do this? What does it tell us about the narrator?
8 What is the answer to the rhetorical question at the end?

9 How does the rest of nature relate to the hills?
10 What is the difference in the way that the cattle-drovers speak and the way the narrator does?

Fourth reading

11 In an earlier version of the poem, Kavanagh used the word 'faith' instead of the word 'heart' in the last line of the poem. Why do you think he made that change? What effect does it have? Do you think that it was a good change to make?
12 In another poem Kavanagh says that 'Naming a thing is the love act and the pledge.' Relate that statement to 'Shancoduff'.
13 'Shancoduff' is a love poem. Do you agree?

Link to language

14 Think of a place you love. Describe it.

A Christmas Childhood

PATRICK KAVANAGH

Prescribed for the Ordinary Level exams in 2007 and 2010

I
One side of the potato-pits was white with frost –
How wonderful that was, how wonderful!
And when we put our ears to the paling-post
The music that came out was magical.

The light between the ricks of hay and straw   **5**
Was a hole in Heaven's gable. An apple tree
With its December-glinting fruit we saw –
O you, Eve, were the world that tempted me

To eat the knowledge that grew in clay
And death the germ within it! Now and then   **10**
I can remember something of the gay
Garden that was childhood's. Again

The tracks of cattle to a drinking-place,
A green stone lying sideways in a ditch
Or any common sight the transfigured face   **15**
Of a beauty that the world did not touch.

II
My father played the melodeon
Outside at our gate;
There were stars in the morning east
And they danced to his music.   **20**

Across the wild bogs his melodeon called
To Lennons and Callans.
As I pulled on my trousers in a hurry
I knew some strange thing had happened.

Outside in the cow-house my mother   **25**
Made the music of milking;
The light of her stable-lamp was a star
And the frost of Bethlehem made it twinkle.

A water-hen screeched in the bog,
Mass-going feet   **30**
Crunched the wafer-ice on the pot-holes,
Somebody wistfully twisted the bellows wheel.

My child poet picked out the letters
On the grey stone,

In silver the wonder of a Christmas townland,   35
The winking glitter of a frosty dawn.

Cassiopeia was over
Cassidy's hanging hill,
I looked and three whin bushes rode across
The horizon – the Three Wise Kings.   40

An old man passing said:
'Can't he make it talk' –
The melodeon. I hid in the doorway
And tightened the belt of my box-pleated coat.

I nicked six nicks on the door-post   45
With my penknife's big blade –
There was a little one for cutting tobacco.
And I was six Christmases of age.

My father played the melodeon,
My mother milked the cows,   50
And I had a prayer like a white rose pinned
On the Virgin Mary's blouse.

▬ Pre-reading

1 The first part of the poem is an evocation of the poet's memories of his own childhood. What are your memories of Christmas time when you were young?

▪ First reading

2 What is the relationship between the narrator and nature?

3 Do you think that the narrator had a happy childhood?

4 Where in the poem does the narrator compare his village with Bethlehem? Why does he do this?

▪▪ Second reading

5 Show how Kavanagh uses religious imagery throughout the poem. What effect does it have? Does the imagery change as the poem progresses?

6 What type of voice does the narrator use?

7 There is awe for the innocence of the past in this poem. Why is this? How is it conveyed?

8 Why is there full rhyme only in the last verse?

▪▪▪ Third reading

9 How does Kavanagh 'wallow in the habitual'?

▪▪▪▪ Fourth reading

10 What is the narrator's standing in relation to everybody else in the poem?

11 Do you think the narrator felt the same way about the subject of the poem when writing the poem as he did when he was young?

On Raglan Road

PATRICK KAVANAGH

Prescribed for the Ordinary Level exams in 2007 and 2010

(Air: 'The Dawning of the Day')

On Raglan Road on an autumn day I met her first and
  knew
That her dark hair would weave a snare that I might
  one day rue;
I saw the danger, yet I walked along the enchanted way,
And I said, let grief be a fallen leaf at the dawning of
  the day.

On Grafton Street in November we tripped lightly along
  the ledge   5
Of the deep ravine where can be seen the worth of
  passion's pledge,
The Queen of Hearts still making tarts and I not making
  hay –
O I loved too much and by such by such is happiness
  thrown away.

I gave her gifts of the mind I gave her the secret sign
  that's known
To the artists who have known the true gods of sound
  and stone   10
And word and tint. I did not stint for I gave her poems
  to say
With her own name there and her own dark hair like
  clouds over fields of May.

On a quiet street where old ghosts meet I see her walking
  now
Away from me so hurriedly my reason must allow
That I had wooed not as I should a creature made of
  clay –   15
When the angel woos the clay he'd lose his wings at the
  dawn of day.

GLOSSARY

Raglan Road: A street off Pembroke Road in Dublin.
Kavanagh lived on Pembroke Road from 1946 to 1958.
He moved to 19 Raglan Road after this.

First reading

1 What is the relationship between the poet and the dark-haired woman?
2 Is there an equal relationship?
3 What is the poet's attitude to love and courtship?
4 How does he think he scared her off? What do you think?

Second reading

5 This poem is also a popular song. Are there any elements of the poem that make this obvious?

Third reading

6 Do you think that the speaker is telling the truth when he says that he 'loved too much'?
7 Trace the images of nature in the poem.
8 What is the effect of putting rhymes in the middle of lines?
9 What part does time play in the poem?

Fourth reading

10 Do you think that the phrase 'it takes two to tango' ever occurred to Kavanagh?
11 Is the poet a misogynist?

Link to language

12 Write an essay beginning with or containing the line 'I saw the danger, yet I walked along'.

On First Looking into Chapman's Homer

JOHN KEATS

Prescribed for the Ordinary Level exams in 2009 and 2010

Much have I travell'd in the realms of gold,
   And many goodly states and kingdoms seen;
   Round many western islands have I been
Which bards in fealty to Apollo hold.
Oft of one wide expanse had I been told   **5**
   That deep-brow'd Homer ruled as his demesne;
   Yet did I never breathe its pure serene
Till I heard Chapman speak out loud and bold:
Then felt I like some watcher of the skies
   When a new planet swims into his ken;   **10**
Or like stout Cortez when with eagle eyes
   He star'd at the Pacific – and all his men
Look'd at each other with a wild surmise –
   Silent, upon a peak in Darien.

GLOSSARY

Looking into: Studying
Chapman's Homer: Translation of the great Greek poet Homer's works by George Chapman, a contemporary of Shakespeare
Realms of gold: World of literature and imagination
Western islands: Britain and Ireland
Bards: Poets
In fealty to: In allegiance to, loyal to
Apollo: God of poetic and musical inspiration
Oft: often
Deep-brow'd: Deep in thought and contemplation
Demesne: Domain, estate

Breathe: Experience
Serene: Calm, clear atmosphere
Watcher of the skies: Astronomer watching the skies
Ken: Knowledge, field of vision
Stout: Strong and brave
Cortez: Spanish explorer who conquered Mexico; Keats is confusing Cortez with Balboa who was the first westerner to see the Pacific
Surmise: Guess, imagine
Darien: Now Panama – narrow stretch of land joining North and South America

JOHN **KEATS**

- Born 1795 in London   • Son of a livery stableman and his wife   • At fifteen was apprenticed to an apothecary-surgeon and went on to further medical training at Guy's Hospital, London   • Once qualified as a surgeon he gave up medicine in favour of poetry   • Belonged to the Romantic movement   • 1818: fell in love with Fanny Brawne but could not marry her because of financial difficulties   • 1819: worked prolifically producing great odes, fine sonnets and several other masterpieces   • 1820: contracted tuberculosis (TB) and travelled to Italy in an attempt to prolong his life   • His mother and brother both died of TB   • Was bitter and angry because his brother had received forged love letters on his death-bed which caused much pain and suffering   • 1821: died in Rome aged twenty-six • Had published only fifty-four poems   • His poetry is an attempt to make sense of a world full of negatives: 'misery, heartache and pain, sickness and aggression'   • Wrote his own epitaph: 'Here lies one whose name was writ in water'

● First reading

1 Chapman has given Keats the opportunity to read the great works of Homer by translating them into English. How do you think Keats feels about this?
2 Keats compares himself in this poem to an astronomer 'watcher of the skies' and to the Spanish explorer Cortez. How is he similar to these people?
3 Before finding Chapman's translation of Homer what does Keats tell us he did?
4 Describe Homer and his works as outlined in lines 5, 6 and 7.
5 Chapman has opened a new door for Keats. Where does this door lead?

●● Second reading

6 This is a Petrarchan sonnet. In what way is the octet (first eight lines) different to the sestet (last six lines)?
7 Do you think the Petrarchan sonnet is a good structure for what Keats has to say in this poem?

8 Is Keats more like an astronomer or an explorer leading men to new lands? Explain your answer.
9 This is a richly musical poem. Examine the words and rhyming within the poem to discuss this comment.
10 Keats begins the poem travelling and exploring and ends it on a note of calmness, silence and stillness. Why does he do this?
11 How would you sum up Keats's attitude to poetry in the whole poem?

La Belle Dame Sans Merci

JOHN KEATS

Prescribed for the Ordinary Level exams in 2009 and 2010

O what can ail thee knight at arms
Alone and palely loitering?
The sedge has withered from the Lake
And no birds sing!

O what can ail thee knight at arms   5
So haggard and so woe begone?
The squirrel's granary is full
And the harvest's done.

I see a lilly on thy brow
With anguish moist and fever dew,   10
And on thy cheeks a fading rose
Fast withereth too –

I met a Lady in the Meads
Full beautiful, a faery's child
Her hair was long, her foot was light   15
And her eyes were wild –

I made a Garland for her head,
And bracelets too, and fragrant Zone:
She look'd at me as she did love
And made sweet moan –   20

I set her on my pacing steed
And nothing else saw all day long
For sidelong would she bend and sing
A faery's song –

She found me roots of relish sweet   25
And honey wild and manna dew
And sure in language strange she said
'I love thee true' –

She took me to her elfin grot
And there she wept and sigh'd full sore   30
And there I shut her wild wild eyes
With kisses four.

And there she lulled me asleep
And there I dream'd – Ah Woe betide!
The latest dream I ever dreamt   35
On the cold hill side.

I saw pale kings and princes too
Pale warriors, death pale were they all;
They cried 'La belle dame sans merci
Thee hath in thrall.'   40

I saw their starv'd lips in the gloam
With horrid warning gaped wide
And I awoke and found me here
On the cold hill's side.

And this is why I sojourn here   45
Alone and palely loitering;
Though the sedge is wither'd from the Lake
and no birds sing.

THE LOVERS.

Pre-reading

1 Describe the person in the title: 'La Belle Dame Sans Merci'.

First reading

2 This poem is a ballad (a song or poem telling a story). What is the story of the poem?

3 Who is telling the story? There are a number of voices in the poem. Identify and describe each speaker.

4 Describe the knight.

5 Describe the beautiful lady.

Second reading

6 There is a lot of suffering in this poem. Where can it be found?

7 Describe the journey made by the knight and the beautiful lady.

8 The last four verses lead us to believe that the knight is doomed. Explain.

9 What message did the 'pale kings and Princes' and 'Pale warriors' have for the knight? Describe what they looked like.

10 The beautiful lady seems to have magical powers – what are they and where can they be seen in the poem?

Third reading

11 It is obvious that the knight is suffering from the same symptoms as a sufferer of TB, of which Keats's mother and brother died and which also killed him. Describe these symptoms.

12 What is the mood of the poem? Does the poet use certain words or phrases or rhymes to conjure up this mood?

13 This poem is essentially about the negative aspects of love. Do you agree? Use evidence from the poem to support your answer.

14 In what season is the poem based? Is this relevant?

15 Is this a love poem or a poem about death?

16 There is a great sense of antiquity about this poem in both the images and the language. Examine the poem for evidence of this.

17 Is this poem simply telling a story or is Keats trying to pass on a message or teach us a lesson?

Night Drive

BRENDAN KENNELLY

Prescribed for the Ordinary Level exam in 2010

I

The rain hammered as we drove
Along the road to Limerick
'Jesus what a night' Alan breathed
And – 'I wonder how he is, the last account
Was poor.'   5
I couldn't speak.

The windscreen fumed and blurred, the rain's spit
Lashing the glass. Once or twice
The wind's fist seemed to lift the car
And pitch it hard against the ditch.   10
Alan straightened out in time,
Silent. Glimpses of the Shannon –
A boiling madhouse roaring for its life
Or any life too near its gaping maw,
White shreds flaring in the waste   15
Of insane murderous black;
Trees bending in grotesque humility,
Branches scattered on the road, smashed
Beneath the wheels.
Then, ghastly under headlights,   20
Frogs bellied everywhere, driven
From the swampy fields and meadows,
Bewildered refugees, gorged with terror.
We killed them because we had to,
Their fatness crunched and flattened in the dark.   25
'How is he now?' Alan whispered
To himself. Behind us,
Carnage of broken frogs.

II
His head
Sweated on the pillow of the white hospital bed.   30
He spoke a little, said
Outrageously, 'I think I'll make it.'
Another time, he'd rail against the weather,
(Such a night would make him eloquent)
But now, quiet, he gathered his fierce will   35
To live.

III
Coming home
Alan saw the frogs.
'Look at them, they're everywhere,
Dozens of the bastards dead.'   40

Minutes later –
'I think he might pull through now.'
Alan, thoughtful at the wheel, was picking out
The homeroad in the flailing rain
Nighthedges closed on either side.   45
In the suffocating darkness
I heard the heavy breathing
Of my father's pain.

BRENDAN **KENNELLY**

- **Born 1936 in Co. Kerry**
- **Professor of English at Trinity College, Dublin**
- **Collections:** *Cromwell*, **1987;** *The Book of Judas*, **1992;** *Familiar Strangers*, **2004**

▪ First reading

1 What is the relationship between Alan and the narrator?
2 What is the purpose of their journey?
3 How do you think the two men feel as they go on their journey?
4 How do their reactions differ?

▪▪ Second reading

5 What is the relationship between the two men and nature?
6 How is the night described?
7 What is the significance of the frogs?
8 How does the tone change in the second verse?
9 Do you get any impression of what type of man the father was?
10 How is the journey home different?
11 Does the road seem different to the narrator?

▪▪▪ Third reading

12 Why does the poet seem to put more emphasis on the journey than on his father's ill health?
13 How does the pace of the poem change throughout?
14 It is rare to see dialogue in poems; what effect does it have?
15 Compare Alan's attitude to the frogs and his attitude to the father.

▦ Fourth reading

16 Kennelly succeeds in building tension expertly. Do you agree?
17 Kennelly has been criticised for being over-sentimental in his poems. Does this poem make you agree with those critics?

▣ Link to language

18 Write a story entitled 'Night drive'.

At Grass

PHILIP LARKIN

Prescribed for the Ordinary Level exams in 2008 and 2009

The eye can hardly pick them out
From the cold shade they shelter in,
Till wind distresses tail and mane;
Then one crops grass, and moves about
 – The other seeming to look on –   5
And stands anonymous again.

Yet fifteen years ago, perhaps
Two dozen distances sufficed
To fable them: faint afternoons
Of Cups and Stakes and Handicaps,   10
Whereby their names were artificed
To inlay faded, classic Junes –

Silks at the start: against the sky
Numbers and parasols: outside,
Squadrons of empty cars, and heat,   15
And littered grass: then the long cry
Hanging unhushed till it subside
To stop-press columns on the street.

Do memories plague their ears like flies?
They shake their heads. Dusk brims the shadows.   20
Summer by summer all stole away,
The starting-gates, the crowds and cries –
All but the unmolesting meadows.
Almancked, their names live; they

Have slipped their names, and stand at ease,   25
Or gallop for what must be joy,
And not a fieldglass sees them home,
Or curious stop-watch prophesies:
Only the groom, and the groom's boy,
With bridles in the evening come.   30

GLOSSARY
Sufficed: Met present needs or requirements
To fable them: To make them legendary
Artificed: Placed skilfully

Almanacked: Placed in a book of records
Prophesies: Predictions

PHILIP **LARKIN**

- Born 1922 in Coventry, England
- His father was the city treasurer
- Educated at Oxford
- Worked as a librarian all his life
- Was the unofficial Poet Laureate of Hull in the 1950s and 60s
- Refused the offer to become official Poet Laureate in 1984
- Was a shy, introverted person who loved reading and writing novels, poetry and jazz reviews
- Awarded the Queen's Gold Medal for Poetry in 1964
- Died of cancer in 1985

First reading

1 What are the horses doing when the poet first sees them?
2 Do they appear like proud racehorses in the first verse?
3 What were the horses like fifteen years ago?
4 What is the atmosphere at the race meeting?
5 How were the horses treated back then?
6 Do you think that the horses do have memories of their glory days?
7 Compare the movement of the horses at the time the poet sees them and fifteen years previously.

Second reading

8 What is the mood of the poem?
9 How does the poet create this mood?

Third reading

10 Fame is a short-lived thing. Do you agree?
11 What does this poem tell us about old age?

Link to language

12 Write a commentary piece for the final stages of a horse race.

An Arundel Tomb

PHILIP LARKIN

Prescribed for the Ordinary Level exams in 2008 and 2009

Side by side, their faces blurred,
The earl and countess lie in stone,
Their proper habits vaguely shown
As jointed armour, stiffened pleat,
And that faint hint of the absurd –   5
The little dogs under their feet.

Such plainness of the pre-baroque
Hardly involves the eye, until
It meets his left-hand gauntlet, still
Clasped empty in the other; and   10
One sees, with a sharp tender shock,
His hand withdrawn, holding her hand.

They would not think to lie so long.
Such faithfulness in effigy
Was just a detail friends would see: 15
A sculptor's sweet commissioned grace
Thrown off in helping to prolong
The Latin names around the base.

They would not guess how early in
Their supine stationary voyage   20
The air would change to soundless damage,
Turn the old tenantry away;
How soon succeeding eyes begin
To look, not read. Rigidly they

Persisted, linked, through lengths and breadths   25
Of time. Snow fell, undated. Light
Each summer thronged the glass. A bright
Litter of birdcalls strewed the same
Bone-riddled ground. And up the paths
The endless altered people came,   30

Washing at their identity.
Now, helpless in the hollow of
An unarmorial age, a trough
Of smoke in slow suspended skeins
Above their scrap of history,   35
Only an attitude remains:

Time has transfigured them into
Untruth. The stone fidelity
They hardly meant has come to be
Their final blazon, and to prove   **40**
Our almost-instinct almost true:
What will survive of us is love.

▪ First reading

1 Describe the scene within the tomb.
2 What is the poet's first impression of the couple?
3 What does he see when he looks at the hands?
4 What role does he attribute to the sculptor?

•• Second reading

5 What happens to the sculpture over time?
6 How do visitors to the tomb treat the entombed couple?
7 How does the poet describe the passing of time?

••• Third reading

8 Are there any particular sounds that dominate the poem?
9 What effect do they have?
10 What is the mood of the poem?
11 What attitude remains?

⠿ Fourth reading

12 Why does he use the phrase 'almost-instinct'?
13 Do you agree that 'What will survive of us is love'?

Ⓛ Link to language

14 Write an essay with the first line 'I thought our love would last forever . . .'

The Explosion

PHILIP LARKIN

Prescribed for the Ordinary Level exams in 2008 and 2009

On the day of the explosion
Shadows pointed towards the pithead:
In the sun the slagheap slept.

Down the lane came men in pitboots
Coughing oath-edged talk and pipe-smoke,   **5**
Shouldering off the freshened silence.

One chased after rabbits; lost them;
Came back with a nest of lark's eggs;
Showed them; lodged them in the grasses.

So they passed in beards and moleskins,   **10**
Fathers, brothers, nicknames, laughter,
Through the tall gates standing open.

At noon, there came a tremor; cows
Stopped chewing for a second; sun,
Scarfed as in a heat-haze, dimmed.   **15**

The dead go on before us, they
Are sitting in God's house in comfort,
We shall see them face to face –

Plain as lettering in the chapels
It was said, and for a second   **20**
Wives saw men of the explosion

Larger than in life they managed –
Gold as on a coin, or walking
Somehow from the sun towards them,

One showing the eggs unbroken.   **25**

GLOSSARY
Slagheap: Pile of waste matter from coal mining etc.

Moleskin: Soft leather-like fabric

First reading

1 What is the mood at the start of the poem?
2 What type of day are the miners having?
3 Describe the men who are walking to work.
4 What happened at noon?
5 How did it affect nature?
6 How did it affect the people?

Second reading

7 What happens to the poem after verse 5?
8 Who is talking in verse 6?

Third reading

9 What is the mood in the poem?
10 How does the poet create this mood?
11 Do you think the poet brings the event alive?

Fourth reading

12 Do you think the poet believes that the dead can communicate with the living?
13 What do you think of Larkin's attitude to death?

Link to language

14 Write a newspaper report that would be written the day after the explosion.

What Were They Like?

DENISE LEVERTOV

Prescribed for the Ordinary Level exam in 2007

1. Did the people of Vietnam
   use lanterns of stone?
2. Did they hold ceremonies
   to reverence the opening of buds?
3. Were they inclined to laughter?   5
4. Did they use bone and ivory,
   jade and silver, for ornament?
5. Had they an epic poem?
6. Did they distinguish between speech and singing?

1. Sir, their light hearts turned to stone.   10
   It is not remembered whether in gardens
   stone lanterns illumined pleasant ways.
2. Perhaps they gathered once to delight in blossom,
   but after the children were killed
   there were no more buds.   15
3. Sir, laughter is bitter to the burned mouth.
4. A dream ago, perhaps. Ornament is for joy.
   All the bones were charred.
5. It is not remembered. Remember,
   most were peasants; their life   20
   was in rice and bamboo.
   When peaceful clouds were reflected in the paddies
   and the water buffalo stepped surely along terraces,
   maybe fathers told their sons old tales.
   When bombs smashed those mirrors   25
   there was time only to scream.
6. There is an echo yet
   of their speech which was like a song.
   It was reported their singing resembled
   the flight of moths in moonlight.   30
   Who can say? It is silent now.

GLOSSARY
Reverence: Respect
Jade: A green semi-precious stone

Illumined: Lit up
Paddies: Fields where rice is grown

76 SIGNS

DENISE **LEVERTOV**

• **Born 1923 in Ilford, Essex, England** • **Worked as a nurse during the war** • **Emigrated to the USA** • **Taught at Stanford University** • **Anti-Vietnam War protestor** • **Collection:** *Breathing the Water*, **1987** • **Died in 1997**

▬ Pre-reading

1 What do you know about the Vietnam War?

▪ First reading

2 What sense of the Vietnamese do we get from the answers that are given?

3 Are there any signs of hope for the future in this poem?

4 How do the priorities of the Vietnamese and the priorities of the questioner differ?

▪▪ Second reading

5 What is the tone of the questions?

6 How does the tone of the answers differ from that of the questions?

7 What is your favourite image or phrase in the poem?

8 Examine each of the metaphors individually: the light, the bud, laughter, decoration, heritage and culture and say how and why each one is used in the poem.

▪▪▪ Third reading

9 Have you ever before read a poem that took the format of a question and answer sequence? What do you think of this format? What do you think is the purpose of this format?

10 What do you think the poet is trying to achieve? Does she achieve this successfully?

11 How important is the last line?

▪▪ Fourth reading

12 Could this poem have been written in a more traditional way? Would it have been as effective?

13 While keeping the integral message and spirit of the poem, rewrite it in a more traditional way.

14 Rewrite this poem in your notebook by putting each answer beneath its question. Does this make the poem easier to follow?

15 Were you moved by this poem? What feelings did you have? Can you explain why?

L Link to language

16 If you were to be put in the questioner's place and had to ask six specific questions to find out 'what they were like', what questions would you ask?

Kidspoem/Bairnsang

LIZ LOCHHEAD

Prescribed for the Ordinary Level exams in 2009 and 2010

it wis January
and a gey dreich day
the first day Ah went to the school
so my Mum happed me up in ma
good navy-blue napp coat wi the rid tartan hood   5
birled a scarf aroon ma neck
pu'ed oan ma pixie an' my pawkies
it wis that bitter
said *noo ye'll no starve*
gie'd me a wee kiss and a kid-oan skelp oan the bum   10
and sent me aff across the playground
tae the place Ah'd learn to say
it was January
and a really dismal day
the first day I went to school   15
so my mother wrapped me up in my
best navy-blue top coat with the red tartan hood,
twirled a scarf around my neck,
pulled on my bobble-hat and mittens
it was so bitterly cold   20
said *now you won't freeze to death*
gave me a little kiss and a pretend slap on the bottom
and sent me off across the playground
to the place I'd learn to forget to say
it wis January   25
and a gey dreich day
the first day Ah went to the school
so my Mum happed me up in ma
good navy-blue napp coat wi the rid tartan hood,
birled a scarf aroon ma neck,   30
pu'ed oan ma pixie an' my pawkies
it wis that bitter.

Oh saying it was one thing
but when it came to writing it
in black and white   35
the way it had to be said
was as if you were posh, grown-up, male, English and dead.

LIZ **LOCHHEAD**

- Born 1947 in Motherwell, Scotland • Studied at Glasgow School of Art • Successful playwright
- Well known for her performance of her poetry
- Love, politics, comedy and childhood are her regular themes • Collection: *Bagpipe Muzak*, 1991

◉ First reading

1 Read the first twelve lines out loud. How much do you understand? Is it easy to assume a Scottish accent when reading the way the words are written? What words and phrases do you not understand? Make a guess at the meanings.
2 Start the poem again and read up to line 24. What has changed in your understanding of the poem?
3 Now read the whole poem from start to finish. What is the poet telling the reader? What is the message of this poem?

◉◉ Second reading

4 Describe the morning of the poet's first day at school.
5 What did the poet learn in school?
6 Does the poet prefer the Scottish way of saying things or the 'proper' way? Find evidence to support your answer.
7 How does the poet feel when she recites the poem 'the way it had to be said'?

◉◉◉ Third reading

8 What features of this poem indicate that it is a 'kidspoem'? What part is written in an adult voice and what part in a child's voice?
9 Is the title 'Kidspoem/Bairnsang' a good indicator of the subject matter? Why does the poet not call it 'Bairnsang/Kidspoem'? Was this just incidental or premeditated?

10 Is the poet proud of her nationality? Is there evidence of this in the poem? Does the poet see herself as Scottish or has her education anglicised her?
11 Poetry appeals, above all else, to the ear. Do you agree with this statement in reference to 'Kidspoem/Bairnsang'?
12 A central theme of this poem is nostalgia. What is the poet nostalgic about?
13 What is the poet's opinion of 'proper' poetry as outlined in the last verse?
14 Describe the poet's style of writing. Is it traditional? Unconventional? Why is all punctuation omitted? Does the absence of punctuation help or hinder your comprehension of the poem?

Wounds

MICHAEL LONGLEY

Prescribed for the Ordinary Level exam in 2010

Here are two pictures from my father's head –
I have kept them like secrets until now:
First, the Ulster Division at the Somme
Going over the top with 'Fuck the Pope!'
'No Surrender!': a boy about to die,   5
Screaming 'Give 'em one for the Shankill!'
'Wilder than Gurkhas' were my father's words
Of admiration and bewilderment.
Next comes the London-Scottish padre
Resettling kilts with his swagger-stick,   10
With a stylish backhand and a prayer.
Over a landscape of dead buttocks
My father followed him for fifty years.
At last, a belated casualty,
He said – lead traces flaring till they hurt –   15
'I am dying for King and Country, slowly.'
I touched his hand, his thin head I touched.

Now, with military honours of a kind,
With his badges, his medals like rainbows,
His spinning compass, I bury beside him   20
Three teenage soldiers, bellies full of
Bullets and Irish beer, their flies undone.
A packet of Woodbines I throw in,
A Lucifer, the Sacred Heart of Jesus
Paralysed as heavy guns put out   25
The night-light in a nursery for ever;
Also a bus-conductor's uniform –
He collapsed beside his carpet slippers
Without a murmur, shot through the head
By a shivering boy who wandered in   30
Before they could turn the television down
Or tidy away the supper dishes.
To the children, to a bewildered wife,
I think 'Sorry Missus' was what he said.

GLOSSARY

Ulster Division: A Division of the British Army
Somme: A river in north-western France. It was the scene of some of the fiercest battles of the First World War
Shankill: A Protestant area of Belfast

Gurkha: A Nepalese soldier
Padre: Priest
Lucifer: An old name for a match
Woodbines: Cigarettes

MICHAEL **LONGLEY**

• Born 1939 in Belfast to English parents   • His father fought in both world wars and his experiences of the horrors of war feature in the poetry of Michael Longley
• Studied the Classics at Trinity College, Dublin
• Worked as a school teacher   • Joined the Arts Council of Northern Ireland in 1970

▬ Pre-reading

1   What images are conjured up by the word 'wounds'? What ideas spring to mind?

◦ First reading

2   The speaker opens the poem by telling us of two pictures from his father's head. These are then described in the first eleven lines. Describe these two pictures.
3   How did the father feel about each of the pictures?
4   What picture of war is portrayed in the first seventeen lines?
5   The father lived for fifty years after the war. What impact did the war have on his life? Has the war anything to do with his death?

◦◦ Second reading

6   Describe the father's burial.
7   What do we learn about the father–son relationship?
8   There are also three soldiers buried beside the poet's father. Describe them.
9   Are there any similarities between these soldiers and the soldiers who fought and died at the Somme?
10   What happened to the bus conductor? Describe the scene.
11   Describe the assassin.

◦◦◦ Third reading

12   What effect does the everyday nature of the scene in line 28, in contrast with the extraordinary nature of the incident, have on the reader?
13   What is the poet's message to the reader in this poem?
14   The effects of war are far-reaching and long-lasting. Discuss this statement in relation to the whole poem.
15   How is the image of the battlefield conveyed in the first verse? What particular words and phrases enhance this image?
16   This is a poem about violence and war. What are the differences between the battlefields in verse 1 (the Somme) and in verse 2 (Northern Ireland in the 1970s)?
17   What are the poet's thoughts on war and violence? Examine the whole poem in your answer and refer to specific images to support your answer.
18   Which images of death do you find most disturbing? Discuss.

L Link to language

19   Write a diary entry of a soldier at the Somme during the First World War or of the assassin mentioned in verse 2.
20   Write a graveside oration you imagine the poet would deliver in memory of his father.

Last Requests

MICHAEL LONGLEY

Prescribed for the Ordinary Level exams in 2009 and 2010

I
Your batman thought you were buried alive,
Left you for dead and stole your pocket watch
And cigarette case, all he could salvage
From the grave you so nearly had to share
With an unexploded shell. But your lungs   **5**
Surfaced to take a long remembered drag,
Heart contradicting as an epitaph
The two initials you had scratched on gold.

II
I thought you blew a kiss before you died,
But the bony fingers that waved to and fro   **10**
Were asking for a Woodbine, the last request
Of many soldiers in your company,
The brand you chose to smoke for forty years
Thoughtfully, each one like a sacrament.
I who brought peppermints and grapes only   **15**
Couldn't reach you through the oxygen tent.

GLOSSARY
Batman: A British military officer's orderly

First reading

1 What happened to the father in the first verse?
2 What did his batman try to do?
3 What does his survival tell us about the father?
4 In the second part, what does the father want?
5 What does the son bring him?
6 What does this tell us about their relationship?

Second reading

7 How does the father treat his cigarette?
8 What is your favourite image in the poem?

Third reading

9 Does the mood change as the poem progresses?
10 How does the poet use irony in the poem?
11 How does the poet feel in the second section?

Link to language

12 Write an essay called 'My last request.'
13 Write a speech on the dangers of smoking.

An Amish Rug

MICHAEL LONGLEY

Prescribed for the Ordinary Level exams in 2009 and 2010

As if a one-room schoolhouse were all we knew
And our clothes were black, our underclothes black,
Marriage a horse and buggy going to church
And the children silhouettes in a snowy field,

I bring you this patchwork like a smallholding   5
Where I served as the hired boy behind the harrow,
Its threads the colour of cantaloupe and cherry
Securing hay bales, corn cobs, tobacco leaves.

You may hang it on the wall, a cathedral window,
Or lay it out on the floor beside our bed   10
So that whenever we undress for sleep or love
We shall step over it as over a flowerbed.

GLOSSARY
Amish: A group of conservative Christians distinguished by plainness in their work and dress

Harrow: A farm machine
Cantaloupe: A small melon

▬ Pre-reading

1 Find out what you can about the Amish people. Perhaps watch the movie *Witness* or do some research on the internet.

▪ First reading

2 What image of the Amish do we get in the first verse?
3 How do you see the rug itself?
4 How does the poet see his marriage?
5 What colours are in the poem?
6 What do they represent?

▪▪ Second reading

7 Is this a sensuous poem?
8 Is there a change of mood in the poem? Where does it happen?
9 How does the poet believe marriage should be treated?

▪▪▪ Third reading

10 Do you think the rug is a good metaphor for marriage? Why?

▣ Link to language

11 Write the speech you would deliver for or against the motion that 'Marriage is an outdated concept'.

Grandfather

DEREK MAHON

Prescribed for the Ordinary Level exams in 2008 and 2009

They brought him in on a stretcher from the world,
Wounded but humorous; and he soon recovered.
Boiler-rooms, row upon row of gantries rolled
Away to reveal the landscape of a childhood
Only he can recapture. Even on cold   5
Mornings he is up at six with a block of wood
Or a box of nails, discreetly up to no good
Or banging round the house like a four-year-old –

Never there when you call. But after dark
You hear his great boots thumping in the hall   10
And in he comes, as cute as they come. Each night
His shrewd eyes bolt the door and set the clock
Against the future, then his light goes out.
Nothing escapes him; he escapes us all.

GLOSSARY
Gantries: Overhead structures with a platform supporting a
travelling crane; an essential tool of shipbuilding

DEREK **MAHON**

- **Born 1941 in Belfast, Northern Ireland**
- **Studied French at Trinity College, Dublin**
- **Travelled through France, Canada and the USA supporting himself through teaching and odd jobs**
- **Worked as a scriptwriter for the BBC and as a freelance writer for a number of newspapers**
- **Writes in a serious tone using specific occurrences to explore wider universal themes**

First reading

1 What do you think that the poet means in the first line of the poem?
2 Can you picture the grandfather in your head? What do you see?
3 What is his daily life like?
4 What was his childhood like?
5 Why does he come in after dark so loudly?

Second reading

6 What does the poet mean by the phrase 'Nothing escapes him'?
7 List the adjectives that are used to describe him. What do they tell us about him?
8 What does the poet mean by the phrase 'he escapes us all'?
9 What is the overall mood of the poem?
10 What sounds help create that mood?

Third reading

11 Do you think the poet wishes he was more like his grandfather?
12 How do you think the speaker in the poem felt about his grandfather?
13 How does the grandfather feel about the future?

Link to language

14 Write a personal essay about a family member who has had a major influence on your life.

After the *Titanic*

DEREK MAHON

Prescribed for the Ordinary Level exams in 2008 and 2009

They said I got away in a boat
And humbled me at the inquiry. I tell you
    I sank as far that night as any
Hero. As I sat shivering on the dark water
    I turned to ice to hear my costly   **5**
Life go thundering down in a pandemonium of
    Prams, pianos, sideboards, winches,
Boilers bursting and shredded ragtime. Now I hide
    In a lonely house behind the sea
Where the tide leaves broken toys and hatboxes   **10**
    Silently at my door. The showers of
April, flowers of May mean nothing to me, nor the
    Late light of June, when my gardener
Describes to strangers how the old man stays in bed
    On seaward mornings after nights of   **15**
Wind, takes his cocaine and will see no one. Then it is
    I drown again with all those dim
Lost faces I never understood, my poor soul
    Screams out in the starlight, heart
Breaks loose and rolls down like a stone.   **20**
    Include me in your lamentations.

GLOSSARY
Pandemonium: Chaos and confusion
Winches: The cranks of wheels

Ragtime: A type of jazz music
Lamentations: Outpourings of grief

▬ Pre-reading

1 What do you know about the *Titanic*? Did you see the movie? Do some research on what happened.

▪ First reading

2 What happened to the speaker in the poem?
3 What happened to the other people on the ship?
4 What does the speaker do now?
5 Why does he stay in bed at this time?
6 Who is the speaker talking to?
7 How is the speaker treated by his community?
8 What does he want the reader to do?

▪▪ Second reading

9 Does the speaker feel sorry for himself?
10 Is he right to?
11 How often does he say 'I' or 'me' in the poem? What does that make us think about him?
12 Which senses are described in the poem?
13 What happens to his senses?

▪▪▪ Third reading

14 Why did the speaker not understand those 'lost faces'?
15 Do you feel sorry for the speaker?
16 Do you think he is a selfish person?
17 The personal tragedy is more difficult than the public. Do you agree?
18 Why do you think the poet gave voice to this man?

Ⓛ Link to language

19 Write a diary entry for a survivor on the *Titanic*, recalling the night of the tragedy.
20 Write a newspaper article about the sinking of the *Titanic* as it would have been written at the time.

Antarctica

For Richard Ryan

DEREK MAHON

Prescribed for the Ordinary Level exams in 2008 and 2009

'I am just going outside and may be some time.'
The others nod, pretending not to know.
At the heart of the ridiculous, the sublime.

He leaves them reading and begins to climb,
Goading his ghost into the howling snow;   5
He is just going outside and may be some time.

The tent recedes beneath its crust of rime
And frostbite is replaced by vertigo:
At the heart of the ridiculous, the sublime.

Need we consider it some sort of crime,   10
This numb self-sacrifice of the weakest? No,
He is just going outside and may be some time –

In fact, for ever. Solitary enzyme,
Though the night yield no glimmer there will glow,
At the heart of the ridiculous, the sublime.   15

He takes leave of the earthly pantomime
Quietly, knowing it is time to go.
'I am just going outside and may be some time.'
At the heart of the ridiculous, the sublime.

GLOSSARY
Sublime: Lofty, majestic
Goading: Urging on
Rime: Frost formed from cloud or fog

Vertigo: Dizziness causing loss of balance
Enzyme: An enzyme causes a living organism to change but is not changed itself

Pre-reading

1 Where is Antarctica?
2 What images does it conjure up for you?
3 Do some research on Scott of the Antarctic and Lawrence Oates.

First reading

4 Where is Oates going in the first line?
5 What will happen to him after he leaves?
6 Does the poet say how Oates should be judged?

Second reading

7 What does an enzyme do?
8 What is Oates trying to do?
9 What is the mood in the poem?
10 How does the repetition help this mood?
11 What effect does the rhyme have on the mood of the poem?

Third reading

12 What does the poet mean by the phrase 'At the heart of the ridiculous, the sublime'?
13 What does the poet mean by the phrase 'earthly pantomime'?

Fourth reading

14 Do you think that Oates was a hero or a fool? Why?
15 What does the poet think?
16 Do you think this is a powerful poem?

Link to language

17 Write Oates' diary entry for the night before he left the camp.

Bearhugs

ROGER McGOUGH

Prescribed for the Ordinary Level exams in 2008 and 2010

Whenever my sons call round we hug each other.
Bearhugs. Both bigger than me and stronger
They lift me off my feet, crushing the life out of me.

They smell of oil paint and aftershave, of beer
Sometimes and tobacco, and of women   **5**
Whose memory they seem reluctant to wash away.

They haven't lived with me for years,
Since they were tiny, and so each visit
Is an assessment, a reassurance of love unspoken.

I look for some resemblance to my family.   **10**
Seize on an expression, a lifted eyebrow,
A tilt of the head, but cannot see myself.

Though like each other, they are not like me.
But I can see in them something of my father.
Uncles, home on leave during the war.   **15**

At three or four, I loved throse straightbacked men
Towering above me, smiling and confident.
The whole world before them. Or so it seemed.

I look at my boys, slouched in armchairs
They have outgrown. See Tom in army uniform   **20**
And Finn in air force blue. Time is up.

Bearhugs. They lift me off my feet
And fifty years fall away. One son
After another, crushing the life into me.

ROGER **McGOUGH**

- **Born 1937 in Liverpool, England**
- **Educated at Hull University**
- **Along with Adrian Henri and Brian Patten, known as the Merseybeat Poets**
- **Well known for the performance of his poetry**
- **Writes funny, accessible poems with real concerns**
- **Recently he has used his poetry to promote human rights**

First reading

1 What is a bearhug?
2 Do you get an impression of the two sons? What do you think they look like? What are their personalities like?
3 Is the poet disappointed that they don't look like him?
4 What type of men were his father and uncles?
5 How do the boys remind the poet of his uncles and father?
6 In what ways are they different?

Second reading

7 How do the 'fifty years fall away'?
8 How does the final verse mirror the first verse? What differences occur?

Third reading

9 How does the poet's time with the sons make him feel?
10 Do you think that there is a hint of regret in the poem? Where might this be?

Link to language

11 Write a story called 'Lost Memories' using the Aesthetic Use of Language.

Buying Winkles

PAULA MEEHAN

Prescribed for the Ordinary Level exam in 2009

My mother would spare me sixpence and say,
'Hurry up now and don't be talking to strange
men on the way.' I'd dash from the ghosts
on the stairs where the bulb had blown
out into Gardiner Street, all relief.   **5**
A bonus if the moon was in the strip of sky
between the tall houses, or stars out,
but even in rain I was happy – the winkles
would be wet and glisten blue like little
night skies themselves. I'd hold the tanner tight   **10**
and jump every crack in the pavement,
I'd wave up to women at sills or those
lingering in doorways and weave a glad path through
men heading out for the night.

She'd be sitting outside the Rosebowl Bar   **15**
on an orange-crate, a pram loaded
with pails of winkles before her.
When the bar doors swung open they'd leak
the smell of men together with drink
and I'd see light in golden mirrors.   **20**
I envied each soul in the hot interior.

I'd ask her again to show me the right way
to do *it*. She'd take a pin from her shawl –
'Open the eyelid. So. Stick it in
till you feel a grip, then slither him out.   **25**
Gently, mind.' The sweetest extra winkle
that brought the sea to me.
'Tell yer Ma I picked them fresh this morning.'

I'd bear the newspaper twists
bulging fat with winkles   **30**
proudly home, like torches.

PAULA **MEEHAN**

- Born 1955 in Dublin
- Grew up in the north inner city area
- Collections: *The Woman Who Was Marked by Winter*, 1991; *Pillow Talk*, 1994; *Dharmyaka*, 2000
- Play: *The Cell*, 1999

▬ Pre-reading

1 What are winkles? Talk to older people in your community and try to find out what they looked like, tasted like etc.

▪ First reading

2 What age do you think the poet was when she was sent to buy the winkles?
3 Where is Gardiner Street?
4 What type of community does she live in?
5 Why is the girl so happy?
6 Describe the scene at the Rosebowl Bar.
7 What impression do you get of this establishment?

▪▪ Second reading

8 What does the girl think of the pub?
9 What age do you think the winkle seller is?

▪▪▪ Third reading

10 Do you think the girl knows how to open the winkles properly?
11 Why does she ask the woman again and again to show her how to open the shell?
12 How does the girl feel on the way home?
13 How does the use of dialogue affect the poem?
14 How does the poet's uses of 'I' affect the mood of the poem?

▦ Fourth reading

15 What is your favourite image in the poem? Why?
16 What does the poem tell us about looking back?
17 How does the speaker feel now about this time?
18 Do you think times have changed from when the poem was set?

My Father Perceived as a Vision of St Francis

For Brendan Kennelly

PAULA MEEHAN

Prescribed for the Ordinary Level exam in 2010

It was the piebald horse in next door's garden
frightened me out of a dream
with her dawn whinny. I was back
in the boxroom of the house,
my brother's room now, **5**
full of ties and sweaters and secrets.
Bottles chinked on the doorstep,
the first bus pulled up to the stop.
The rest of the house slept

except for my father. I heard **10**
him rake the ash from the grate,
plug in the kettle, hum a snatch of a tune.
Then he unlocked the back door
and stepped out into the garden.

Autumn was nearly done, the first frost **15**
whitened the slates of the estate.
He was older than I had reckoned,
his hair completely silver,
and for the first time I saw the stoop
of his shoulder, saw that **20**
his leg was stiff. What's he at?
So early and still stars in the west?

They came then: birds
of every size, shape, colour; they came
from the hedges and shrubs, **25**
from eaves and garden sheds,
from the industrial estate, outlying fields,
from Dubber Cross they came
and the ditches of the North Road.
The garden was a pandemonium **30**
when my father threw up his hands
and tossed the crumbs to the air. The sun

96 SIGNS

cleared O'Reilly's chimney
and he was suddenly radiant
a perfect vision of St Francis,
made whole, made young again,
in a Finglas garden.

35

⦿ First reading

1 The poet wakes up to a variety of sounds. What are they? Why does the poet appeal to our sense of sound instead of our other senses?

2 How does the poet feel when she wakes up? Why does she feel like this?

3 Everyone is asleep except the poet and her father. Describe what each does.

4 Describe the poet's father.

5 Is this person she sees as her father familiar to her?

6 A fantastic scene unfolds in the back garden. Describe it.

⦿⦿ Second reading

7 There is a spiritual aspect to what the father does in the back garden. What is it? How does the poet create this effect?

8 Describe the setting of the poem. Is the setting important to your understanding of the overall poem?

9 Discuss the significance of the title.

10 It is not the setting but what happens there that is important in this poem. Discuss.

⦿⦿⦿ Third reading

11 Paula Meehan has said that the joy of writing poetry is 'getting the right word in the right place, at manipulating the rhythm, at swinging the sentence around the lines, at pushing my own breath into patterns that enact the emotional state I'm expressing'. Does she achieve these ideals in this poem?

When I Consider

JOHN MILTON

Prescribed for the Ordinary Level exam in 2010

When I consider how my light is spent,
E're half my days, in this dark world and wide,
And that one Talent which is death to hide,
Lodg'd with me useless, though my Soul more bent
To serve therewith my Maker, and present   **5**
My true account, least he returning chide,
Doth God exact day-labour, light deny'd,
I fondly ask; But patience to prevent
That murmur, soon replies, God doth not need
Either man's work or his own gifts, who best   **10**
Bear his milde yoak, they serve him best, his State
Is Kingly. Thousands at his bidding speed
And post o're Land and Ocean without rest:
They also serve who only stand and waite.

GLOSSARY

Consider: Think about, ponder
My light is spent: My eyesight is gone
One talent: His writing talent (referring to the Parable of Talents in the Bible: a servant buries the talent God gives him instead of using it and making the most of it. He is punished by God)
Lodg'd: God lodged (invested) a talent in Milton
More bent: Determined

My maker: God
Chide: Scold, give out to
Day-labour: A full day's work
Fondly: Foolishly
Bear his milde yoak: Put up with the little burdens
Murmur: Quiet complaint
His bidding: Doing what he asks

JOHN **MILTON**

- **Born 1608 in London** • **Educated at St Paul's School and Christ Church College, Cambridge receiving a BA in 1629 and an MA in 1632** • **Received the nickname 'The Lady of Christ's' in Christ Church College for his long flowing hair and his gentle, mannerly and polite ways** • **Early attempts at poetry consisted in paraphrasing the psalms** • **Wrote in English and in Latin** • **Predominantly religious themes** • **Travelled to France and Italy where he met Galileo** • **Became politically motivated on his return to England, commenting on the religious and political upheaval and the Civil War** • **Wrote pamphlets in support of divorce after his hasty marriage to Mary Powell in 1642** • **Rejoined her in 1645** • **Supporter of Oliver Cromwell and of the execution of King Charles in 1649** • **Became Cromwell's secretary for foreign tongues in 1649** • **Became blind in 1652; Mary died having borne him three daughters** • **Married Katherine Woodstock in 1655 but she died in childbirth in 1658** • **His political career ended in 1660 with the return of the monarchy** • **Returned to writing poetry and wrote his two great masterpieces:** *Paradise Lost*, **1667 and** *Paradise Regained*, **1671** • **Died in 1674**

Pre-reading

1 Do you think God would be happy with how you have used the talents given to you?

2 What is your impression of God / a higher being? From where is this impression formed? What influences our view of God? Parents? The Bible? Television?

First reading

3 Milton is concerned that God will be angry with him for not making full use of his talent for writing. Why has he not fully used his talent? Where in the poem do you see this?

4 What is Milton's impression of the world?

5 Milton compares his relationship with God in banking terms: 'lodg'd' and 'my true account'. Explain these terms and Milton's use of them.

6 Where does Milton refer to his blindness?

7 What is the message of this poem?

Second reading

8 What are the main questions Milton is asking in the octet?

9 Trace the development of thought through the full poem. Where are there changes?

10 What is your impression of Milton? What words or images support your view?

11 What kind of picture does Milton present of God? Is this how you see God / a higher being?

12 Is the message of this poem a modern topic or is it a topic firmly rooted in the past?

Third reading

13 What evidence is there in the poem of the poet's profound religious faith?

14 What is the meaning of the final line?

15 Light, banking and a divine king are three dominant images in this poem. Discuss each one using words and phrases to build your picture of each.

16 Outline the use Milton makes of the Petrarchan sonnet form in this poem.

The Locket

JOHN MONTAGUE

Prescribed for the Ordinary Level exams in 2007 and 2009

Sing a last song
for the lady who has gone,
fertile source of guilt and pain.
The worst birth in the annals of Brooklyn,
that was my cue to come on,　　　　　　　　　　　**5**
my first claim to fame.

Naturally, she longed for a girl,
and all my infant curls of brown
couldn't excuse my double blunder
coming out, both the wrong sex,　　　　　　　　　**10**
and the wrong way around.
Not readily forgiven.

So you never nursed me
and when all my father's songs
couldn't sweeten the lack of money,　　　　　　　**15**
when poverty comes through the door
love flies up the chimney,
your favourite saying.

Then you gave me away,
might never have known me,　　　　　　　　　　　**20**
if I had not cycled down
to court you like a young man,
teasingly untying your apron,
drinking by the fire, yarning

Of your wild, young days　　　　　　　　　　　　　**25**
which didn't last long, for you,
lovely Molly, the belle of your small town,
landed up mournful and chill
as the constant rain that lashes it,
wound into your cocoon of pain.　　　　　　　　　**30**

Standing in that same hallway,
don't come again, you say, roughly,
I start to get fond of you, John,
and then you are up and gone;
the harsh logic of a forlorn woman　　　　　　　**35**
resigned to being alone.

And still, mysterious blessing,
I never knew, until you were gone,
that, always around your neck,
you wore an oval locket
with an old picture in it,
of a child in Brooklyn.

40

JOHN **MONTAGUE**

- **Born 1929 in Brooklyn, New York, USA**
- **Raised by his aunts on a farm in Garvaghy, Co. Tyrone**
- **Educated at University College, Dublin, Yale and Berkeley, California**
- **Taught at University College, Cork and in America**
- **Collections: *The Rough Field*, 1973; *The Dark Kingdom*, 1984**

Pre-reading

1 What does a locket represent to you?

First reading

2 From your reading of the poem, in what type of family life did the poet grow up?
3 How do you think the poet's mother felt about the birth?
4 How does the poet reflect on his own birth?
5 What happened to the poet?

Second reading

6 How did he become close to his mother again?
7 How did the mother react to his visits?
8 What was his mother's youth like?

Third reading

9 What surprise did he get after her death?
10 How did he feel about this?
11 Is this poem a good tribute to his mother?
12 This is a poem about hope. Do you agree?

Link to language

13 Write the poet's speech at his mother's burial.

Like dolmens round my childhood...

JOHN MONTAGUE

Prescribed for the Ordinary Level exams in 2007, 2008 and 2009

Jamie MacCrystal sang to himself,
A broken song without tune, without words;
He tipped me a penny every pension day.
Fed kindly crusts to winter birds.   **5**
When he died, his cottage was robbed,
Mattress and money box torn and searched.
Only the corpse they didn't disturb.

Maggie Owens was surrounded by animals,
A mongrel bitch and shivering pups,   **10**
Even in her bedroom a she-goat cried.
She was a well of gossip defiled,
Fanged chronicler of a whole countryside;
Reputed a witch, all I could find
Was her lonely need to deride.   **15**

The Nialls lived along a mountain lane
Where heather bells bloomed, clumps of foxglove.
All were blind, with Blind Pension and Wireless,
Dead eyes serpent-flicked as one entered
To shelter from a downpour of mountain rain.   **20**
Crickets chirped under the rocking hearthstone
Until the muddy sun shone out again.

Mary Moore lived in a crumbling gatehouse,
Famous as Pisa for its leaning gable.
Bag-apron and boots, she trampled the fields   **25**
Driving lean cattle from a miry stable.
A by-word for fierceness, she fell asleep
Over love stories, Red Star and Red Circle,
Dreamed of gypsy love rites, by firelight sealed.

Wild Billy Eagleson married a Catholic servant girl   **30**
When all his Loyal family passed on:
We danced round him shouting 'To Hell with King Billy',
And dodged from the arc of his flailing blackthorn.
Forsaken by both creeds, he showed little concern
Until the Orange drums banged past in the summer   **30**
And bowler and sash aggressively shone.

Curate and doctor trudged to attend them,
Through knee-deep snow, through summer heat,

From main road to lane to broken path,
Gulping the mountain air with painful breath.
Sometimes they were found by neighbours,
Silent keepers of a smokeless hearth,
Suddenly cast in the mould of death.

Ancient Ireland, indeed! I was reared by her bedside,
The rune and the chant, evil eye and averted head,
Fomorian fierceness of family and local feud.
Gaunt figures of fear and of friendliness,
For years they trespassed on my dreams,
Until once, in a standing circle of stones,
I felt their shadow pass

Into that dark permanence of ancient forms.

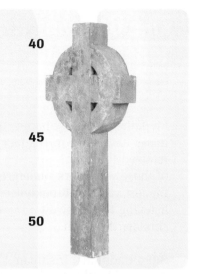

40

45

50

GLOSSARY

Mongrel: Cross-breed
Defiled: Tainted or contaminated
Chronicler: One who keeps a record

Deride: To mock or ridicule
Miry: Muddy or mucky
Fomorian: Demons or evil gods of ancient Ireland

▬ Pre-reading

1 Find a Junior Certificate History book and research dolmens. Where were they found? What was their function?

▪ First reading

2 According to the poet, what was Jamie MacCrystal like?
3 How did he die?
4 Did he deserve to die this way?
5 How did it affect the poet?
6 How did the local community see Maggie Owens?
7 What did the poet see in her?
8 How did people use the Nialls?
9 How did Mary Moore's public perception and the private reality differ?
10 How did the locals treat Billy Eagleson?
11 How did he treat the locals?
12 Was there more to him than his religion?

▪▪ Second reading

13 What do all these people have in common?

14 How did these people die?
15 How did they affect the poet in later years?

▪▪▪ Third reading

16 What is the poet's mood in the last verse?
17 What sounds dominate this verse?
18 What effect does this have on the poem?

▦ Fourth reading

19 How does the poet leave these people behind?
20 Where does he think they belong now?

Ⓛ Link to language

21 Can you think of an unusual character in your own area? How are they treated? Has this poem changed your way of thinking about them?
22 Write a description of this person.

The Cage

JOHN MONTAGUE

Prescribed for the Ordinary Level exams in 2007, 2008 and 2009

My father, the least happy
man I have known. His face
retained the pallor
of those who work underground:
the lost years in Brooklyn   5
listening to a subway
shudder the earth.

But a traditional Irishman
who (released from his grille
in the Clark St I.R.T.)   10
drank neat whiskey until
he reached the only element
he felt at home in any longer:
    brute oblivion.

And yet picked himself
up, most mornings,   15
to march down the street
extending his smile
to all sides of the good,
all-white neighbourhood
belled by St Teresa's church.   20

When he came back
we walked together
across fields of Garvaghy
to see hawthorn on the summer
hedges, as though   25
he had never left;
a bend of the road

which still sheltered
primroses. But we
did not smile in   30
the shared complicity
of a dream, for when
weary Odysseus returns
Telemachus should leave.

Often as I descend   35
into subway or underground
I see his bald head behind
the bars of the small booth;
the mark of an old car
accident beating on his   40
ghostly forehead.

Pre-reading

1 What kind of poem do you expect to follow the title 'The Cage'? What thoughts enter your mind when you think of a cage?

First reading

2 What did the speaker's father look like? Where did he work?

3 'My father, the least happy man I have known.' Is this sentiment obvious all through the poem?

4 Are we told, in the poem, what has caused and contributed to the speaker's father's unhappiness?

5 The speaker's father had a public face and a private face. What was the difference between the two?

6 Describe the father's visit home to Garvaghy.

Second reading

7 In verse 5 there is a reference to the Greek tale of Odysseus and Telemachus. Why has this reference been included in the poem?

8 What was the state of the father–son relationship in this poem? Are they close?

9 The poet's father had a hard life; the poet describes it as 'the lost years'. Describe his life in Brooklyn. What images does the poet create? What are the sights and sounds of New York?

10 What did the father do to escape his torment?

Third reading

11 What does the poet feel about his father? Are his feelings complex or straight-forward? Do his feelings change? Discuss.

12 What is the poet's mood as he remembers his father's life?

13 Look again at your answer to question one. Is the title 'The Cage' appropriate to the content of this poem? Explain your answer.

14 The title 'The Cage' not only refers to the father's job but also to his sense of imprisonment. Discuss the importance of the title to the overall effect of the poem.

15 Discuss each of the following in the context of the poem: emigration, poor working conditions, loneliness, father–son relationships, public persona / private pain.

16 This poem is racked with pain and torment. Who is suffering? The father? The son? Discuss.

17 What, in your view, is the most vivid and memorable image in the poem?

Strawberries

EDWIN MORGAN

Prescribed for the Ordinary Level exam in 2007

There were never strawberries
like the ones we had
that sultry afternoon
sitting on the step
of the open french window   5
facing each other
your knees held in mine
the blue plates in our laps
the strawberries glistening
in the hot sunlight   10
we dipped them in sugar
looking at each other
not hurrying the feast
for one to come
the empty plates   15
laid on the stone together
with the two forks crossed
and I bent towards you
sweet in that air
in my arms   20
abandoned like a child
from your eager mouth
the taste of strawberries
in my memory
lean back again let me love you   25

let the sun beat
on our forgetfulness
one hour of all
the heat intense
and summer lightening   30
on the Kilpatrick hills

let the storm wash the plates

EDWIN **MORGAN**

- **Born 1920 in Glasgow, Scotland**
- **Taught for many years at Glasgow University**
- **Has translated poetry from many languages**
- **He was first published in 1952**
- **Collection: *Selected Poems*, 1985**

🔲 First reading

1 Describe the scene of the poem in your own words.
2 What is the mood of the two people?
3 What type of relationship do they have?
4 Why were there never strawberries like the ones they had that day?
5 What happens as the poem develops?

🔲 Second reading

6 How does the weather affect their mood?
7 What is your favourite image in the poem?
8 What are the dominant sounds in the poem?
9 How do they affect the mood?

🔲 Third reading

10 Why is the last line left on its own?
11 Why doesn't the poet use punctuation?
12 What effect does this have?

🔲 Fourth reading

13 In this poem the poet doesn't try to make a message as much as a mood. Do you agree?

🔲 Link to language

14 Write a story containing the line 'that sultry afternoon sitting on the step of the French window'.

Anseo

PAUL MULDOON

Prescribed for the Ordinary Level exams in 2007 and 2008

When the Master was calling the roll
At the primary school in Collegelands,
You were meant to call back Anseo
And raise your hand
As your name occurred.   **5**
Anseo, meaning here, here and now,
All present and correct,
Was the first word of Irish I spoke.
The last name on the ledger
Belonged to Joseph Mary Plunkett Ward   **10**
And was followed, as often as not,
By silence, knowing looks,
A nod and a wink, the Master's droll
'And where's our little Ward-of-court?'

I remember the first time he came back   **15**
The Master had sent him out
Along the hedges
To weigh up for himself and cut
A stick with which he would be beaten.
After a while, nothing was spoken;   **20**
He would arrive as a matter of course
With an ash-plant, a salley-rod.
Or, finally, the hazel-wand
He had whittled down to a whip-lash,
Its twist of red and yellow lacquers   **25**
Sanded and polished,
And altogether so delicately wrought
That he had engraved his initials on it.

I last met Joseph Mary Plunkett Ward
In a pub just over the Irish border.   **30**
He was living in the open,
In a secret camp
On the other side of the mountain.
He was fighting for Ireland,
Making things happen.   **35**
And he told me, Joe Ward,
Of how he had risen through the ranks

To Quartermaster, Commandant:
How every morning at parade
His volunteers would call back Anseo   **40**
And raise their hands
As their names occurred.

PAUL **MULDOON**

- **Born 1951 in Portadown, Co. Armagh**   • **Raised in a
small village called The Moy featured in many of his
poems**   • **Educated at Queen's University, Belfast**
• **Worked for the BBC**   • **Works as a university lecturer
in the USA**   • **Collections:** *Quoof*, **1984;** *Madoc*, **1990**
• **Opera:** *Shining Brow*

⊟ Pre-reading

1 What are your own memories of primary
   school, your teachers, friends, characters
   in your own class, especially the ones that
   got into a lot of trouble?

⊡ First reading

2 What does the word *anseo* mean? When
   was it used in school?
3 Describe the master. What does his title
   say about him?
4 Why are Ward's forenames important?
5 What is Ward's life like at the end of the
   poem?
6 What do you imagine his soldiers' lives are
   like under his command?

⊡⊡ Second reading

7 Why does Ward take such care with the
   stick?
8 The narrator of the poem and the master

use puns. Isolate each pun and explain to
what they are referring.

⊡⊡⊡ Third reading

9 The tone in the first verse is very
   unemotional. What effect does this have
   on your reading of the poem? Does the
   tone change later on? If so, how?
10 What contradictions are there in the
    poem?
11 How do the first and last verse mirror
    each other? Why does the poet do this?

⊞ Fourth reading

12 'What goes around comes around'. Do
    you think that this saying is relevant to this
    poem?
13 W. H. Auden said that 'Poetry makes
    nothing happen'. Compare that idea to
    Ward's statement that he was 'making
    things happen'.

The Reading Lesson

RICHARD MURPHY

Prescribed for the Ordinary Level exams in 2007 and 2008

Fourteen years old, learning the alphabet,
He finds letters harder to catch than hares
Without a greyhound. Can't I give him a dog
To track them down, or put them in a cage?
He's caught in a trap, until I let him go,   **5**
Pinioned by 'Don't you want to learn to read?'
'I'll be the same man whatever I do.'

He looks at a page as a mule balks at a gap
From which a goat may hobble out and bleat.
His eyes jink from a sentence like flushed snipe   **10**
Escaping shot. A sharp word, and he'll mooch
Back to his piebald mare and bantam cock.
Our purpose is as tricky to retrieve
As mercury from a smashed thermometer.

'I'll not read anymore.' Should I give up?   **15**
His hands, long-fingered as a Celtic scribe's,
Will grow callous, gathering sticks or scrap;
Exploring pockets of the horny drunk
Loiterers at the fairs, giving them lice.
A neighbour chuckles. 'You can never tame   **20**
The wild duck: when his wings grow, he'll fly off.'

If books resembled roads, he'd quickly read:
But they're small farms to him, fenced by the page,
Ploughed into lines with letters drilled like oats:
A field of tasks he'll always be outside.   **25**
If words were bank-notes, he would filch a wad;
If they were pheasants, they'd be in his pot
For breakfast, or if wrens he'd make them king.

GLOSSARY
Pinioned: Bound
Snipe: A long-billed bird like a woodcock

Filch: Steal

RICHARD **MURPHY**

- **Born 1927 in Co. Mayo**
- **Lives in Co. Dublin**
- **Collections:** *The Battle of Aughrim*, 1968; *High Island*, 1974; *The Mirror Wall*, 1989 • **Autobiography:** *The Kick*, 2001

First reading

1 What is the boy's background? Can you tell from the evidence in the poem?
2 Does the boy fit a stereotype?
3 What is the relationship between the two in the poem? Is it equal?
4 Do you think the boy will give up?
5 Do you think the narrator will?

Second reading

6 Will learning to read really change the boy's life?
7 How does the narrator feel about the exercise?
8 Do you think the neighbour is right? Do you think a wild duck should be tamed?

Third reading

9 Why does the poet use so many nature-related metaphors in the poem?
10 What do you think of the dialogue used in the poem?
11 How does the last verse change the tone of the poem?
12 In the second verse the boy's reactions are compared to animals'. Do you think these descriptions are delivered well? Are they fair?

Fourth reading

13 With whom of the two main characters in the poem do you empathise most? Why?

Wolves in the Zoo

HOWARD NEMEROV

Prescribed for the Ordinary Level exams in 2007 and 2010

They look like big dogs badly drawn, drawn wrong.
A legend on their cage tells us there is
No evidence that any of their kind
Has ever attacked man, woman, or child.

Now it turns out there were no babies dropped   **5**
In sacrifice, delaying tactics, from
Siberian sleds; now it turns out, so late,
That Little Red Ridinghood and her Gran

Were the aggressors with the slavering fangs
And tell-tale tails; now it turns out at last   **10**
That grey wolf and timber wolf are near extinct,
Done out of being by the tales we tell

Told us by Nanny in the nursery;
Young sparks we were, to set such forest fires
As blazed from story into history   **15**
And put such bounty on their wolvish heads

As brought the few survivors to our terms,
Surrendered in happy Babylon among
The peacock dusting off the path of dust,
The tiger pacing in the stripéd shade.   **20**

HOWARD **NEMEROV**

- Born 1920 in New York, USA
- Served in the Canadian and American air forces in the Second World War
- Was US Poet Laureate from 1988–90
- Has been compared to Robert Frost
- Died in 1991

First reading

1 What does the first line tell us about the wolves?
2 Does the second sentence surprise you? Why?
3 What is the story that the poet refers to at the start of the second verse?
4 Why does he call Red Ridinghood and her Gran 'aggressors'?
5 Where are the wolves now?

Second reading

6 What has the overall effect of all the fairytales been on wolves?
7 What does the poet mean when he says 'brought the few survivors to our terms'?
8 Which sounds dominate the poem? What effect do they have?
9 How does the poet use alliteration in the poem?

Third reading

10 Do you think that humans have given wolves a fair deal throughout history?

Link to language

11 Write an article for a tabloid newspaper about a celebrity who has been harmed by rumours.

The Great Blasket Island

JULIE O'CALLAGHAN

Prescribed for the Ordinary Level exams in 2009 and 2010

Six men born on this island
have come back after twenty-one years.
They climb up the overgrown roads
to their family houses
and come out shaking their heads.   5
The roofs have fallen in
and birds have nested in the rafters.
All the white-washed rooms
all the nagging and praying
and scolding and giggling   10
and crying and gossiping
are scattered in the memories of these men.
One says, 'Ten of us, blown to the winds –
some in England, some in America, some in Dublin.
Our whole way of life – extinct.'   15
He blinks back the tears
and looks across the island
past the ruined houses, the cliffs
and out to the horizon.

Listen, mister, most of us cry sooner or later   20
over a Great Blasket Island of our own.

JULIE O'CALLAGHAN

- Born 1954 in Chicago, USA
- Lives in Naas, Co. Kildare
- Also writes for young people
- Collections: *Edible Anecdotes*, 1983; *What's What*, 1992
- Collection for young people: *Taking My Pen for a Walk*, 1988

▬ Pre-reading

1 Where is the Great Blasket Island?
2 What do you know about it or what would your impressions of it be before you read the poem?

● First reading

3 Why did the men return?
4 Was their childhood a happy time all the time?
5 What does one of the men say?
6 What does he get wrong?
7 What is the significance of this exaggeration?

●● Second reading

8 What else could they have exaggerated?
9 Does the poet have sympathy for the men?
10 What does the poet mean by the last two lines?
11 Why did it take the men twenty-one years to return?

●●● Third reading

12 What does the poet think of nostalgia?
13 What does she think of the men?
14 'Get over it!' Is this the central message of the poem?

L Link to language

15 Write a dialogue between the men on their trip to the island and on the way home.

Gunpowder

BERNARD O'DONOGHUE

Prescribed for the Ordinary Level exams in 2009 and 2010

In the weeks afterwards, his jacket hung
Behind the door in the room we called
His study, where the bikes and wellingtons
Were kept. No-one went near it, until
Late one evening I thought I'd throw it out.   5
The sleeves smelled of gunpowder, evoking . . .
Celebration – excitement – things like that,
Not destruction. What was it he shot at
And missed that time? A cock pheasant
That he hesitated too long over   10
In case it was a hen? The rat behind
The piggery that, startled by the bang,
Turned round to look before going home to its hole?

Once a neighbour who had winged a crow
Tied it to a pike thrust into the ground   15
To keep the others off the corn. It worked well,
Flapping and cawing, till my father
Cut it loose. Even more puzzlingly,
He once took a wounded rabbit off the dog
And pushed it back into the warren   20
Which undermined the wall. As for
Used cartridges, they stood well on desks,
Upright on their graven golden ends,
Supporting his fountain-pen so that
The ink wouldn't seep into his pocket.   25

GLOSSARY
Graven: Carved

BERNARD O'DONOGHUE

- Born 1945 in Cullen, Co. Cork
- Educated at Lincoln College, Oxford
- Fellow of Wadham College, Oxford
- Editor of *The English Review*
- Many works of criticism
- Collection: *Gunpowder*, 1996

First reading

1 The poem begins mysteriously with the phrase 'In the weeks afterwards'. After what, do you think?
2 Why didn't anybody go near the jacket?
3 Why do you think the father kept missing things when he was shooting at them?
4 What happened with the pheasant?
5 Why did he release the rat?

Second reading

6 What do these incidents tell us about the father?
7 Explain what happened to the crow.
8 Explain the father's reaction.
9 Why do you think he put the rabbit back in the warren?
10 What did he use the bullet shells for?
11 What does this tell us about him?

Third reading

12 Do you think that the father belonged in the country? Why?
13 Do you think the son respected his father's choices? Why?

Fourth reading

14 Read Seamus Heaney's poem 'Death of a Naturalist'. Compare the sentiments in the two poems.

Link to language

15 Write a character description of the father, based on the evidence.

Looking at Them Asleep

SHARON OLDS

Prescribed for the Ordinary Level exams in 2008 and 2009

When I come home late at night and go in to kiss the children,
I see my girl with her arm curled around her head,
her face deep in unconsciousness – so
deeply centered she is in her dark self,
her mouth slightly puffed like one sated but   5
slightly pouted like one who hasn't had enough,
her eyes so closed you would think they have rolled the
iris around to face the back of her head,
the eyeball marble-naked under that
thick satisfied desiring lid,   10
she lies on her back in abandon and sealed completion,
and the son in his room, oh the son he is sideways in his bed,
one knee up as if he is climbing
sharp stairs up as into the night,
and under his thin quivering eyelids you   15
know his eyes are wide open and
staring and glazed, the blue in them so
anxious and crystally in all this darkness, and his
mouth is open, he is breathing hard from the climb
and panting a bit, his brow is crumpled   20
and pale, his long fingers curved,
his hand open, and in the center of each hand
the dry dirty boyish palm
resting like a cookie. I look at him in his
quest, the thin muscles of his arms   25
passionate and tense, I look at her with her
face like the face of a snake who has swallowed a deer,
content, content – and I know if I wake her she'll
smile and turn her face toward me though
half asleep and open her eyes and I   30
know if I wake him he'll jerk and say Don't and sit
up and stare about him in blue
unrecognition, oh my Lord how I
know these two. When love comes to me and says
Who do you know, I say This girl, this boy.   35

GLOSSARY
Sated: Satisfied

SHARON **OLDS**

- **Born 1942 in the USA**
- **Professor of creative writing at New York University**
- **Works with physically disabled people**
- **Collection:** *The Wellspring*, 1996

 ## First reading

1 In your own words describe how the girl sleeps.

2 In your own words describe how the boy sleeps.

 ## Second reading

3 What does the way they sleep tell us about each one's character?

4 How different do you think the two children are?

5 What is your favourite image from the descriptions of the two children?

6 How would each one react upon being awakened?

Third reading

7 How close is the mother to her children?

8 Make a list of all the adjectives in the poem and decide which ones are the most effective at describing the children.

9 What does the poet mean in the last three lines?

Link to language

10 Pick a child you know and write a physical description of them without using colours. Try to invent images to describe them.

The Present Moment

SHARON OLDS

Prescribed for the Ordinary Level exam in 2007

Now that he cannot sit up,
now that he just lies there
looking at the wall, I forget the one
who sat up and put on his reading glasses
and the lights in the room multiplied in the lenses.   **5**
Once he entered the hospital
I forgot the man who lay full length
on the couch, with the blanket folded around him,
that huge, crushed bud, and I have
long forgotten the man who ate food –   **10**
not dense, earthen food, like liver, but
things like pineapple, wedges of light,
the skeiny nature of light made visible.
It's as if I abandoned that ruddy man
with the swollen puckered mouth of a sweet-eater,   **15**
the torso packed with extra matter
like a planet a handful of which weighs as much as the earth, I have
left behind forever that young man my father,
that smooth-skinned, dark-haired boy,
and my father long before I knew him, when he could   **20**
only sleep, or drink from a woman's
body, a baby who stared with a steady
gaze the way he lies there, now, with his
eyes open, then the lids start down
and the milky crescent of the other world   **25**
shines, in there, for a moment, before sleep.
I stay beside him, like someone in a rowboat
staying abreast of a Channel swimmer,
you are not allowed to touch them, their limbs
glow, faintly, in the night water.   **30**

First reading

1 Who are the people in the poem?
2 What is their relationship?
3 What condition is the man in?
4 Was he always this way? What was he like before this?

Second reading

5 Describe each phase of his life as described in the poem.
6 How does the narrator feel about her father now?
7 Did she always feel this way?
8 How does she feel about their relationship?
9 Why does she feel that she is 'not allowed to touch'?
10 There are many impressions of him given. Which one strikes you the most?

Third reading

11 Of which impression is the narrator fondest?
12 'S' sounds dominate this poem. Why is this sound used? What effect does it have?
13 Examine the effectiveness of each of the metaphors: the glasses, the band, the food, the planet, the swimmer etc.

Fourth reading

14 This poem is about regret. Do you agree?
15 For whom do you think the poet wrote the poem?
16 Is there an overall theme in this poem or is the poet just describing a situation?

Child

SYLVIA PLATH

Prescribed for the Ordinary Level exams in 2007 and 2008

Your clear eye is the one absolutely beautiful thing.
I want to fill it with color and ducks,
The zoo of the new

Whose names you meditate –
April snowdrop, Indian pipe,   5
Little

Stalk without wrinkle,
Pool in which images
Should be grand and classical

Not this troublous   10
Wringing of hands, this dark
Ceiling without a star.

SYLVIA **PLATH**

- Born 1932 in Boston, USA
- Studied at Smith College and then at Cambridge
- Married the poet Ted Hughes in 1956
- Suffered from depression and had an unstable life
- Hughes left her and her two young children in 1962
- She killed herself on 11 February 1963

First reading

1 What does the poet wish for her child?

Second reading

2 Why does she want to 'fill it [his eye] with color and ducks'?

3 What do the ducks and the zoo represent to you?

4 April Snowdrop and Indian Pipe are flowers. Why does she put these in the poem?

5 What does she mean by grand and classical images?

6 What do you think about the first line?

7 Think of all these images together. What do they represent now?

Third reading

8 How do you think the child was feeling before the poem was written?

9 Do you think the poet's strategy would work?

Fourth reading

10 What is the atmosphere in the poem?

11 Do you think she is a good mother?

The Arrival of the Bee Box

SYLVIA PLATH

Prescribed for the Ordinary Level exams in 2007 and 2008

I ordered this, this clean wood box
Square as a chair and almost too heavy to lift.
I would say it was the coffin of a midget
Or a square baby
Were there not such a din in it.   5

The box is locked, it is dangerous.
I have to live with it overnight
And I can't keep away from it.
There are no windows, so I can't see what is in there.
There is only a little grid, no exit.   10

I put my eye to the grid.
It is dark, dark,
With the swarmy feeling of African hands
Minute and shrunk for export,
Black on black, angrily clambering.   15

How can I let them out?
It is the noise that appals me most of all,
The unintelligible syllables.
It is like a Roman mob,
Small, taken one by one, but my god, together!   20

I lay my ear to furious Latin.
I am not a Caesar.
I have simply ordered a box of maniacs.
They can be sent back.
They can die, I need feed them nothing, I am the owner.   25

I wonder how hungry they are.
I wonder if they would forget me
If I just undid the locks and stood back and turned into a tree.
There is the laburnum, its blond colonnades,
And the petticoats of the cherry.   30

They might ignore me immediately
In my moon suit and funeral veil.
I am no source of honey
So why should they turn on me?
Tomorrow I will be sweet God, I will set them free.   **35**

The box is only temporary.

First reading

1 What opinion does the poet have of the box when she sees it first?
2 What is her initial impression of the bees themselves?
3 What does she see when she looks into the box?
4 How does she feel in the fifth verse?
5 Do her feelings change in the sixth verse?
6 If so, why?
7 What does she decide to do?

Second reading

8 Describe the sounds the bees make.
9 How do these sounds make her feel?
10 What is your favourite image in the poem?

Third reading

11 What do you think would happen if she 'just undid the locks and stood back and turned into a tree'?
12 Why do you think the poet wrote this poem?
13 Why do you think that the last line is on its own?
14 What does the poet mean by the phrase 'I will be sweet God'?

Aunt Jennifer's Tigers

ADRIENNE RICH

Prescribed for the Ordinary Level exams in 2008, 2009 and 2010

Aunt Jennifer's tigers prance across a screen,
Bright topaz denizens of a world of green.
They do not fear the men beneath the tree;
They pace in sleek chivalric certainty.

Aunt Jennifer's fingers fluttering through her wool   5
Find even the ivory needle hard to pull.
The massive weight of Uncle's wedding band
Sits heavily upon Aunt Jennifer's hand.

When Aunt is dead, her terrified hands will lie
Still ringed with ordeals she was mastered by.   10
The tigers in the panel that she made
Will go on prancing, proud and unafraid.

GLOSSARY
Topaz: Yellow
Denizens: Those that frequent a particular place

Chivalric: Noble, honourable

ADRIENNE **RICH**

• Born 1929 in Baltimore, Maryland, USA
• Collections: *A Change of World*, 1951; *The Fact of a Doorframe*, 1984 and 2002; *An Atlas of a Difficult World*, 1991; *Midnight Salvage*, 1999; *Fox*, 2001; and *The School Among the Ruins*, 2004

First reading

1 What are Aunt Jennifer's tigers?
2 Describe what they are like.
3 What do they tell us about Aunt Jennifer?
4 What picture of Aunt Jennifer do you have in your head after the first verse?
5 Do you get a physical image of her from the second verse?
6 How do the two images differ?

Second reading

7 Why does Aunt Jennifer make her tapestries?
8 Do you think Aunt Jennifer had a happy life?

Third reading

9 What do you think of the simple rhyming scheme the poet uses?
10 What effect does this have on your reading of the poem?

Fourth reading

11 Art lives on after the artist. Do you think this is a fair summary of this poem?

Link to language

12 Write a speech promoting your favourite hobby to your classmates.

Power

ADRIENNE RICH

Prescribed for the Ordinary Level exams in 2008 and 2009

Living   in the earth-deposits   of our history

Today a backhoe divulged   out of a crumbling flank of earth
one bottle   amber perfect   a hundred-year-old
cure for fever   or melancholy   a tonic
for living on this earth   in the winters of this climate   **5**

Today I was reading about Marie Curie:
she must have known she suffered   from radiation sickness
her body bombarded for years   by the element
she had purified
It seems she denied to the end   **10**
the source of the cataracts on her eyes
the cracked and suppurating skin   of her finger-ends
till she could no longer hold   a test-tube or a pencil

She died   a famous woman   denying
her wounds   **15**
denying
her wounds   came   from the same source as her power

GLOSSARY

Backhoe: An implement for digging the ground
Divulged: Revealed
Flank: Side
Amber: Precious orange-coloured stone with mythological healing powers

Melancholy: Depression
Cataracts: A disease of the eye
Suppurating: Weeping

■ Pre-reading

1 Do some research on Marie Curie. Find out about her life and her work.

▪ First reading

2 What does the first line do? What does it tell us about what is to come?
3 What happened during the excavation?
4 What was the significance of the find?
5 What does the poet say that the amber did?
6 How was Marie Curie affected by her own work?

▪▪ Second reading

7 Is there any rhythm in the poem?
8 What effect does this have?
9 Examine the detail of what happened to Marie Curie. Why does the poet use such harsh detail?

▪▪▪ Third reading

10 In your opinion, why did Marie Curie continue her work?
11 What does the poem tell us about creativity?
12 What does the poem tell us about denial?

L Link to language

13 Imagine you are Marie Curie; write a diary of the last days of your life.

Storm Warnings

ADRIENNE RICH

Prescribed for the Ordinary Level exams in 2008, 2009 and 2010

The glass has been falling all the afternoon,
And knowing better than the instrument
What winds are walking overhead, what zone
Of grey unrest is moving across the land,
I leave the book upon a pillowed chair   **5**
And walk from window to closed window, watching
Boughs strain against the sky

And think again, as often when the air
Moves inward toward a silent core of waiting,
How with a single purpose time has traveled   **10**
By secret currents of the undiscerned
Into this polar realm. Weather abroad
And weather in the heart alike come on
Regardless of prediction.

Between foreseeing and averting change   **15**
Lies all the mastery of elements
Which clocks and weatherglasses cannot alter.
Time in the hand is not control of time,
Nor shattered fragments of an instrument
A proof against the wind; the wind will rise,   **20**
We can only close the shutters.

I draw the curtains as the sky goes black
And set a match to candles sheathed in glass
Against the keyhole draught, the insistent whine
Of weather through the unsealed aperture.   **25**
This is our sole defense against the season;
These are the things that we have learned to do
Who live in troubled regions.

GLOSSARY

The undiscerned: Those who can't perceive
Polar realm: Near the north or south pole

Sheathed: Covered
Aperture: Opening

First reading

1 What is the poet doing at the start of the poem?
2 What distracts her?
3 What does she see outside?
4 What does she say in the last line of the second verse?
5 Why does she cover the candles with a glass?

Second reading

6 What does she say can be done to stop the storm from coming?
7 What does she say can be done to prevent time from moving on?

Third reading

8 What is the mood in the poem?
9 How does the poet create this mood?
10 How does the mood of the poem contrast with the weather outside the house?

Fourth reading

11 Why do you think the poet wrote this poem?
12 What does the poem tell us about love and time?

Link to language

13 Write a story containing the line 'I draw the curtains as the sky goes black'.

Remember

CHRISTINA ROSSETTI

Prescribed for the Ordinary Level exams in 2007 and 2008

Remember me when I am gone away,
Gone far away into the silent land;
When you can no more hold me by the hand,
Nor I half turn to go, yet turning stay.
Remember me when no more day by day   5
You tell me of our future that you plann'd:
Only remember me; you understand
It will be late to counsel then or pray.
Yet if you should forget me for a while
And afterwards remember, do not grieve: 10
For if the darkness and corruption leave
A vestige of the thoughts that once I had,
Better by far you should forget and smile
Than that you should remember and be sad.

CHRISTINA **ROSSETTI**

- **Born 1830 in London**
- **Sister of painter and poet Dante Gabriel Rossetti**
- **Member of the High Anglican movement**
- **Heavily influenced by the Bible**
- **Collections:** *Goblin Market*, **1862;** *The Face of the Deep*, **1892**
- **Died in 1894**

First reading

1 What does the poet mean by the phrase 'Gone far away into the silent land'?
2 Do you know any other words or phrases for death?
3 Who do you think she is writing to?
4 How close were they?
5 Make a list of all the things that the two people in the poem can no longer do together.

Second reading

6 Why does the poet repeat the word 'remember' so often?
7 What does the poet mean in the last two lines?
8 Describe the rhyming scheme in the poem.

Third reading

9 This is a sonnet. Why do you think the poet uses this format?
10 How does the poem make you feel? Why?
11 How do you think the person for whom the poem was written felt when he/she first read this poem?

Link to language

12 Write your own epitaph.

On Passing the New Menin Gate

SIEGFRIED SASSOON

Prescribed for the Ordinary Level exams in 2008 and 2009

Who will remember, passing through this Gate,
The unheroic Dead who fed the guns?
Who shall absolve the foulness of their fate, –
Those doomed, conscripted, unvictorious ones?
    Crudely renewed, the Salient holds its own.   **5**
    Paid are its dim defenders by this pomp;
    Paid, with a pile of peace-complacent stone,
    The armies who endured that sullen swamp.

Here was the world's worst wound. And here with pride
'Their name liveth for ever,' the Gateway claims.   **10**
Was ever an immolation so belied
As these intolerably nameless names?
Well might the Dead who struggled in the slime
Rise and deride this sepulchre of crime.

GLOSSARY

Menin Gate: In Ypres, Belgium. A gate on which 54,889 names of soldiers who died in the First World War are carved. Every night a trumpet sounds the last post and a name is read from the list
Absolve: Clear of blame or guilt
Foulness: Disgusting, horrible
Fate: Destiny, what is ahead
Conscripted: Called up for compulsory military service
Unvictorious: Not having gained or won
Crudely: Vulgarly, indecently

Renewed: Replaced
Salient: Very noticeable
Pomp: Splendid display of glory
Complacent: Smug and self-satisfied
Endured: Tolerated
Sullen swamp: Gloomy, boggy marsh – the trenches
Immolation: Kill as a sacrifice
Belied: Failed to confirm
Deride: Scoff at, jeer, laugh at
Sepulchre: Tomb, grave

SIEGFRIED **SASSOON**

• Born 1886 in Kent, England • Educated at Clare College, Cambridge • Early life involved moving in fashionable literary circles and travelling to his family's country home • He enlisted in the Royal Welsh Fusiliers at the outbreak of the First World War • By 1917 he was disillusioned with the war and protested openly, complaining about those in power and their lack of concern for the men fighting on the front line • His poetry is mostly anti-war, revealing the absolute horror of life in the trenches and castigating those who had the power or influence to save the lives of soldiers • Died in 1967

● First reading

1 What is the message of this poem?
2 Is this an anti-war poem? Is there any evidence of this?

●● Second reading

3 The poet is talking about the thousands of soldiers who died during the First World War. He calls them 'unheroic', 'doomed', 'conscripted', and 'unvictorious'. What does he think of these men?
4 When these men perished they were 'crudely renewed'. What does the poet mean by this? Does he agree with a policy of renewal of soldiers?
5 What is the poet's impression of those directing the war? Where is this to be seen?

●●● Third reading

6 Is the New Menin Gate a fitting memorial to the war dead according to Sassoon?
7 Why does he refer to the names of the dead as 'nameless names'?
8 What image of life in the trenches is presented in this poem? How does Sassoon create an image of the trenches? What words and phrases does he employ?

9 Why would the dead 'rise and deride' this monument?

Link to language

10 Imagine you have been commissioned to design a fitting memorial for the war dead. Write a description of what you would build and explain why.

Fear No More the Heat o' the Sun

WILLIAM SHAKESPEARE

Prescribed for the Ordinary Level exams in 2008 and 2009

Guiderius:
Fear no more the heat o' the sun,
Nor the furious winter's rages;
Thou thy worldly task hast done,
Home art gone, and ta'en thy wages:
Golden lads and girls all must,   5
As chimney sweepers, come to dust.
Arviragus:
Fear no more the frown o' the great;
Thou art past the tyrant's stroke;
Care no more to clothe and eat;
To thee the reed is as the oak: 10
The sceptre, learning, physic must
All follow this and come to dust.
Guiderius:
Fear no more the lightning-flash,
Arviragus:
Nor the all-dreaded thunder-stone;
Guiderius:
Fear no slander, censure rash;   15
Arviragus:
Thou hast finish'd joy and moan:
Both:
All lovers young, all lovers must
Consign to thee and come to dust.
Guiderius:
No exorciser harm thee!
Arviragus:
Nor no witchcraft charm thee!   20
Guiderius:
Ghost unlaid forbear thee!
Arviragus:
Nothing ill come near thee!
Both:
Quiet consummation have;
And renownèd be thy grave!

This poem is from the play 'Cymbeline', one of Shakespeare's last plays. It is a lament or dirge – a song or poem expressing grief and mourning after a death. It is a lament for a young boy named Fidele who is presumed dead. Fidele is actually the King's disowned daughter, Imogen, who has been travelling in disguise through a forest. Guiderius and Arviragus find her and do not recognise her as their sister. They begin this lament at the loss of the young 'boy' who appears to be dead.

Rages: Storms
Home art gone: Gone to heaven
Ta'en thy wages: Taken what you earned
Tyrant's stroke: Wicked ruler's hand / touch

The reed as the oak: Reeds and rushes are the same to you now as the mighty oak
Sceptre: Ruling power (ceremonial staff held by kings and queens)
Physic: Doctor; medicine
Slander: False, malicious statement
Censure rash: Severe criticism
Consign to thee: Join up with
Exorciser: Person who can drive out evil spirits by religion
Forbear: Refrain from, leave alone
Consummation: Death
Renowned: Well known

WILLIAM **SHAKESPEARE**

- **Born 1564 in Stratford-upon-Avon, England**
- **Background not very clear** • **Father was a local mayor and Justice of the Peace** • **Educated at the King's New School** • **Trained in formal classical Roman literature**
- **Joined a group of travelling actors in London and became known both as a good actor and playwright**
- **Was part of the most successful theatrical company of his time** • **Married Anne Hathaway in 1582; she remained in Stratford while he returned to London**
- **Wrote thirty-seven plays – comedies, tragedies and histories; 154 sonnets and was part-owner of the Globe Theatre** • **Died in 1616**

First reading

1 Why should Imogen 'Fear no more the heat o' the sun'?
2 What aspects of life does one not need to fear once one is dead?
3 Does the reader need a little background information to understand this poem or can it stand alone?

Second reading

4 What is the poet's message about death as outlined in the poem?
5 How do Guiderius and Arviragus view life? Is it good, enjoyable, sad, satisfying, difficult? Discuss.

6 What image of kings and rulers do we get from the poem?
7 What are Guiderius' and Arviragus' hopes for the deceased in the final six lines?
8 'Everyone must eventually die' seems to be the dominant message of this poem. Where in the poem is this most apparent?

Third reading

9 What is the tone of this poem? Find a quotation to support your view.
10 Is this an optimistic or pessimistic poem? Refer to the poem to support your answer.

Ozymandias

PERCY BYSSHE SHELLEY

Prescribed for the Ordinary Level exam in 2008

I met a traveller from an antique land
Who said: Two vast and trunkless legs of stone
Stand in the desert . . . Near them, on the sand,
Half sunk, a shattered visage lies, whose frown,
And wrinkled lip, and sneer of cold command,   5
Tell that its sculptor well those passions read
Which yet survive, stamped on these lifeless things,
The hand that mocked them, and the heart that fed:
And on the pedestal these words appear:
'My name is Ozymandias, king of kings: 10
Look on my works, ye Mighty, and despair!'
Nothing beside remains. Round the decay
Of that colossal wreck, boundless and bare
The lone and level sands stretch far away.

GLOSSARY

Ozymandias: Ramses II – Pharaoh of Egypt in the thirteenth century BC
Antique: Ancient
Vast: Huge
Trunkless: Without a trunk (body)
Visage: Face
Sneer: Scornful expression, show of hatred and contempt
Cold command: Unfeeling, ruthless control and authority

Pedestal: Base
Despair: Feeling of complete lack of hope
Collosal: Gigantic, huge, immense
Boundless: Cannot see any borders or boundaries. Nothing except sand for as far as the eye can see
A narrative: A poem telling a story or account of events
A sonnet: A fourteen-line poem, Petrarchan in form (divided into octet and sestet)

PERCY **BYSSHE SHELLEY**

- **Born 1792 in Sussex, England** • **Son of an English well-to-do conservative gentleman** • **Educated at Eton and Oxford** • **Expelled for refusing to retract a pamphlet he wrote called** *The Necessity of Atheism* • **Held anti-religious and anti-monarchy views** • **Spoke out about the need for reforms in society and in political spheres** • **Saw the role of poet as important in society** • **Married a young schoolgirl in 1811 but eloped to Europe with Mary Wollstonecraft Godwin (author of** *Frankenstein***)** • **Had few admirers in his lifetime but is much respected now** • **Drowned age thirty in a boating accident** • **A Romantic – not a writer of love poetry but instead someone who reacted against formality and restraint. Romantics believed that the individual's feelings and imagination were important and that society was a corrupting influence. Romantics celebrated art and nature over city life and civilisation**

▬ Pre-reading

1 Say the word 'Ozymandias' aloud or in your head. What does the word conjure up for you? If a person was called Ozymandias in what period of history do you think they would have lived? What would they have been like?

● First reading

2 After you read this poem for the first time divide it into sentences, writing out each one. Now re-read it and see does the poem become easier to read and understand?
3 Describe the statue the speaker saw in the desert.
4 What state was it in?
5 How did it come to be in that state?
6 Describe the Pharaoh and say what kind of person you imagine Ozymandias was.
7 How did the Pharaoh want to be remembered? What does his epitaph on the pedestal tell us about him?
8 Why was the statue of Ozymandias originally constructed?

●● Second reading

9 What do we learn about the sculptor? Was he good at his job?
10 What does the poet mean in the line 'The hand that mocked them, and the heart that fed:'?
11 Why does the poet talk about the sand?
12 How important to the poem is the image of the desert?

●●● Third reading

13 Nature is more powerful than any one man. Do you think that this is one of the messages of the poem?
14 What does this poem tell the reader about power?
15 What do you think was Shelley's attitude to the statue as it lay wrecked in the sand?
16 There are three voices in the poem; name them and state what does each have to say? Which voice is the most powerful? Why?
17 As the huge statues of Saddam Hussein were pulled down all over Iraq in 2003 are there any similarities or conclusions we can draw?

The Hunchback in the Park

DYLAN THOMAS

Prescribed for the Ordinary Level exams in 2009 and 2010

The hunchback in the park
A solitary mister
Propped between trees and water
From the opening of the garden lock
That lets the trees and water enter   5
Until the Sunday sombre bell at dark

Eating bread from a newspaper
Drinking water from the chained cup
That the children filled with gravel
In the fountain basin where I sailed
     my ship   10
Slept at night in a dog kennel
But nobody chained him up.

Like the park birds he came early
Like the water he sat down
And Mister they called Hey mister   15
The truant boys from the town
Running when he had heard them clearly
On out of sound

Past lake the rockery
Laughing when he shook his paper   20
Hunchbacked in mockery
Through the loud zoo of the willow
     groves
Dodging the park keeper
With his stick that picked up leaves.

And the old dog sleeper   25
Alone between nurses and swans
While the boys among willows
Made the tigers jump out of their eyes
To roar on the rockery stones
And the groves were blue
     with sailors   30

Made all day until bell time
A woman figure without fault
Straight as a young elm
Straight and tall from his crooked
     bones
That she might stand in the night   35
After the locks and the chains

All night in the unmade park
After the railings and shrubberies
The birds the grass the trees the lake
And the wild boys innocent as
     strawberries   40
Had followed the hunchback
To his kennel in the dark.

GLOSSARY
Sombre: Dark and gloomy
Truant: Student who skips school without permission

Grove: Group of trees

DYLAN **THOMAS**

- Born 1914 in the Welsh seaport of Swansea
- No formal third level education   • Worked in the local newspaper offices and headed for London in 1934
- Worked as a broadcaster, prose writer, poet and lecturer
- Drank excessively and lived a tumultuous life
- His poetry often reflects his life and is full of energy and burning intensity   • 'My poetry is the record of my individual struggle from darkness towards some measure of light.'   • Died in 1953 in New York, USA during a poetry-reading tour

Pre-reading

1   What is a 'hunchback'? Describe the physical appearance of a 'hunchback'. Is it acceptable to label people because of physical features?

First reading

2   Describe the park. What words and phrases help build the image of the park?
3   Describe the hunchback as he is presented to us in the poem.
4   How does the hunchback spend his day? What kind of life does he lead?
5   What image is portrayed of the 'truant boys'? How do they relate to the hunchback?

Second reading

6   Where does the hunchback go at night?
7   Describe the woman mentioned in lines 32–6. Who is she? Is she real or imaginary? Does she give comfort to the hunchback?
8   Describe the hunchback's emotional state. Is there a note of mental instability apparent in the poem? Where do you find this?
9   Do you pity the hunchback?

Third reading

10   There are some words and phrases which seem unusual and don't appear to fit in with the rest of the poem:
'Like the water he sat down'
'Alone between nurses and swans'
'And the groves were blue with sailors'
'And the wild boys innocent as strawberries'
What do you think the poet means in these lines?
11   In spite of the many mentions of chains and locks and bells the hunchback seems to live a free and uncontrolled life. Discuss.
12   Even after the park has been shut up for the night and everyone has gone home, the hunchback is haunted by visions. What does he see? What effect do they have on him?

Link to language

13   Imagine you were a visitor to the park. You watch the hunchback as he makes his way along, encounters the 'truant boys', eats and drinks and passes the day. Write a diary entry describing the whole scene and how it affects you.

Adlestrop

EDWARD THOMAS

Prescribed for the Ordinary Level exam in 2007

Yes, I remember Adlestrop –
The name, because one afternoon
Of heat the express-train drew up there
Unwontedly. It was late June.

The steam hissed. Someone cleared his throat.   **5**
No one left and no one came
On the bare platform. What I saw
Was Adlestrop – only the name

And willows, willow-herb, and grass,
And meadowsweet, and haycocks dry,   **10**
No whit less still and lonely fair
Than the high cloudlets in the sky.

And for that minute a blackbird sang
Close by, and round him, mistier,
Farther and farther, all the birds   **15**
Of Oxfordshire and Gloucestershire.

GLOSSARY
Unwontedly: Unusually
Haycock: Small haystacks

Whit: The least possible amount

EDWARD **THOMAS**

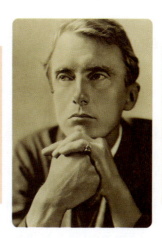

- **Born 1878 in the London district of Lambeth**
- **Educated at Lincoln College, Oxford**
- **Often felt drained and depressed as a result of a strenuous and exhausting workload**
- **Was a prolific writer more as a result of a large demanding family than inspiration**
- **Joined the army in 1915 and was killed in the battle of Arris in 1917**

▬ Pre-reading

1 Think of a town that you have passed through but didn't know well. What were your impressions of it?
2 What does the name 'Adlestrop' suggest to you?

▪ First reading

3 Why did the train stop?
4 Describe what the poet sees.
5 Describe how the poet feels.

▪▪ Second reading

6 What is the mood in the poem?
7 Which is your favourite image in the poem?
8 What sounds dominate the poem?

▪▪▪ Third reading

9 Why do you think the poet wrote this poem?
10 What does he want to remember?

L Link to language

11 Write a review for your school magazine of your favourite holiday destination.

Peace

HENRY VAUGHAN

Prescribed for the Ordinary Level exams in 2007 and 2010

My Soul, there is a Countrie
Far beyond the stars,
Where stands a winged Centrie
All skilfull in the wars,
There above noise, and danger   5
Sweet peace sits crown'd with smiles,
And one born in a Manger
Commands the Beauteous files,
He is thy gracious friend,
And (O my Soul awake!)   10
Did in pure love descend
To die here for thy sake,
If thou canst get but thither,
There growes the flowre of peace,
The Rose that cannot wither,   15
Thy fortresse, and thy ease;
Leave then thy foolish ranges;
For none can thee secure,
But one, who never changes,
Thy God, thy life, thy Cure.   20

GLOSSARY
Centrie: A guard or protector
Gracious: Kind, polite and pleasant

Thither: There
Fortresse: Castle

144 SIGNS

HENRY **VAUGHAN**

- **Born 1622 in Wales**
- **Studied at Oxford**
- **Practised as a doctor**
- **Fought in the English Civil War on the Royalist side**
- **A profound religious experience made him stop writing
  love poetry and devote himself to writing for God**
- **Died in 1695**

◘ First reading

1   What does the poet mean by the phrase
    'a Countrie / Far beyond the stars'?
2   Who is the poet describing in the poem?
3   Who is the poet talking to in the poem?
4   What does he want the reader to do?

◘◘ Second reading

5   How many sentences are in the poem?
6   Does the answer surprise you?
7   How does this rhythm affect the poem's
    mood?

◘◘◘ Third reading

8   Examine the militaristic images in the
    poem. Why does the poet use them?
9   What sounds dominate the poem?

▦ Fourth reading

10 Do you think the poet is someone 'at
    peace' with himself?
11 After studying this poem do you agree
    with the poet's ideas about peace?

Ⓛ Link to language

12 Write an essay entitled 'Peace'.

To Norline

DEREK WALCOTT

Prescribed for the Ordinary Level exams in 2009 and 2010

This beach will remain empty
for more slate-coloured dawns
of lines the surf continually
erases with its sponge,

and someone else will come   **5**
from the still-sleeping house,
a coffee mug warming his palm
as my body once cupped yours,

to memorize this passage
of a salt-sipping tern,   **10**
like when some line on a page
is loved, and it's hard to turn.

GLOSSARY

Norline: Norline Metivier – a dancer. The poet's wife from 1976. Divorced in 1993 after a separation of many years

Tern: Seabird with long wings

DEREK **WALCOTT**

- **Born 1930 on the West Indian island of St Lucia**
- **Educated at the University of West Indies, Jamaica**
- **Moved to Trinidad where he worked as a reviewer, art critic, playwright and artistic director of a theatre workshop**
- **Currently teaches at Boston University having been poet in residence at a number of American institutions**
- **Awarded the Nobel Prize for Literature in 1992**

◖ First reading

1 The poem is dedicated to the poet's ex-wife. Where can she be seen in the poem?
2 How do you feel after reading the poem?
3 Are there any references to their relationship? Where can this be seen?
4 Describe the image of the beach as outlined in verse 1.

◖◖ Second reading

5 How is the atmosphere of calm created?
6 Describe the poet's mood.
7 Why, in verse 3, might someone want to memorise the beach scene?
8 What is the theme of this poem?
9 'Empty', 'erases', 'someone else', 'once', 'memorize', 'it's hard to turn' are all key words to your understanding of the poem. What do these words indicate?

◖◖◖ Third reading

10 Why is it hard to turn a page containing a line that is loved? To what does he compare this?

⌊ Link to language

11 'Moving on', 'Memories', 'Leaving Love' are some suggested alternative titles for this poem. Compose your own title and explain your choice.

Summer Elegies

DEREK WALCOTT

Prescribed for the Ordinary Level exams in 2009 and 2010

Cynthia, the things we did,
our hands growing more bold as
the unhooked halter slithered
from sunburnt shoulders!

Tremblingly I unfixed it   **5**
and two white quarter moons
unpeeled there like a frisket,
and burnt for afternoons.

We made one shape in water
while in sea grapes a dove   **10**
gurgled astonished 'Ooos' at
the changing shapes of love.

Time lent us the whole island,
now heat and image fade
like foam lace, like the tan   **15**
on a striped shoulder blade.

Salt dried in every fissure,
and, from each sun-struck day,
I peeled the papery tissue
of my dead flesh away;   **20**

it feathered as I blew it
from reanointed skin,
feeling love could renew itself, and a new life begin.

A halcyon day. No sail.   **25**
The sea like cigarette paper
smoothed by a red thumbnail,
then creased to a small square.

The bay shines like tinfoil,
crimps like excelsior;   **30**
All the beach chairs are full,
but the beach is emptier.

The snake hangs its old question
on almond or apple tree;
I had her breast to rest on,
the rest was History.   35

▪ First reading

1 Where is the poem set?
2 Who are the people in the poem?
3 What is their relationship?
4 What happens to them as the poem
   develops?

▪▪ Second reading

5 How important is the setting in this poem?
6 What colours are in the poem? Are they
   implied or named? What effect do they
   have?
7 What is the mood of the poem?
8 What is the pace of the poem?
9 Which sounds dominate the poem? What
   effect do they have?

▪▪▪ Third reading

10 What does the poet mean by the
    lines 'All the beach chairs are full, /
    but the beach is emptier'?
11 Do you think there is a lot
    of regret in the final verse?

L Link to language

12 Write an article for the travel section of a
    Sunday newspaper about the beach in
    the poem.

The Young Wife

For Nigel

DEREK WALCOTT

Prescribed for the Ordinary Level exam in 2010

Make all your sorrow neat.
Plump pillows, soothe the corners
of her favourite coverlet.
Write to her mourners.

At dusk, after the office, **5**
travel an armchair's ridge,
the valley of the shadow in the sofas,
the drapes' dead foliage.

Ah, but the mirror – the mirror
which you believe has seen **10**
the traitor you feel you are –
clouds, though you wipe it clean!

The buds on the wallpaper
do not shake at the muffled sobbing
the children must not hear, **15**
or the drawers you dare not open.

She has gone with that visitor
that sat beside her, like wind
clicking shut the bedroom door;
arm in arm they went, **20**

leaving her wedding photograph in
its lace frame, a face smiling at
itself. And the telephone
without a voice. The weight

we bear on this heavier side **25**
of the grave brings no comfort.
But the vow that was said
in white lace has brought

you now to the very edge
of that promise; now, for some, **30**
the hooks in the hawthorn hedge
break happily into blossom

and the heart into grief.
The sun slants on a kitchen floor.
You keep setting a fork and knife   **35**
at her place for supper.

The children close in the space
made by a chair removed,
and nothing takes her place,
loved and now deeper loved.   **40**

The children accept your answer.
They startle you when they laugh.
She sits there smiling that cancer
kills everything but Love.

First reading

1 What has happened to the wife?
2 What are the rituals that the husband is
   going through?
3 How does each of his chores remind him
   of his wife?
4 How does this affect him?

Second reading

5 What does the mirror tell him?
6 What does the poet mean by the phrase
   'the very edge of that promise'?
7 Why does nothing take her place?
8 What is the 'deeper love'?

Third reading

9 Which images from nature does the poet
   use?
10 What effect do they have?
11 Which sounds dominate
   the poem?
12 What effect do
   they have?

Fourth reading

13 What do you think of the last line? Are
   there any signs of hope in the poem?
14 Did you find this poem moving? How did
   the poem affect you?

The Pardon

RICHARD WILBUR

Prescribed for the Ordinary Level exam in 2008

My dog lay dead five days without a grave
In the thick of summer, hid in a clump of pine
And a jungle of grass and honeysuckle-vine.
I who had loved him while he kept alive

Went only close enough to where he was   **5**
To sniff the heavy honeysuckle smell
Twined with another odour heavier still
And hear the flies' intolerable buzz.

Well, I was ten and very much afraid.
In my kind world the dead were out of range   **10**
And I could not forgive the sad or strange
In beast or man. My father took the spade

And buried him. Last night I saw the grass
Slowly divide (it was the same scene
But now it glowed a fierce and mortal green)   **15**
And saw the dog emerging. I confess

I felt afraid again, but still he came
In the carnal sun, clothed in a hymn of flies,
And death was breeding in his lively eyes.
I started in to cry and call his name,   **20**

Asking forgiveness of his tongueless head.
. . . I dreamt the past was never past redeeming:
but whether this was false or honest dreaming
I beg death's pardon now. And mourn the dead.

GLOSSARY
Emerging: Coming into view
Carnal: Of the body or flesh, worldly

Redeeming: Making up for faults or mistakes

RICHARD **WILBUR**

• Born 1921 in New York City, USA   • Raised in New Jersey, USA   • Enlisted in the army in 1942 and worked as a cryptographer   • Started writing in the army in an effort to rationalise his feelings during wartime   • Returned home and taught in many universities   • Has written poetry, literary essays, children's books and translations of classic works   • His poetry shows a love of the world around him   • Won the Pulizter Prize in 1956   • Became US Poet Laureate in 1987

Pre-reading

1 What are the different meanings of the word 'pardon'?

First reading

2 What images are strongest in this poem? Imagine you have to paint three pictures telling the story of this poem – describe each picture.
3 Why does the poet specify that the dog had been missing for five days? Is this relevant to the poem?
4 Describe the child as he discovers the body of the dead dog. How does he feel? Imagine his body language. Describe his fear. What other emotions is he feeling?

Second reading

5 Tell the story of this poem in your own words.
6 Examine the poem verse by verse picking out all the words and phrases describing the hot summer weather. Using these words and phrases write a descriptive paragraph detailing Wilbur's summer at the age of ten.
7 How did Wilbur feel about his dog when he was alive? How did he feel about him when he was dead?

8 This poem appeals heavily to the senses – sight, sound and smell. Examine the images under these three headings.
9 'And I could not forgive the sad or strange / In beast or man.' Explain what Wilbur is trying to say here.
10 In verse 4 the dog is coming back to haunt Wilbur in horrific, grotesque and vivid nightmares. Describe the dog now.
11 How does Wilbur react to the reappearance of the dog?
12 What lesson has Wilbur learned?
13 Has Wilbur's view of death changed from the beginning to the end of the poem?

Third reading

14 Is the title of this poem, 'The Pardon', appropriate to the subject matter? Explain.
15 Is this poem a true reflection of how a child would react to a traumatic incident?
16 How do you feel about Wilbur as a child of ten and Wilbur the adult?

The Red Wheelbarrow

WILLIAM CARLOS WILLIAMS

Prescribed for the Ordinary Level exam in 2010

so much depends
upon

a red wheel
barrow

glazed with rain   **5**
water

beside the white
chickens

WILLIAM CARLOS **WILLIAMS**

• Born 1883 in New Jersey, USA   • Studied medicine
• Lived and practised in Rutherford, New Jersey   • Also
wrote fiction, drama and essays   • Was concerned with
creating a distinctly American form of art
• His philosophy of writing was summed up by his phrase
'No ideas but in things'   • Died in 1963

▬ Pre-reading

1 What do you think a poet could possibly
have to say about a red wheelbarrow?
2 Who would write a poem about a wheelbarrow?

▪ First reading

3 How does the poet convey the message
that he is talking about something very
important?
4 What is your initial reaction to this poem?
5 Does the poet follow his opening statement by telling us what is so significant
about the red wheelbarrow?

⁚ Second reading

6 Why does the poet mention the 'white
chickens'? Why are we told it is raining?
7 From your reading of this poem do you
agree that poets look at ordinary things in
an extraordinary way? Discuss.
8 This poem leaves the reader with more
questions than answers. What questions
would you like to ask the poet?
9 What makes a piece of writing into a
poem? Is this a poem? How does 'The
Red Wheelbarrow' compare with other
poems on your course?
10 Imagine that this poem, as it is printed
above, is just a skeleton and you can add
words and phrases to enhance and
embellish it. What would you add and
why?

⌶ Link to language

11 Write a letter to the poet asking the questions you feel would help a Leaving
Certificate student better understand this
poem.

Composed upon Westminster Bridge

WILLIAM WORDSWORTH

Prescribed for the Ordinary Level exam in 2009

Earth has not anything to show more fair:
Dull would he be of soul who could pass by
A sight so touching in its majesty:
This City now doth, like a garment, wear
The beauty of the morning; silent, bare,   **5**
Ships, towers, domes, theatres, and temples lie
Open unto the fields, and to the sky;
All bright and glittering in the smokeless air.
Never did sun more beautifully steep
In his first splendour, valley, rock, or hill;   **10**
Ne'er saw I, never felt, a calm so deep!
The river glideth at his own sweet will:
Dear God! the very houses seem asleep;
And all that mighty heart is lying still!

GLOSSARY

Majesty: Grandeur and magnificence – like royalty
Doth: Does

Steep: Soak or bathe in liquid
Glideth: Glides

WILLIAM **WORDSWORTH**

- **Born 1770 in Cockermouth, Cumberland, north of the Lake District, England** • **Educated at St John's College, Cambridge** • **Lived with his sister, Dorothy, in the Lake District** • **Published *Lyrical Ballads* (one of the most important works in the history of English literature) with Samuel Taylor Coleridge in 1798** • **Believed that poetry should be 'language really used by men'. He wanted poetry to be real and everyday, not just for the elite** • **He became a republican and supporter of the French Revolution** • **Challenged epics and other traditional forms of poetry** • **Became Poet Laureate in 1843 but died seven years later**

◾ Pre-reading

1 Imagine your home town, city or village at night or in the early morning. Describe it. How is it different to during the day?

◾ First reading

2 What does Wordsworth think of London? What words and images stand out in his description?

3 In lines 3 and 4 he says 'Dull would he be of soul who could pass by / A sight so touching in its majesty:' What does Wordsworth mean in these lines? Who is 'he'?

4 In lines 10 and 12 Wordsworth mentions 'he' and 'his', different to the 'he' in line 2. Who is he referring to in lines 10 and 12? Is 'he' important in Wordsworth's opinion? How is this portrayed?

5 How do we know Wordsworth is enjoying the scene before him?

◾ Second reading

6 What will the city be like later in the day? Examine each peaceful image in the poem and discuss the changes that may occur.

7 Will Wordsworth enjoy the scene later on in the day?

8 This poem opens with a bold statement challenging the reader to think of anything on earth 'more fair' than the scene he is about to describe. Is this a good opening? Explain your answer.

9 The words 'Dear God!' and the exclamation mark seem out of place in the flow of peacefulness and calmness. Why have they been included in the poem and why in the second-last line?

◾ Link to language

10 Write a promotional yet informative piece on your home place under the following headings:
   How to get there
   Places of interest / main attractions
   Accommodation
   Eating out
   Night life
   Local history
   Amenities
   Festivals / Dates of importance
   Traditions / Culture

11 Write a composition entitled either
   'My Home Place'
   or
   'The Place I Call Home'

Request to a Year

JUDITH WRIGHT

Prescribed for the Ordinary Level exams in 2009 and 2010

If the year is meditating a suitable gift,
I should like it to be the attitude
of my great-great-grandmother,
legendary devotee of the arts,

who, having had eight children   5
and little opportunity for painting pictures,
sat one day on a high rock
beside a river in Switzerland

and from a difficult distance viewed
her second son, balanced on a small ice-floe,   10
drift down the current towards a waterfall
that struck rock-bottom eighty feet below,

while her second daughter, impeded,
no doubt, by the petticoats of the day,
stretched out a last-hope alpenstock   15
(which luckily later caught him on his way).

Nothing, it was evident, could be done;
and with the artist's isolating eye
my great-great-grandmother hastily sketched the scene.
The sketch survives to prove the story by.   20

Year, if you have no Mother's day present planned;
reach back and bring me the firmness of her hand.

JUDITH **WRIGHT**

- **Born 1915 in Armidale, New South Wales, Australia**
- **Educated at Universities of Sydney and Queensland**
- **Active anti-war campaigner in the 1960s** • **Became a conservationist** • **Loved nature, animals and the land. She worked on the land on her family's ranch at Willamumba during the Second World War** • **Wrote not only poetry but also criticism, fiction and children's fiction •** **Collections:** *Collected Poems*, **1975;** *The Double Tree: Selected Poems*, **1978;** *Phantom Dwelling*, **1986** • **Died in 2000**

Pre-reading

1 If you had an opportunity to ask the coming year for something – a wish, a request – what would you ask for?

First reading

2 To whom is the poet speaking?
3 What do we learn about the poet's 'great-great-grandmother'?
4 Why did the poet's 'great-great-grandmother' not have much opportunity to paint?
5 What did her children do as she painted pictures in Switzerland?
6 Is this poem written in the modern day or is it in the past? What evidence can you find to support your answer?

Second reading

7 What would the poet like the Year to provide for her?
8 What near-disaster occurs?
9 How do the individual characters in the poem react to this near-disaster?
10 Is the poet's great-great-grandmother's reaction one you would expect of a mother? Why?
11 What is meant by the phrase 'artist's isolating eye'? Is there evidence of this in the poem?

Third reading

12 Picture the scene. Describe the whole location and event in detail.
13 How does the poet feel about her great-great-grandmother? Where in the poem can this be seen?
14 Does the poet expect us to believe that this really happened? Are there any signs in the poem that the poet expects us to question this story?
15 Is this a light and funny poem or is there a serious dark side to it?

Link to language

16 Imagine it is New Year's Eve; write a letter to the new year with your list of requests.

The Lake Isle of Innisfree

W. B. YEATS

Prescribed for the Ordinary Level exams in 2007 and 2010

I will arise and go now, and go to Innisfree,
And a small cabin build there, of clay and wattles made:
Nine bean-rows will I have there, a hive for the honey-bee,
And live alone in the bee-loud glade.

And I shall have some peace there, for peace comes dropping slow,   **5**
Dropping from the veils of the morning to where the cricket sings;
There midnight's all a glimmer, and noon a purple glow,
And evening full of the linnet's wings.

I will arise and go now, for always night and day
I hear lake water lapping with low sounds by the shore;   **10**
While I stand on the roadway, or on the pavements grey,
I hear it in the deep heart's core.

W. B. **YEATS**

- William Butler Yeats, born 1865 in Dublin of a Co. Sligo family • Moved to London at the age of two and back to Dublin in his teens • His poetry shows an interest in Irish mysticism, mythology, history, folklore and superstitions • Was one of the founders of the Abbey Theatre, Dublin in 1904 • Wrote plays as well as poetry • His brother Jack B. Yeats was a well-known Irish artist • Had a fixation and great love for Maud Gonne who refused to marry him on many occasions but he remained obsessed with her all through his life • Became a senator in 1922 and had an active public life • Awarded the Nobel Prize for Literature in 1923 • Died in 1939 in Rome and his body could not be returned to Ireland until after the war

⊟ Pre-reading

1 This is one of the most famous Irish poems ever written. Have you ever read or heard it before?
2 Where is Innisfree?

⊡ First reading

3 In your own words, what will the poet do when he gets to Innisfree?
4 Why does he want to keep bees?
5 What does he see and hear when he thinks of Innisfree?
6 How does this place affect him when he is no longer there?

⊡⊡ Second reading

7 How does the poet create such a peaceful atmosphere in the poem?
8 Contrast the roadway and the grey pavements with the island.
9 What sounds help in the poem?
10 How does the rhyming help with creating the atmosphere?

⊡⊡⊡ Third reading

11 What is your favourite image in the poem?
12 Why do you think Yeats loved this place so much?

🄻 Link to language

13 Do you have a favourite place? Write a poem or a paragraph about it.

The Wild Swans at Coole

W. B. YEATS

Prescribed for the Ordinary Level exams in 2007 and 2010

The trees are in their autumn beauty,
The woodland paths are dry,
Under the October twilight the water
Mirrors a still sky;
Upon the brimming water among the stones   **5**
Are nine-and-fifty swans.

The nineteenth autumn has come upon me
Since I first made my count;
I saw, before I had well finished,
All suddenly mount   **10**
And scatter wheeling in great broken rings
Upon their clamorous wings.

I have looked upon those brilliant creatures,
And now my heart is sore.
All's changed since I, hearing at twilight,   **15**
The first time on this shore,
The bell-beat of their wings above my head,
Trod with a lighter tread.

Unwearied still, lover by lover,
They paddle in the cold   **20**
Companionable streams or climb the air;
Their hearts have not grown old;
Passion or conquest, wander where they will,
Attend upon them still.

But now they drift on the still water,   **25**
Mysterious, beautiful;
Among what rushes will they build,
By what lake's edge or pool
Delight men's eyes when I awake some day
To find they have flown away?   **30**

▬ Pre-reading

1   Where is Coole?

▪ First reading

2   Describe the scene painted by Yeats with his words in the first six lines.
3   What has he seen there every year for the last nineteen years?
4   What has happened to him since the first time he went there?
5   What has happened to the swans since the first time he saw them?
6   What question does he ask in the final verse?

▪▪ Second reading

7   Do you think that the poet is jealous of the swans?

8   Which images in the poem are your favourites?
9   Make a list of the verbs that Yeats uses. What mood do they help create in the poem?
10 What sounds dominate the poem?

▪▪▪ Third reading

11 How are the swans presented throughout the poem?
12 What does the poet tell us about himself in the poem?

▪▪▪▪ Fourth reading

13 Do you think the poet has a lot of regrets about his life?
14 Do you think the poet spends too much time looking backwards to the past?

An Irish Airman Foresees His Death

W. B. YEATS

Prescribed for the Ordinary Level exams in 2007 and 2010

I know that I shall meet my fate
Somewhere among the clouds above;
Those that I fight I do not hate,
Those that I guard I do not love;
My country is Kiltartan Cross,   5
My countrymen Kiltartan's poor,
No likely end could bring them loss
Or leave them happier than before.
Nor law, nor duty bade me fight,
Nor public men, nor cheering crowds,   10
A lonely impulse of delight
Drove to this tumult in the clouds;
I balanced all, brought all to mind,
The years to come seemed waste of breath,
A waste of breath the years behind   15
In balance with this life, this death.

▬ Pre-reading

1 After reading the title, what did you expect from this poem?

▪ First reading

2 Why do you think the speaker is so definite in the first two lines?
3 What is the speaker saying in lines 3 and 4?
4 What do you expect him to tell us later on?
5 What is his relationship with the people of Kiltartan Cross?
6 How was the war affecting them?

▪▪ Second reading

7 Why was war not an attractive option for the speaker in the poem?
8 What were his reasons for going to fight?

▪▪▪ Third reading

9 What do you think the speaker's frame of mind was when he decided to go to war?
10 How does the poet use rhyme in the poem?
11 How does the poet use repetition in the poem?
12 What effect does this have?

L Link to language

13 Write the diary entries of the airman in the days before his death.

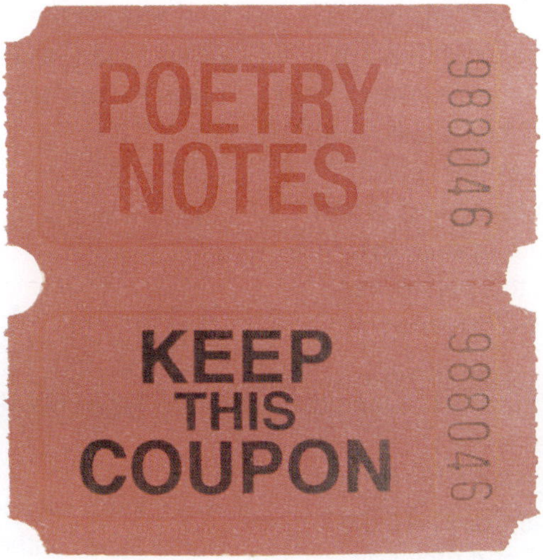
POETRY
NOTES
988046
KEEP
THIS
COUPON
988046

Fleur Adcock
For Heidi with Blue Hair

THIS IS A poem about teenage rebellion, refusal to conform and what happens when there is a clash with adults. The poet is addressing this poem directly to Heidi, her niece. She speaks *to* her: 'When *you* dyed *your* hair . . . *you* were sent home from school'. The story is told in a straightforward and clear way. Heidi, in an act of freedom of expression, dyes her hair blue. There is a vivid description of the hair – ultramarine on the short, clipped sides and jet black on the spiky top. Heidi is then sent home from school. The headmistress is not impressed, and we can almost hear her tone as she chastises 'apart from anything else'. She cannot send Heidi home just because she dyed her hair, as this is not against the school rules. Instead Heidi is sent home because her hair is not dyed in the school colours. Heidi takes this punishment badly; there are tears and we can imagine quite a scene.

In complete contrast to the strict and rigid headmistress, Heidi's father is 'freedom-loving'. He rings the school and supports his daughter, explaining that Heidi and he discussed the hair-dying before she did it, and they also checked the school rules. He may be 'freedom-loving' but he still encourages Heidi to stay within the boundaries. He continues to defend his daughter, saying that her image may be punk but it is only an image, and her behaviour does not match the image. We see she has a clean record and has never been in trouble before – 'The school had nothing else against you'.

Heidi is adamant that she will not change back her hair, for a number of reasons. She says it cost twenty-five dollars, and also it is a permanent colour and will not wash out. She refuses to conform. The poem then reveals something significant about Heidi's past. In verse 5 we learn that Heidi's mother has died and this shimmers like a ghost behind all the arguments. It is not discussed in great detail but it is very much an issue and wins our sympathy for Heidi. We see her as young and vulnerable and dealing with the huge issue of her mother's death, and this shows just how ridiculous the hair issue is in the bigger scheme of things. The teachers are portrayed as silly and frivolous as they 'twitter' and give in to the argument.

In the final verse we learn that Heidi's black friend continues to challenge the school authorities and dyes her hair in the school colours. This is a show of support for Heidi and adds to the feeling of victory; it is unnecessary, as Heidi has already won the battle to display her individuality.

•

Maya Angelou
Phenomenal Woman

REVIEWER MONICA STARK described this poem as 'an anthem of women's strength in their own womanhood'. It is indeed a poem full of confidence, self-love and pride. The title, 'Phenomenal Woman', encapsulates everything the poet is attempting to say in the poem – that she is a phenomenal woman.

The poem opens with a straightforward statement that pretty women, obviously intimidated yet intrigued by the speaker, question her about her secret – how she became and is so phenomenal. She tells us that she is not the traditional female icon – neither cute nor thin. The answer the speaker gives is unsatisfactory to the 'pretty women'. They cannot believe that her phenomenal status is based simply on her arms, hips, walk and the curl of her lip. Of course the message here is simple. The speaker is phenomenal because she is herself. Lines 14–20 tell us the effect she has on men – they find her irresistible – they stand or fall and swarm around her like bees around honey. Women question her but men adore her.

The short, simple sentences and childish rhyming scheme make the speaker's message very clear and matter-of-fact. There are no hidden meanings. One element is essential in promoting yourself to the heights of being a Phenomenal Woman, and that is self-belief. The speaker repeats her message – each verse ends with the refrain 'I'm a woman / Phenomenally. / Phenomenal Woman, / That's me' – to emphasise her point, to repeat and reiterate her message. She is extraordinary, exceptional and sensational because she is herself – 'That's me'. The poem exudes confidence and self-assurance. Here is a woman who knows herself well, is at peace with herself and knows the effect she has on those around her.

This poem is a celebration of what it means to be a woman, not a stick-thin model or a manufactured 'nipped and tucked' airbrushed woman, but an ordinary, simple woman. It is a poem about being comfortable with your own self-image and sexuality. It is a poem about accepting and rejoicing. She exposes her inner strength, which is her femininity. She does not brag or boast, she hopes that others will see her and that they too will celebrate – 'It ought to make you proud'. Every move she makes, every step she takes shows that she is in full control, she knows what she is doing and everything is intentional. She is brimming over with confidence and happiness because she is a 'phenomenal woman'.

Simon Armitage
It Ain't What You Do, It's What It Does to You

THE TITLE OF this poem outlines the whole message of the poem. The poet's message is clear and simple; he promotes the belief that it is not what you do, it is the feeling you get when doing it that matters. He gives us a number of examples of exotic, extraordinary things people do and he contrasts them with ordinary, banal, everyday things that he has done. His conclusion is that the outcome – the feeling – is just the same.

In verse 1 he shows that he did not need to bum across America with just a dollar and a knife to get a feeling of adventure and excitement. Instead he 'lived with thieves in Manchester'. In verse 2 he admits that he has not walked through the Taj Mahal in India, so focused and meditative that he could hear the soft padding every time his foot hit the marble floor. Instead he has experienced the intense serenity of skimming stones across a lake in Lancashire. He was so at one with nature at that moment that he could feel the stone losing power, slowing down and finally sinking.

Finally in verse 3 Armitage tells us that he has not felt the rush of adrenalin from sitting on the edge of a small plane playing with the parachute cord that could ultimately save his life. He declares that he has felt this adrenalin rush, this heightened sense of excitement and fulfilment, from helping a physically handicapped child. He has experienced these feelings by holding the child's 'wobbly head' and by rubbing his 'fat hands'.

In conclusion, the last four lines reveal just what these emotions feel like. He describes a tightness in his throat and an overwhelming, flowing sensation deep inside. This feeling is 'something else', not usual, not ordinary and can be achieved without doing the very adventurous and exotic things.

W. H. Auden
Funeral Blues

THIS POEM IS most recognisable as it was recited in the movie *Four Weddings and a Funeral* by a character mourning the death of a loved one. The speaker calls for the world to stop as he feels he cannot continue because of the overwhelming grief he feels at the loss of his beloved.

This poem can be read as an elegy as the poet is rendered completely helpless by the death of his loved one. He wants time to stop, he wants to sever all communication with the outside world, he wants to quieten the dog by giving him a juicy bone. No music is to be played; the only sound acceptable to the speaker is the 'muffled drum' heralding the arrival of the coffin and the mourners. All of these feelings can be accepted as those of someone recently bereaved. Verse 2, however, takes the mourning process a step further. The speaker calls for aeroplanes to circle in the sky transmitting the message 'He Is Dead'. He would like to put ribbons on the public doves and replace the traffic policemen's white gloves with black ones as a mark of respect. Verse 2 shows how irrational the speaker feels with loss, how exaggerated he makes his expression of sorrow in an attempt to communicate how deeply he feels the grief, pain and loss.

Verse 3 tells what the deceased meant to the speaker. He was his direction in life, he filled his thoughts always during work and rest – he was his everything. He believed that love was forever and is now completely devastated to find that there is no forever – love has ended.

Verse 4 shows the raw grief felt at the death of his partner as he faces the world alone. He no longer needs things of beauty (the stars, sun, moon, ocean, wood) as alone he cannot appreciate beauty. The future is bleak: 'For nothing now can ever come to any good.'

This poem can also be read as a satire as the poet is ridiculing the public for their exaggerated outpourings of grief at the death of a public figure. The images are outlandish and lavish; the speaker's requests are over-the-top and at times ridiculous.

Whichever way the reader chooses to interpret it, this poem reflects feelings of grief, desolation and heartbreak, whether deeply felt at the loss of a soul mate, or felt by an ordinary member of the public at the loss of a much-loved popular figure.

·

Patricia Beer
The Voice

THIS SENTIMENTAL LYRIC is written in memory of a sad, eccentric aunt who suffers the tragedy of losing a son. When this happens a kind neighbour gives her a gift of a parrot. The aunt takes to the parrot immediately and buys a beautiful cage to keep it in. She behaves just like an eager mother who rushes out to buy a cot for a new baby.

When he first arrives, the parrot doesn't seem to fit in. He takes adjusting to. His colours make him stand out for a while. He doesn't make any noises at all and this is disconcerting. Parrots are usually associated with lots of noise but this one has to be taught what to say. 'He came from silence but was ready to become noise.'

The aunt teaches him to talk gradually using nursery rhymes just like she would with a child. The parrot becomes part of her, takes on all her idiosyncrasies and adds some of his own for good measure. He even takes on the aunt's Devon accent. In the end 'He fitted in.'

He also gets old. Eventually just before he dies he loses his memory and descends into parrot senility. He starts to get his nursery rhymes mixed up. This is distressing for the aunt. Eventually, just like Jill in the nursery rhyme, he 'tumbled after'.

Much humour is used throughout the poem especially in the way the poet uses colour, and in the way she uses nursery rhymes to illustrate the bird's speech, but the poem is dominated by the sadness and regret in the final verse. The poet tells us that her aunt died soon after her pet with little left to hang on to. She has lost her husband, her son, her companion and her pride. The poet tells us that she can no longer hear her aunt's voice but she can still recall the parrot's. The poet ends on a slightly more positive note by reminding us of the thing that gave her aunt purpose in her last years.

Elizabeth Bishop
The Fish

THIS IS A very long but straightforward poem telling of the poet's experience while out fishing. Immediately she tells us she catches a 'tremendous' fish. He isn't just big, he is amazing and fascinating. She does not bring the fish into the boat immediately, she holds him half out of the water and sees that her hook is firmly fixed in the side of his mouth. The fish does not battle to go free. On first sight she sees that the fish is very battered and worthy of her respect, but also plain and ordinary. His skin reminds the poet of old wallpaper in pattern, but in texture the poet tells us the fish is speckled with barnacles, growths of lime and sea lice and that strips of green weed trail under him. The poet pays particular attention to the fish's gills that gulp in oxygen – dangerous to the fish. The gills appear frightening as they are very sharp and look 'fresh and crisp with blood'.

The poet looks beyond the fish's external appearance; she imagines the meat – 'white flesh' inside the fish's body packed piece on top of piece like tightly packed feathers. She thinks of the fish's intestines – red and black and pink. In his eyes she can see a blankness; he does not return her stare. She admiringly examines his face and the structure of his jaw. She notices five pieces of fishing line and describes each in detail. They remind her of medals worn proudly after a war, or of a wise old man's beard trailing from his sore and aching jaw.

A sense of victory fills the boat as she examines the fish, like the rainbow colours of spilt engine oil. Everything is then transformed. Overwhelmed by this feeling the poet releases the fish to fight another battle. She feels she should not be the one to end the life of such a worthy soldier who has fought so many battles and always won. She respects the fish's courage and rewards him with another chance of freedom and it is the poet who then feels a great sense of achievement. The victory and exultation spreads from the warrior fish through the boat and into the poet. The victory is not the usual victory of a fisherman who catches a big fish, instead it is the feeling of releasing your great catch back into the wild.

Elizabeth Bishop
The Filling Station

BISHOP RECREATES IN minute detail a visit to a petrol filling station. What is a routine everyday experience is transformed as she looks into the situation and dissects it to see the human side of a dirty, greasy petrol station.

The poem opens unexpectedly with an exclamation: 'Oh, but it is dirty!' She was not expecting the extent of the filth and is surprised when she sees it up close. The title of the poem places us firmly in the scene and the rest of the poem is spent delving beneath the dirty surface. The poet investigates who lives there, imagines what goes on, sees that somebody cares and slaves away to make the petrol station somewhere special to live. There is a hint of danger (or is it humour?) in line 6 – 'Be careful with that match!'.

The filling station, usually a male-dominated location, seems to have evidence of a woman's touch. There are many indications that it is more than a place of work – it is a home. The dirt has character; there is something endearing in it; we see that it belongs to somebody and that makes it special – maybe it is the father's or the son's or even the dog's. The only deviations from the blackness and dirt are the presence of comic books and a doily. Someone, it seems, is aiming at something higher than grease and dirt; someone is making an effort to improve the surroundings. This 'somebody' makes little changes so that the ever-present dirt is forgotten, as there is an effort to enhance and refine the filling station.

There is a beautiful softness in the lines

. . . Somebody
arranges the rows of cans
so that they softly say:
ESSO-SO-SO-SO

This sibilant 's' sound is calming and soothing and creates a sense of tranquillity and peacefulness in a place of 'high-strung automobiles'.

•

Eavan Boland
Child of Our Time

THIS POEM WAS written after the poet saw a press photograph of a fire-fighter carrying a child from the wreckage of the Dublin bombings. The poem is an elegy written to the child, and is an apology from the poet for the behaviour of adults who have cost the child his life.

Immediately the poet tells us that she has been made to change her way of thinking by the events that she has witnessed in the photograph. She has had to look within herself to force out a poem that could justifiably reflect what she has seen. She says the tone of the poem will be set by 'your final cry'. The poet recognises the contradiction in what she attempts to do when she cries out for the child's 'unreasoned end', and she says that this will inspire her. In fact she says that this poem must be written because of what happened. She says that she does not have a choice in the matter. The death of the child is pushing the very rhythm, and driving her motives for writing the poem.

Its rhythm from the discord of your murder
Its motive from the fact you cannot listen.

In the second verse she tells the child that adults have a duty to teach children peaceful things about animals and nursery rhymes; that adults should protect children. Children should learn from adults. In this case however, the adults have to learn from the death of this young child. She insists that they must 'for your sake' find 'a new language'.

•

Eavan Boland
This Moment

THIS BRIEF LYRIC creates an immediate atmosphere within its own brevity. The poet creates a scene and allows us to view it much in the same way that we would view a picture or a painting. The poet is sparing with her detail, yet because of this every detail that she does give gains more importance. There is nothing extra in this lyric. In some of the sentences she does not even bother with verbs.

The poet begins with the place and time. However, they are both vague at best. They are delivered staccato-like as if they were secrets that were not to be uncovered except to a select few.

She follows with more mystery. Something is about to 'happen / out of sight'. She is not telling us what. There is anticipation everywhere, even in nature itself. Things are coming to life and having their moment while everybody else goes to sleep and stops. There is always something happening whether we are aware of it or not.

Then she introduces two people: a mother and a child. They perform a simple act. The child runs into the mother's arms. She continues mothering no matter what time it is nor what place it is, no matter what is or isn't going on outside. The poet reminds us that nature goes on too:

Stars rise.
Moths flutter.
Apples sweeten in the dark.

This is a simple poem about the simplicity of life, the continuing circle of nature and of motherhood and the idea that what may seem banal has its own importance.

•

Rosita Boland
Naming My Daughter

ROSITA BOLAND WROTE this fictional poem after reading a Caribbean novel featuring a character called 'Rain'. She loved the idea that a name could represent so much and so constructed this poem around it.

It is a beautiful poem telling of the halcyon days of hope and anticipation before the birth of a baby, replaced by heartbreak and death, finally ending with acceptance and contentment. This is a very controlled poem telling the story of a mother trying to pick a name for her unborn child. It is very simple and honest. She has pinned up a list of possible names and added to it as time passed. The months leading up to the birth of a child are full of planning and preparation, and expectant parents are always asked if they have picked a name. The speaker deliberates over her choice, and the passing of time is marked by the beautiful alliteration of the line 'As the months swelled slowly on.'

The next line is stark and bare and the speaker does not, or maybe cannot, comment or discuss it further. The baby is born dead – 'She was born without colour'. All around there are colours blooming – 'the yellow daffodils / And the greening trees'. It is a wet March and the rainwater gives life to the flowers and the trees, leading to a display of lushness all around. But in total contrast to the exploding colours and life outside, her daughter is colourless. The words have been stripped bare as the speaker cannot allow even a hint of emotion, for fear of breaking down.

The poem does not descend into darkness and depression at the death of the baby. Instead there is a note of optimism as the speaker searches to find a suitable name for her daughter. She is adamant that the names she had been considering no longer seem appropriate: 'I chose none of those names for my daughter.' She looks again at names and decides on a Caribbean name, 'Rain'. The speaker finds solace in this name as she sees it as something 'soft, familiar and constant'. She does not want a name lacking significance and meaning so 'Rain' is perfect. Her child may be beneath a 'thin coverlet of earth', but she has become part of nature. The speaker finds it comforting that her daughter will always be touched and have a connection with the living world.

Paddy Bushe
Midwife

THIS LYRIC IS written to a daughter, explaining an accident that happened to her and the effect that it had on her father. There are only two sentences in the whole poem. They take up one verse each. This has a swirling effect on the reader. It shows the desperation of the father as he struggles to come to terms with the accident, and his feelings as the accident is taking place.

The event is very simple. The daughter, aged two, is walking along the bank of the Caragh River. She loses her footing and falls. The father can see this happen 'in slow motion' but feels helpless. The river seems very loud and dangerous. He describes it as 'black and white'. The daughter is terrified and her 'wide eyes pleaded for breath'. As the daughter hits the water the father sees it as the death of her innocence, and he runs through all his emotions in the few seconds of it happening.

In the second verse, the poet describes his struggle as he tries to grip his daughter by the hair, her slipping away from him twice and eventually his pulling her to safety. This is when the midwife metaphor of the title comes in. She is crying even though she is not hurt. It is the fear of the panic all around her. She is swaddled like a newborn as everybody looks on. The father finishes with a deep breath as he exclaims 'o daughter', and says that he feels he has got her back again to treasure and take care of like a new child.

Paddy Bushe
Jasmine

THIS POEM IS about the decay of a father as he gets older and starts losing his memory, possibly through Alzheimer's disease or maybe just through senility. The father has been taken from his children by his illness. This poem discusses how this makes the children feel.

The father asks the simple question 'What colour is jasmine?'. The question does not pose a difficulty for his children. What does cause difficulty is the idea of how that question raised itself in the mind of the father in the first place. They are not sure how the question made its way to their father's mind or where it was going to next.

> . . . we couldn't recognise the road
> your question had travelled, nor sound the
>   extent
> of the blue void to which it would return.

We get the feeling that the question stopped them in their tracks as the ward had to come back to normality and the 'hum / of conscientious care'.

They decide that thinking about that question in a literal way isn't an option. So they 'took the long way home'.

In the final couplet the poet ties the metaphor with the rest of the poem. He asks that the question may bring his father to a kind of peace, just like a climbing plant such as jasmine can pull a broken piece of trellising together. It can climb among the broken pieces and allow them to stay tied to the wall even if they have come away. This is what the speaker wishes for his father: that he will be able to keep himself together.

The poet creates the mood in this poem by using sensuous language. The language is designed to appeal to the senses by using soft 's' sounds. There is an atmosphere of compassion and of wonder.

Colour is used to give life to the poem. As well as the colours in the flower itself, he also uses the 'blue from your wheelchair' and the 'blue void' most effectively.

The poem ends in an upbeat fashion. The poet is toasting his father by beginning the couplet with a salutary 'And may . . .'.

Overall this is a poem that is searching for understanding. It is one that is still asking questions about the significance of what occurred. There is almost a sense of hope in not knowing the answers, yet knowing that there is still activity in the father's mind.

•

John Donne
The Flea

'THE FLEA' IS a courting poem where the speaker in the poem tries, through his various twistings of the metaphor of the flea, to get his lover to sleep with him. Like 'Valentine' by Carol Ann Duffy, it is a *metaphor-based* poem. One metaphor is explored and made to suit the poet's situation in a variety of ways. He also uses it as a *conceit*. A conceit was a metaphysical term that poets of the time used. It involved using a far-flung idea and linking it to something far more immediate.

The poem begins with the poet telling his lover to notice the flea. He points to its size and says that it is just as small as the thing that he is being denied. He points out that the flea has bitten him and the lover. Their blood has already been intermingled, so why does the lover have a problem with pushing this even further? He says that he is jealous of the flea as the insect gets to enjoy this mingling of their blood, but the poet himself does not get to.

In the second verse he asks his lover not to kill this flea since the flea represents their love, and to kill one would also mean the death of the other. The poet expands on this in the verse by explaining that the mixing of their blood is sacred, just like marriage. He concludes that since they have already mixed their blood within the flea they are already practically married. To kill the flea would be to kill their 'marriage'. This would undoubtedly be a sin. He says that she would also be committing suicide. Another sin. So he presents another reason why they should make love.

> Though use make you apt to kill me,
> Let not to this, self-murder added be,
> And sacrilege, three sins in killing three.

The final verse begins with condemnation of the lover for killing the flea. Donne seems to be beaten in his advances towards her, so he asks her what she had to gain in the death of so small a creature as the flea. 'In what could this flea guilty be . . .?' He says that all it can do is give her some small triumph over him and that she is being petty.

However, he hasn't given up. In a complete reversal of everything he has previously said, he says that the flea's life is worthless and it is not worth worrying about. Just like she should not waste any time fretting about giving in to the poet and just give in!

•

John Donne
Song: Go, and Catch a Falling Star

THIS POEM USES a listing style to express the poet's point. The tasks that he lists are impossible to do, which proves, he believes, that his request in the poem will also be impossible to fulfil. He tells us first of all that honesty is difficult to track down, and secondly that an honest and faithful woman is completely impossible to find.

He starts by listing the tasks: catching a falling star, finding magical flowers, seeing the devil, hearing mermaids sing and not feeling jealous. Some of these may seem frivolous and strange but then he introduces a very serious turn. He asks can that which inspires honesty be found. This is a rhetorical question and the answer in his mind is that it cannot.

> And find
> What wind
> Serves to advance an honest mind.

In the second verse he sets the tasks as something even more difficult. He says that even if you were a magical person with great powers who could see the invisible, no matter how far you went, even if you travelled for 'ten thousand days and nights', when you returned you would swear that

> No where
> Lives a woman true, and fair.

This seems a very extreme and downhearted thing for Donne to say. Indeed, the first two verses are full of heightened emotion and would lead the reader to question what it was that put Donne into this frame of mind.

The final verse at least begins in a more considered tone. He says that if you do find a 'woman true, and fair' then let him know. Although even if she lived next door to him, he would not meet her. He ends with a tough caveat. He tells the reader that between the time of writing the letter and Donne's receiving it she will probably have been unfaithful already.

This poem is quite depressing in some ways. Donne sees no hope for honesty in a relationship and is quite unrelenting in his ways of getting this point across.

•

Carol Ann Duffy
Valentine

THIS IS A love poem but it is not a straight-forward, slushy, romantic love poem. Indeed, in the first line we see that the poet is putting great emphasis on the fact that her love (the emotion and the person) is not ordinary and therefore the poet is not going to give a traditional gift for Valentine's day, such as a 'red rose or a satin heart'. Instead the poet is going to give her lover an onion.

The rest of the poem explains why she feels she should give an onion to her lover. The onion becomes an *extended metaphor*.

She points out that the onion can give light in a time of darkness just like the moon. She examines the erotic nature of an onion. She compares the onion to a lover who brings out the truth regardless of the price. She says that a love affair, like an onion, can make the protagonists see sides of themselves that they'd rather not see.

She talks about how its taste is difficult to shift, but like the taste of an onion a love affair can eventually end as well. Then she compares the inside of an onion to a wedding ring, but says that this is lethal.

All of these images are harsh, and in a way they are cold. The poet seems to be bringing a 'wake-up call' to her lover. The implication could be that they do not have a traditional romantic relationship and therefore to give a traditional romantic present would be the wrong thing to do, and would be dishonest.

At the end she adds her own caution: getting too close is dangerous, and says that love can be 'lethal'.

She uses a forceful, matter-of-fact tone. There is little ambiguity. Note her use of the definite 'It will' and 'I give' instead of 'It could' or 'I offer'. There is a sense that these are the facts; if you don't like them – 'tough', although there is a little hint of teasing in the poem as well.

She uses very few formal, traditional poetic devices although she is careful with her use of sound, especially in lines such as 'Its fierce kiss will stay on your lips'.

The metre in the poem seems to be purpose-built. She varies her line lengths a lot, even including one-word lines. What do you think the significance of these short lines is?

Paul Durcan
Going Home to Mayo, Winter, 1949

IN THIS CONVERSATIONAL narrative Durcan uses an event from his childhood in the winter of 1949 to outline the main differences between city life and life in the countryside, and expresses his feelings on both. The poem opens with father and son escaping the 'alien, foreign city of Dublin'. We are left in no doubt but that young Durcan does not feel he fits in in Dublin. This is a special, magical occasion and Durcan remembers it in great detail. He remembers driving 'through the night in an old Ford Anglia' with a 'rexine seat of red leatherette'. Durcan absorbs every little detail of this memorable journey. He enjoys the trip and the game he plays with his father. As the moonlight shines through the windscreen his childish exuberance explodes, and he cries out 'Daddy, Daddy . . . pass out the moon'. There is a sense of closeness between father and son as they share the journey westwards. They speed onwards towards their destination and the young Durcan remembers in wonderment the place names of all the towns they pass through; each one a marker telling them they are getting closer to 'home'.

Although they cannot pass out the moon he is not disappointed. A bigger and better prize awaits him when they arrive in Turlough 'in the heartland of Mayo'. Durcan now feels at home, in the heart of his family. This is a homely place dominated by women. His bedroom is over the pub, and in the morning his ears are filled with the sounds of country animals waking up – 'cattle-cries and cock-crows'. Movement and comfort, noise and life surround him. Life here is like an endless, expansive piece of material that has no beginning and no end. Durcan and his father are close and enjoy a relaxed relationship in Mayo. They go walking and talking 'in the high grass down by the river'. They connect in a way that would never happen in Dublin.

From line 21 onwards the picture becomes bleak and desolate. Durcan is disillusioned as he tells us that 'home was not home' and although Mayo was where the heart was it was not where they lived. The image of Dublin is stark and glaring in the daylight. It is like a waking 'nightmare', and he attempts to deal with his return to Dublin in the same way he dealt with not being able to outrun the moon. He cannot fight it so he grudgingly accepts it.

The return journey is in stark contrast to the journey west. There is no fun, no games, no closeness, no communication and no connection. The journey is slow and impersonal and they reluctantly 'chug' down by the canal into the city. As they pass every lock gate on the canal it seems to be a bell tolling a death march as they return to the drabness and dullness of Dublin. Durcan registers and despises every detail of this journey –

> And railings and palings and asphalt and traffic lights,
> And blocks after blocks of so-called 'new' tenements

These images are heavy with misery and gloom. He feels imprisoned by the railings and palings. The final three lines are dark and depressing as they point to death. Every step of the journey seems to indicate a cross, marking out loneliness and despair for his father. This all culminates in the expansive image of a 'wide, wide cemetery'. Like life in Mayo, life in Dublin is seamless; it seems to have no beginning and no end, but in a negative, deathly manner.

T. S. Eliot
Preludes

THE POEM 'PRELUDES' resembles a film snatching snapshots of people's lives in an urban setting. There are four sections to the poem and each unveils a different character. The common thread running through all four is a sense of staleness, hopelessness and emptiness as day repeats day in a never-ending continuum.

Prelude I shows the personification of a winter evening; it 'settles down' after a hard day's work. But on returning home there is nothing to lift the spirits; the cramped corridors are suffocatingly stale with the smell of cooked food. Eliot again appeals to our sense of smell in line 4 as he presents to us 'The burnt-out ends of smoky days'. The cheerlessness and drabness is further reinforced as a 'gusty shower' of rain completely envelops the character, wrapping litter and withered leaves around his feet.

There is a feeling that at the end of the day there is no reassuring hug and kiss from a loved one, instead this character is embraced by the cold and rain and all that has been discarded onto the streets. He is not alone. The shower beats down on others like him, and the glumness of the situation touches many. It even affects a lonely horse impatiently waiting on a street corner. Line 13 introduces a glimmer of hope: 'And then the lighting of the lamps', but this potential is never followed through and the desolation is felt even deeper.

Prelude II tells the tale of morning time. Again the time of day is personified as it 'comes to consciousness'. Sleep is not refreshing and regenerative, and Eliot emphasises the staleness and banality by again appealing to our sense of smell: 'faint stale smells of beer'. The snapshots of life displayed here are dull and humdrum:

'sawdust-trampled street', 'muddy feet', 'coffee-stands'. Morning lacks enthusiasm and there is no evidence of eagerness as people journey to work. Eliot sees it as 'masquerades', dressing up and pretending. Each person is no longer an individual but part of a mass movement locked in a mundane routine tediously starting each day as they did the last. This verse borders on becoming claustrophobic as the contamination and pollution suppress all freshness and invigoration.

Prelude III directly addresses the character, 'You'. He addresses everyone caught up in the rat race of urban life. The pace is sluggishly slow, lacking energy, fervour or gusto. The character kicks off a blanket but remains slumped in bed 'and waited'. Waiting for what? Sleep is not restorative as she tosses and turns fitfully playing seedy and 'sordid' images over in her mind like movie clips.

Morning light is unwelcome as it trespasses between the shutters. The dawn chorus lacks harmony as the birds are in the gutter also. The character here seems artificial and lacks wholesomeness. Her hair is curled around papers, her skin is discoloured and the image is unattractive and disgusting. She goes through the motions as if in a trance, without being invigorated in any way. She is a hollow shell lacking a personality and a spiritual dimension.

Prelude IV does nothing to lift the tone of the poem. Again the character's thoughts are projected upwards, this time onto the sky where they fade and disintegrate into city life. Time passes and is of no consequence: 'At four and five and six o'clock'. Each hour is the same as the one before and days pass in a similar fashion.

Line 48 tells us that the poet is moved as he watches the characters gently suffering the journey through life. The final three lines reflect on the sentiments of the previous preludes as the poet encourages us to laugh at these people locked in the never-ending routine of daily drudgery. The world continues turning just as ancient women continued looking for firewood where there was none. Life, it seems, is futile, and the effort expended leads only to emptiness and disappointment.

·

T. S. Eliot
Aunt Helen

THIS POEM IS Eliot's negative reaction to the genteel society in Boston to which his Aunt Helen belonged. He is showing, through humour and satire, a great concern for the moral emptiness and sense of self-importance felt by people like his Aunt Helen. Although it is his aunt who has died he is not mourning her death, and he shows us that no one else is either. He is detached and informative, lacking the personal touch of such a close relative.

Eliot sets about mocking his aunt and her ways. He comments on her immediately – she was unmarried, and although her house was small it was 'near a fashionable square'. She was looked after by 'servants to the number of four'. These quotes seem to echo his aunt's exact sentiments and words; she was concerned about public image, was proper and to the point and completely lacked any personal touches when dealing with her staff. In lines 4 and 5 we see that her death has brought both her street and heaven to a state of silence. Silence on her street would be an appropriate mark of respect for the deceased, but surely heaven should have been rejoicing the arrival of such a fine and upstanding lady. Silence in heaven indicates God's dissatisfaction with how Aunt Helen lived her life, and we see that there were no celebrations to greet her at the gates of heaven.

As a further mark of respect the window shutters are closed and the undertaker still wipes his feet even though the lady of the house is no longer there to reprimand him. There is obvious sarcasm as Eliot tells us that the undertaker 'was aware that this sort of thing had occurred before'. People of Aunt Helen's high standing were human after all, and did eventually, in spite of their sense of self-importance, die!

The final part of the poem reveals more about the kind of person Aunt Helen was. She left a 'handsome' amount to her dogs. There is no mention of her looking after the people who had cared for her, or indeed charities. It appears that those she really cared about were animals. Aunt Helen's taste for the finer things in life is shown in the line 'The Dresden clock continued ticking' unaware that its owner had died. Time goes on no matter who has died – even Aunt Helen. The things of importance to Aunt Helen, her small house, being close to a 'fashionable square', her dogs, a 'Dresden clock', are all mentioned by Eliot and held up for ridicule. This is all she cared about in life.

The footman shows no respect for his mistress, her property or her high standards and values.

We feel a sense of release and freedom when we see him sitting on the dining table with the 'second housemaid' on his knee. She is not referred to by name, again an echo of Aunt Helen, as that would not have been the 'proper' way to deal with staff members. Although the shutters have been closed as a mark of respect, we feel that the windows have been thrown open to release the servants from the stuffiness of refined confinement. The servants most certainly did not carry on like this in Aunt Helen's time; they 'had always been so careful'. They knew that she would have been disapproving.

Robert Frost
Out, Out—

THIS SAD NARRATIVE tells of a horrific accident that leads to the death of a young boy. The title of the poem comes from Shakespeare's tragedy *Macbeth*. When Macbeth is told that his wife is dead he cries

> Out, out, brief candle!
> Life's but a walking shadow, a poor player
> That struts and frets his hour upon the
>   stage,
> And then is heard no more.

The title emphasises how short life is and how it can be ended as easily as the blowing out of a candle. This poem is based on an event that occurred in New Hampshire, America in 1910. A young boy was cutting wood with a chainsaw when it hit a loose pulley and severed his hand. The boy died of shock, blood loss and heart failure. The incident made a tremendous impression on Frost. The poem opens with vivid images comparing the saw to vicious creatures. It buzzes threateningly like a swarm of bees, it snarls like a savage animal and it rattles like a venomous rattlesnake. There is a sense of unease, and the scene is set for disaster as the saw fiercely reduces the wood to dust. There is a sense of foreboding and dread.

The tone changes and the scene becomes tranquil and homely. The wood is fragrant and a light breeze blows. The scenery is picturesque as the sun sets behind the mountains. Although the setting sun is a romantic and beautiful image we cannot forget that darkness then follows. Line 7 reminds us of the menacing saw as it 'snarled and rattled, snarled and rattled'. The danger and threat is emphasised. It was a day when 'nothing happened' and the poet wishes it had remained like that: 'Call it a day, I wish they might have said'. In retrospect, had the boy been released from work a half-hour early the disaster would have been avoided and the boy would have been delighted to be given the half-hour.

We are reminded that this is a domestic scene by the arrival of the boy's sister wearing an apron and announcing supper. Line 16 begins the tragedy. The saw leaps from the boy's hand and the hand is severed. The poet is shocked and exclaims 'But the hand!' This short simple phrase reflects the shock and fright felt by all present. The boy's reaction is at first a regretful laugh but as the reality of the situation becomes clear he helplessly swings around appealing for help as he tries to keep the blood and the life from spilling from his wound. The boy is old enough to grasp the severity of the situation but is childish enough to beg his sister not to allow the doctor to remove his hand completely.

The word 'So' followed by a full stop has a daunting sense of finality about it. The shortening lines and quickening pace of the poem mirror the rising tension and the feeling that everything is happening very quickly. The line 'But the hand was gone already', is purely factual and reserved. It seems the poet cannot reveal any emotion for fear of breaking down. He purely relays the story from here on as he has removed himself from the scene. The doctor in this story does not symbolise hope; he can do nothing except drug the boy in an attempt to dull the pain and the reality. Then the unexpected happens: 'No one believed' – the boy's heart stops, and he dies. Again the sentences are short and informative hiding all emotion. Everyone turns 'to their affairs'; the boy is dead. The last line is vague. Does everyone continue with their daily chores because they are dazed with shock or because they realise there is nothing now to be done except survive and carry on as best they can?

Robert Frost
The Road Not Taken

THIS IS POSSIBLY Frost's best-known poem. It is both personal and universal as he tells of a dilemma: the inability to make a decision without regretting the outcome. He invites the reader in and makes us question our own decision-making skills.

It is morning and the poet sets the scene. He is in a yellow wood at autumn time. Looking at the seasons as symbols of stages in our lives, autumn is seen as a time to take stock, a time of wisdom and maturity before facing the bleakness of winter. The first sentence extends to line 12, which reflects the poet's meandering and pondering. Frost is at a fork in the road and would dearly love to travel down both roads. He sees that this is impossible as he is only 'one traveler'. He ponders and deliberates which direction he should choose. He chooses the road he feels 'wanted wear' and appears to have been less travelled. It was a difficult decision as the other road was 'just as fair'. Two lines later, however, he admits that both roads were really about the same. He says he will save the other road for another day, but he knows that in life one journey leads to another and he doubts he will ever return. He feels regret that he will never return, and knows that someday in the future he will look back 'with a sigh'. The contra-diction is obvious. The poet chose one road over the other as it was less travelled, but later he tells us both were 'about the same' and 'both that morning equally lay'.

It is irrelevant which road he chose and which he leaves; the poem is about the poet's feelings on making a decision and the regret involved in passing up on an opportunity. We learn all about the decision and nothing about what happens after he made the decision.

Robert Frost
Acquainted with the Night

THIS IS A dark poem; not only is the poet depicting night-time but also he reveals an inner loneliness and depression. For the poet it is dark both on the inside and the outside. It is a deeply personal poem as it exposes his innermost feelings. The first to the fifth and the seventh lines all begin with 'I', making this an overwhelmingly powerful expression of personal emotion.

This poem tells the story of loneliness, depression, isolation and unhappiness. The poet feels that he is cut off from life, he does not belong, he stands alone and apart. The weather seems to sympathise with his plight as it is always raining when he goes out walking. It also feels his pain – an example of *pathetic fallacy* (attributing human feeling or behaviour to nature).

The poet has walked further than the city boundaries and has still found only darkness. He has looked down the saddest side streets, passed a night watchman and avoided communication by averting his eyes. He does not want to explain himself. There are many signs of life around him: footsteps, an interrupted cry, houses, streets; but he feels no connection to them. 'One luminary clock', maybe the moon, signals the passing of time, but time means nothing. There never seems to be a right or a wrong time – only time. The poet repeats the first line again emphasising his plight:
'I have been one acquainted with the night.'

He is not an intimate friend of the night, he is merely an acquaintance, and this is a passing phase of his life. It is not permanent and there is a hint of hope that it will progress into a happier state. This poem is set in an urban environment reinforcing the belief that one does not need to be alone to be lonely.

He feels friendless, desolate and isolated even though he is surrounded by people. In this poem the poet is not looking for answers or dissecting the issue, he is merely reporting it.

•

Eamonn Grennan
Taking My Son to School

THIS SIMPLE LYRIC details a delicate moment between a father and a son. It is the son's first day of school but there seems to be more fear in the father than the son. The poem is presented in a series of staccato-like short sentences and phrases presenting an image of great apprehension on behalf of the father.

The poem begins in the family garden. Nature, and particularly flowers, dominate the imagery of the poem. The garden represents a place where the father and son are able to be together. It is a joint family area where they can bond. The father is afraid that this bond is about to be broken. The poet mentions taking a picture of his son: 'Catching him, as it were, in flight'. He fears that his son is flying away from him.

The son's excitement is obvious in the second verse. He is chattering and singing, hyperactive as the tension builds within him. We still see the father's anxiety as he talks about the lack of maps and the 'wilderness we enter'. Again nature-related images are given here. When they arrive at the school, the other children are gathered around the teacher; they are described as being like geese around the teacher. The father's trepidation seems justified as he sees his son: 'Silent, he stands on their border' (more garden images). When he hands the teacher the flowers, she doesn't have a chance to react to them yet. The son is disenchanted, his 'Head drooping, a flower after rain.'

The father is devastated for his son. He sees him alone on the edge of the group and miserable. The father wants to save him from his misery. But when he finally drives away he sees the son much more settled. 'His red hair blazes.' The father is resigned to keeping his memories of when the child was younger. He has to share him from now on.

•

Kerry Hardie
May

THIS IS A simple and concise poem about the beauty of nature in the month of May. There is a stretch in the daylight hours introducing a sense of ease, a freedom from worry, distress and burden. The poet uses short simple sentences to bombard the reader with images of beauty, calmness and ease. The hills are reflecting the sky, the seeds are bursting open, and the air is soft and fragrant. The birds' song is rebounding from the sky, and there is peacefulness and an air of relaxation in the meadows as the cows lie down so contented that they forget to feed. The horses exude relaxation and light-heartedness as they swish their tails. There is a vivid shot of colour near the hill as the furze (gorse) flares forth its bright yellow flowers. Everywhere is light and airy, carefree and bright.

The final two lines seem discordant with the rest of the poem. There is disharmony as the poet tells us that life was not always peaceful and easy. The winter, now forgotten, was full of hardship, hunger and betrayal. The final line expresses a sense of expectation. There is a belief that from this point on there will always be hope and forgiveness. There is a darkness here which hints at suspicion – why was winter so difficult? What betrayal or treachery occurred? What is there to forgive? There are no answers to these questions. There is only the statement that May and summer are very welcome and restorative and have brought a much-hoped-for release from the hardship of winter.

•

Seamus Heaney
Postscript

Note: A postscript is an additional paragraph at the end of a letter; an afterthought.

READING THIS POEM it feels as if we have just joined in a conversation with the poet Seamus Heaney and he is giving us some holiday advice.

> And some time make the time to drive out west
> into County Clare, along the Flaggy Shore,

He has obviously driven this route many times and is very impressed by the inspiring vista that greets him. He even suggests that September or October are the best times to appreciate the views, showing that he has travelled time and time again to enjoy this landscape. This drive can offer everything. On the one side is the ocean described in magical and powerful terms: 'wild / With foam and glitter'.

On the other side is more water: a lake, but it is in complete contrast with the untamed and wild ocean. The lake is dead flat and calm, it is 'slate-grey', dignified and tranquil. The lake is not lit by the sun nor the moon but is illuminated by a flock of swans. Heaney uses the unusual but very effective image of 'earthed lightning' in an attempt to convey the brightness and power of the swans. They are powerful and commanding creatures 'roughed and ruffling'. They are dominating the scene with both their striking colour, 'white on white', and their 'fully grown headstrong-looking heads'.

Heaney's voice reappears in line 12, having been lost as he immersed himself in the description of the lake and the swans, and he again offers the reader some advice. He says it is pointless stopping on this journey in the hope of absorbing the scene 'more thoroughly'. The initial sighting will fill your senses with all you need to fully appreciate the scene. Stopping for further appreciation is futile.

In line 13 the poet tells us 'You are neither here nor there', referring maybe to the isolation of the area, or indeed telling the reader that you are not part of this beautiful scene and stopping to investigate it closer will not involve you any more than if you just drive on by. This is a scene apart; it overwhelms the onlooker as if the car were pounded by strong gusts of wind: 'big soft buffetings'. 'Flaggy Shore' is off the beaten track, its beauty will catch you 'off guard', and your heart will be blown open with the grandeur and majesty of the swans and the splendour and loveliness of the whole scene.

·

Elizabeth Jennings
One Flesh

THIS POEM IS a meditation by the poet on her parents and their relationship. She examines her parents in old age and ponders on whether or not they were always like this.

To do this she pictures them in bed.

The poet goes straight in to the poem: immediately the parents are presented as being in two beds in the same room, the father reading to himself and the mother tossing and turning. They are both trying to get to sleep. They have come to a pragmatic arrangement to facilitate this. Their sleeping apart should mean that they will sleep more easily but it doesn't work. Instead they both lie in silence and 'it is as if they wait / Some new event'.

The poet does not comprehend how her parents can have drifted so far apart, 'like flotsam from a former passion'. She is fascinated by the way 'They hardly ever touch' and finds that if they do it is done with hesitancy and fear. The parents' lives seem to have come full circle. They have returned to the chaste lives that they may have had before they were married.

In the last verse the poet points out the contradiction in the parents' relationship, and sees that they are 'Strangely apart, yet strangely close together'. She sees that the silence is their way of communicating now as they are slowly but surely ageing like 'a feather / Touching them gently'.

Finally the poet comes to the conclusion that they may not even be conscious of the differences that are emerging in their relationship; they may not be fully aware that

These two who are my father and my mother
Whose fire from which I came, has now grown cold?

This may seem at first like a rhetorical question but it may not be. The poet may genuinely not know how her parents, who were once in love, can seemingly live so seperately, especially since they are still together.

Elizabeth Jennings
The Ladybird's Story

THIS POEM, AS the title suggests, is written in the voice of a ladybird. The ladybird is walking along the crevices of somebody's hand, finding 'So many meeting-places and directions'. Even when the hand is moved, the ladybird hangs on bravely. When she hears the person speak the ladybird does not understand the old proverb. When the hand is lifted up so that the person can see the insect properly, fear enters the ladybird's mind for the first time.

The ladybird describes the person's face perfectly but in a new and refreshing way:

> I watched the beak, the peak of your huge
>   nose
> And the island of your lips.

The ladybird does not know what her fate is to be. She admits that she is in no position to protect herself like other insects are. She expects to be blown away, but the proverb that she heard earlier saves her: 'A ladybird. Good luck. Perhaps some money.' Instead, the person holds her hand still and guides the ladybird gently towards safety. However, the ladybird is a realist and knows that the person is not an insect-rights activist:

> . . . it was not I you cared about but
>   money.
> You see I have watched you with flies.

Patrick Kavanagh
Shancoduff

ACCORDING TO THE critic Antoinette Quinn, 'Shancoduff is a north-facing hill farm depicted at its wintry worst, frostbound, starved of grass, swept by sleety winds.' Yet this is a love poem to it. Kavanagh had a love/hate relationship with the countryside of his youth. One of his most famous poems is 'Stony Grey Soil'. In that poem the poet accused the area where he was reared of burgling 'his bank of youth'. He describes the area as being one that is lifeless and soulless, and he questions how he managed to survive in a place where even plant life struggled to maintain an existence.

Yet in this poem his attitude is different. He is more interested in finding the good in his 'black hills'. He turns any notion of something negative into something positive. He transforms the faults of Shancoduff in the same way that a lover transforms his partner's faults into something to be loved. The immediate question that must be asked is why would anybody write a love poem to Shancoduff?

The answer must be because it is his. He claims ownership four times. He calls them '*My* black hills' twice in the first verse and then '*My* hills' and '*my* Alps'. Possession of this land is obviously very important to Kavanagh. After all, the hills are eternal. Shancoduff will last long after he has gone, and more importantly, it will still be there after the people who sneer at it are gone. He also personifies the hills. They are given a personality like a lover would have. The hills can 'look', they are 'incurious', they are 'happy', they 'hoard'.

Kavanagh relishes their drabness. Anything that might be confused as being negative can be construed into a positive. For example the fact that the hills are so incurious or inactive that they can't even be bothered to look at the sun is seen as a good thing when Kavanagh compares it with the fate of Lot's wife, who was turned to salt for looking back as she left Sodom and Gomorrah.

Kavanagh places a lot of emphasis on the local place names. He lists them with pride: Glassdrummond, Rocksavage, Featherna Bush; these are as important as the Alps. The names themselves have mythic qualities. They sound tough and treacherous. They have the resonance of something from an action movie where a hero stands proud above the hills. They all have a grandness granted to them by being multi-syllabic.

Kavanagh's own importance in the poem is also highlighted here as the person who has

> . . . climbed the Matterhorn
> With a sheaf of hay for three perishing
> calves

This act itself seems heroic, as if he had climbed the most dangerous mountain-face in the world, whereas all he has done is walk up a hill to feed the cows. This use of hyperbole shows the love that Kavanagh has for this place.

The rebellious nature of the hills is also shown as the hills refuse to conform to the usual structures of nature. They are oblivious to the changes in the seasons and the weather. Their immortality is stressed by the fact that they are unchanged by the travails of time. Spring time cannot catch up with them as his

> . . . hills hoard the bright shillings of
> March
> While the sun searches in every pocket.

The poem turns at this point; the poet has come to the realisation, albeit after being told so, that his mountains are not the glorious thing of beauty that he may have thought they

were. The farmers who are in a more sheltered, wealthier place sneer at him. Even though his hills are personified with their 'rushy beards', nobody else declares them worth looking after. When he is acknowledged as a poet, it is almost done as a form of derision. A poet may be someone who is seen as poor.

Kavanagh departs with a rhetorical question that is forced on him by the comments of the other men. This affects him deeply, just as if his wife or lover were to be described as ugly or disgusting. He asks himself 'is my heart not badly shaken?'. The love that he felt for the hills is broken by the reality forced on him.

Patrick Kavanagh
A Christmas Childhood

IN 'A CHRISTMAS Childhood', Kavanagh seems to be very conscious of his voice and the voice that he is using in the poem. Kavanagh adopts an innocent, naive attitude in this poem and this seems to be central to both the style and the substance. It is this merging of what he is saying and how he is saying it that gives this poem real quality. It uses simple, direct language and this simplicity is also important in what the poet is attempting to say. This is, however, in this reader's eyes a poem of two halves, to use the football cliché. Indeed this poem was originally published as two separate pieces; the first part was published in 1943, the second part was published a full three years earlier.

PART I
The poem begins with a simple description of a potato field where one side was in the sun and was beginning to thaw out. The other side

was still frozen over and 'white with frost'. Nature dominates everything; it takes over and liberates inanimate objects. The paling post that was once merely supporting a fence now sends music out through it:

> And when we put our ears to the paling-
>   post
> The music that came out was magical.

The way that nature attacks all the senses is important to Kavanagh. He goes through sight, taste and hearing in order to give us a holistic vision of how the Christmas spirit invades everything.

He then inserts an over-the-top repetition of his emotions. Hyperbole pervades through this part with even the fence providing 'magical' music. He continues with this mixture of the simple and the marvellous when comparing a gap of light with 'a hole in Heaven's gable'. Even an apple tree reminds him of the temptation of Adam. The death of innocence and a longing to return to innocence is a familiar theme in Kavanagh's poetry, and this reinforces it. The world has taken him, like Eve took Adam, from what he supposed was a better life.

> O you, Eve, were the world that tempted
>   me
> To eat the knowledge that grew in clay
> And death the germ within it!

He then sets up the second part of the poem by leaving us tranquil symbols of the 'gay / Garden that was childhood's', the most important being the final image 'Of a beauty that the world did not touch.'

There is a longing here to return to a better time for himself. In that time people were more dependent on nature. This closer interaction with nature is epitomised and made clearer by the amount of religious imagery that runs through the first section. There is plenty of religious imagery present such as 'Heaven's gable' and Eve and the apple. The time was more sacred to Kavanagh; he saw it as a time that was also good and holy.

PART II

The second part of the poem continues with the religious imagery, and makes striking comparisons between an Irish town and Bethlehem with its 'stars in the morning east'. There is a genuine excitement pervading this part, and it is less diluted by an adult knowingness than the first part. There are simple descriptions of what was going on in his childhood, and this allows him to retain an attitude of child-like wonder. The voice in the second half of the poem is certainly clearer.

The setting for the second half of the poem is almost completely outdoors, and this natural, open setting allows him to go from the local to the universal or even biblical with ease. There is a seamless intertwining of the personal and the public. Again the significance of the fact that the father was playing his music outdoors can not be underplayed. He finds harmony with nature and allows it to influence his playing. The stars manage to recognise his father's music, and are so captivated that they decide to dance to it.

Rapidly Kavanagh brings us back to his own townland and remarks on the unspoken signs between the families. Whereas in 'Epic' he describes local rivalries, here the unspoken language of music is a uniting force as 'his melodeon called / To Lennons and Callans'. Kavanagh remarks that he 'knew some strange thing had happened'. The harmonising power of his father's music is highly significant when one reflects on the first verse, where the music from the paling-post is described as magical.

His mother's daily ritual of milking the cows becomes inspired by 'the frost of Bethlehem'. The religious imagery continues here. Bethlehem brought new hope to people, and this time of year, with its sense of a new start, also suggests rebirth. Nature in the form of ice and wind and the water-hen is recalled. It is the sense of 'wonder of a Christmas townland' where even the dawn is personified and winks. Yet again Kavanagh tries to show how all of the senses are affected. *Sight* with the 'child-poet [who] picked out letters', the *sound* of the melodeon and when the 'water-hen screeched in the bog' and the

Mass-going feet
Crunched the wafer-ice on the potholes

In the sixth verse Kavanagh shows exquisite skill at mixing the northern constellation Cassiopeia with 'Cassidy's hanging hill', using run-through lines with clever use of alliteration to expose the child's sense of awe at Christmas. This also introduces the religious notion again, and suggests the northern star that guided the three wise men towards the birth of Christ; instead the stars guide people towards his father's house.

There is one wise man who proves his intelligence by commenting on the poet's father's melodeon playing. His father is working just like nature when the inanimate is brought to life as the man says 'Can't he make it talk'.

Pleasant childhood memories of Christmas are exposed graciously throughout the poem; his father's way of making the melodeon talk, his mother's commitment to the daily work on the farm, his presents and an overall satisfaction that nature has provided all of these things.

Patrick Kavanagh
On Raglan Road

Note: This poem is better known as a song. It was made famous by Luke Kelly of the Dubliners. It is worth the reader's effort to hear a recorded version of this song.

THIS IS A love poem. It is a love poem tinged with regret. Kavanagh sometimes prided himself on his innocence in his poems. Indeed in a number of them he advocated a sensibility that encouraged it. In this poem he expects the reader to see him as completely naive.

He begins the poem with a specific place. This is very similar to many of his poems. Of the poems in this anthology, however, this is the first poem set in Dublin rather than Monaghan. When Kavanagh names a place he does so not only because 'Naming these things is the love act' ('The Hospital') but also because the naming of these places helps to ground the poems. It allows the reader to believe them and him. The perception may be that if this is a real place and time ('an autumn day') then it must be true.

From the beginning of the poem, Kavanagh puts himself in the place of an innocent who has been dragged into a situation that he did not want but that could not be avoided. Kavanagh sees the inevitable pitfalls ahead but cannot resist. He admits that he

. . . **knew**
That her dark hair would weave a snare
 that I might one day rue

He acknowledges that he 'saw the danger' yet still walked into her path. Indeed the image created by Kavanagh of himself is of an innocent who is hypnotised by a medusa-like creature who forces him to do her will.

Kavanagh admits to giving into temptation, but like Othello he admits in his own way that he 'did not love too wisely but too well'. Kavanagh says that he 'loved too much and by such by such is happiness thrown away'.

The Queen of Hearts image is a curious one. There is a suggestion here that Kavanagh was gambling and it didn't pay off. He certainly didn't end up 'making hay'. He seems to be complaining that the woman was too quiet and spent her time doing homely things rather than making hay with him.

In the third verse he declares that he gave and she took. This may seem like an arrogant attitude to a contemporary reader.

> I gave her gifts of the mind I gave her the
>   secret sign that's known
> To the artists who have known the true
>   gods of sound and stone
> And word and tint.

He declares that he has brought her to Parnassus and has given her that which every intelligent person would want: an insight into his mind. He was even gracious enough to name her in some of his poems. What more could any woman want:

> . . . I did not stint for I gave her poems to
>   say
> With her own name there

He does this even though she may have ruined his talent and killed the sunshine that should have fallen on him:

> . . . her own dark hair like clouds over
>   fields of May.

In the fourth verse Kavanagh sees his 'ex' and rationalises why she would turn away from him. He comes to the final damning conclusion that she did not deserve his love. He describes himself as an angel and his 'ex' as a gargoyle.

The angel made too much of a sacrifice by trying to love somebody so base that they are made of clay. The net result of this encounter was inevitable: the angel was injured.

> . . . I had wooed not as I should a
>   creature made of clay—
> When the angel woos the clay he'd lose
>   his wings at the dawn of day.

As a poem, 'On Raglan Road' is certainly presented from the poet's point of view. Should he be expected to give more balance? He is not writing a piece of journalism. Poetic license with the truth is allowable but it is important to see that this is one side of the argument and maybe Kavanagh loses some of the impact that he might have had.

Some of the imagery that Kavanagh uses is worth remarking upon. He seems to be referring to himself in a passive mode and as somebody who is angelic and taken by nature, whereas the woman in the poem is associated with darkness. 'her dark hair', 'the deep ravine', 'clouds over fields of May', 'made of clay'.

The long, winding lines of the poem are often associated with poetry written *as gaeilge*, and fit in with many of the poems written in the bardic tradition. Many of these poems were also about women, but any woman in a vision poem was presented as someone who was pure, representing Ireland to the poet and encouraging him to eulogise rather than lament. (Although Kavanagh's lament seems to be more for himself.) These long lines fit into the pattern of the song-line. They flow dreamily and sweetly.

He also uses a lot of mid-line rhyme in this poem which also encourages a lament-like air. There are examples of this all the way through the poem. In the first verse: 'hair' and 'snare', 'grief' and 'leaf'. In the second verse he uses 'ravine' and 'seen', 'Hearts' and 'tarts' and 'much' and 'such'. The third verse has 'mind' and 'sign', 'tint' and 'stint' and 'there' and 'hair'.

Finally the fourth verse has 'street' and 'meet', 'me' and 'hurriedly', 'wooed' and 'should' and 'woos' and 'lose'.

•

John Keats
On First Looking into Chapman's Homer

THIS POEM EXPLAINS how Keats felt on reading George Chapman's translations of Homer's great works from Greek into English. Keats informs us that he has travelled and has experienced much of the world of literature in Britain and Ireland ('western islands'). He has encountered many bards (poets) who are loyal to the god of poetic inspiration, Apollo. He had been told of the vast works written by a deep-browed Homer but he could never study them, as he did not understand Greek. He compares Homer's work to a place he has not been able to visit.

Now that Keats has discovered Chapman's translations, Homer's work speaks to him 'loud and bold'. His eyes have been opened to the greatness of Homer and he feels the excitement like an astronomer who discovers a new planet. He also compares his joy and excitement to that of the great explorer Cortez when he first sets eyes on the Pacific Ocean. (He has actually confused Cortez with another adventurer, Balboa, who was the first Westerner to see the Pacific.) Chapman has opened up a new world for Keats and he can now experience what was once alien to him.

This is a Petrarchan sonnet divided into an octet (eight lines) and a sestet (six lines). The octet tells of his travelling and experience and the sestet tells how he feels on reading Chapman's translations of Homer's great works.

John Keats
La Belle Dame Sans Merci

THIS BALLAD TELLS of the plight of a young knight. The poem starts with an anonymous narrator speaking directly to the knight. He asks why the knight is alone and loitering, looking pale and sickly. The vegetation at the side of the water has withered and there are no birds singing. Winter is coming, heralding death. The language is plain and simple and the image is portrayed vividly. The knight is also withering and dying like nature around him.

In verse 2 the narrator continues to question the knight in an effort to find out what is wrong with him. The knight is now 'haggard' and 'woe begone'. Autumn is definitely at an end and nature prepares for the season of no growth. The squirrel has stashed away his food for hibernation and the farmer has completed the harvest. The images portray a bare, lifeless and empty landscape and this is clearly a reflection of the knight's physical state.

In verse 3 the knight takes on the colours of the flowers, but this does not indicate health or beauty. The colours he assumes are the colours of the lily and the rose – both flowers associated with funeral wreaths. He is as pale as the lily and the natural rosy glow of his cheeks is fading. The knight is in a state of severe mental and physical anguish and pain. The use of metaphors (lily and rose) is powerful as we see the knight withering like a delicate flower.

Verse 4 begins the knight's own story. He met a beautiful lady in a meadow; she had long hair and wild eyes and reminded him of a fairy's child. He wove a garland of flowers for her head and adorned her wrists and waist with chains of flowers. She looked lovingly at him and whispered into his ear. We do not know what she said or asked but his response was immediate. He put her on his 'pacing' horse and was totally consumed by her. He admits that the rest of the day disappeared as he she bent towards him and sang a magical song. She found food and drink from nature for him and as time passed he fell deeper and deeper under her spell.

Up to this point he was a willing partner to this beautiful, magical woman and we hear that she spoke to him in a strange language telling him of her true love. The final five verses show the demise of the knight. The beauty brought him to her grotto and cried and sighed. The knight tried to reassure her with kisses and she lulled him to sleep. It was not a comforting sleep as distressing dreams haunted him. He saw kings, princes and warriors and they were deathly pale. They cried out that they had been spellbound by 'La belle dame sans merci'. The knight saw their faces clearly and observed their wide, gaping lips. He awoke and it was twilight. Here ends the knight's story but the real conclusion is his impending death, and he awaits his demise alone and pale in the cold, bare and birdless twilight.

·

Brendan Kennelly
Night Drive

THIS IS A narrative poem. It tells of three separate scenes; firstly the journey from Dublin to Limerick taken by the poet and Alan, his brother perhaps. The second part tells us what they find when they get there. The third part describes the journey home.

Their journey to Limerick is done in a night when the weather is madness. Alan does all the talking on the journey while the poet is unable to say a word. Most of this section describes the weather. He describes the

weather as being like a mad, rabid animal. He shows the wind trying to lift the car and move it. He shows the river breaking its banks and grabbing the car. He shows the trees reaching out from the side of the road and breaking their journey. Then the strangest thing happens: the frogs are forced out of the marshland by the weather and onto the road.

Section two is set in the hospital where the poet's father is lying still, yet sweating. There is serenity in this part of the poem compared to the madness and wildness in the first section. The colours are white; the pillow and the 'white hospital bed'. The contrast is striking. Their father tries to fight back the inevitable and succeeds temporarily at least. He has been reduced by his battle however; he is no longer able to 'rail against the weather'.

The third section allows time for reflection. Darkness returns in this last piece. The brothers have been made sombre by their experience and death is the first thing to greet them as they make their journey home. Alan is distracted by having to focus on his driving and does not have as much room to contemplate as his brother does. He shows his optimism when he suggests 'I think he might pull through now'.

On the other hand, nature has left the poet in a more pessimistic mode as he is haunted:

> In the suffocating darkness
> I heard the heavy breathing
> Of my father's pain.

Nature has become overwhelming.

·

Philip Larkin
At Grass

THE BEAUTIFULLY EVOCATIVE title, 'At Grass', conveys the relaxation and winding-down of the retirement period for racehorses after a career filled with competitiveness and time pressures.

The poem opens in a quiet and subtle manner reflecting the mood of the horses. The speaker is anonymous and there does not appear to be any human involvement in the tranquil scene. 'The eye', not 'my' eye, introduces the scene and searches for the two horses concealed in the shade. They seem to have blended into the landscape as they shelter from the cold. There is no movement until line 3 when the wind 'distresses tail and mane'. 'Distresses' is an unusual choice of word as it has such negative connotations in such a peaceful setting. Coupled with the mention of a 'cold shade' the reader cannot help but see a shadow of death lurking in the background. But that does not concern these horses, as they seem to be enjoying their anonymity. There is no structure to their time as they crop grass and move about in a leisurely, relaxed manner.

Verses 2 and 3 look into the past and see that fifteen years ago all it took was 'two dozen distances' to transform these horses into legendary heroes. All the great race meetings 'Of Cups and Stakes and Handicaps' are hazy and 'faint' and blend together into one long catalogue of racing paraphernalia: 'silks', 'parasols', 'empty cars' and 'littered grass'. These were triumphant, sunny summer days in many Junes when these horses' names became immortal.

Verse 4 begins with the speaker musing – do the memories of these great successes hum in the horses' ears like flies buzzing in the open air? Humorously the horses shake their heads as if to answer 'No'. As dusk fills the shadows and the bright lights fade, the summers 'stole away' and soon the glory days are in the past. The names of these great giants of horse racing continue to attract glory but the horses have moved on; they enjoy their retirement in the meadows. They have slipped out of their former identities and now live lives separate from their famous names. They 'stand at ease'; gone are the pressures of chomping at the bit at the start line. The grass no longer symbolises human interference and drive; the grass is now 'unmolesting', it does not bother them. They gallop when they feel like it 'for what must be joy'. No one scrutinises their every move through binoculars or assesses their race times with stop watches. The only human intervention is the appearance of the groom and his assistant in the evenings.

This is an exceptional poem cleverly considering the concept of standing outside of your successes and glories, leaving the hugely sought-after spotlight and immersing yourself in lush green fields of total anonymity.

Philip Larkin
An Arundel Tomb

THIS POEM DESCRIBES a stone grave that the poet has visited. In the tomb lie the stone shapes of two bodies lying horizontally next to each other. The poet, when he sees it, regards it as curious and examines it in this poem. He is interested in the nature of this commemoration and the life that the people in the tomb might have lived.

The first thing that he notices on his initial viewing is how everything seems to be quite simple. The faces are blurred without showing any real detail of their original character. He tells us of their regal stature; they were an earl and a countess. He points out the fact that their clothes have become almost one garment in the way they were sculpted. Then he points out the little dogs under their feet, which he regards as merely eccentric.

He initially dismisses this as nothing to be worried about until he notices one small detail. The earl has his hand taken out of his glove and instead it is placed in his wife's. They are holding hands. This gives him 'a sharp tender shock'. He goes on to examine this in more detail. He says that nobody would ever lie together as long as these have. He says that when this sculpture was originally made, the couple might have commissioned it to be made this way but they would not have expected it to be seen like this for so long and by so many people. He wonders why it was done at all.

He believes that the couple could not have imagined the changes that would come to the world as they lay there together hand in hand. He says that they could not foresee how they would be made so public; after all it was such a private gesture between them, they could not know the different attitudes that would be shown to royalty in general and to them in particular throughout the centuries.

Larkin describes the changes that nature brings to the world around them, yet they still lie there hand in hand in an unending gesture of love. He points out all the people who would come and visit their final resting place down the ages and barely know anything about them. He says the times and people have changed so much that 'Only an attitude remains'.

He says that perhaps time has made them seem to represent something that they did not intend. They have become a pure symbol of love and of the idea that no matter what we go through, it is only our love for others that can go on living after us.

Philip Larkin
The Explosion

THIS LYRIC TELLS the story of an accident at a mine in England when many people were killed. It is said to be based on real events. It describes two groups of people. The first five verses describe a group of miners on their way to work on the day of the explosion. The rest of the poem looks at the wives they leave behind, their reaction to the catastrophe and the choices that they face for the future.

The first part of the poem is told in a passive, objective voice. It is very matter of fact. The poet is not a part of this community. He talks about 'men' and 'they'. The first sign gives nature an ominous role as the 'shadows pointed' at the scene of the impending doom, giving a feeling inevitability. The men are shown without too much emotion. They are simple men making their way to work without any awareness of what is coming for them. '. . . men in pitboots / Coughing oath-edged talk and pipe-smoke'. There is innocence in the men. They chase rabbits and examine birds' eggs like children might. This innocence is soon to be lost. They are part of a community; 'Fathers, brothers, nicknames'; a community soon to be torn apart.

When the explosion happens, Larkin gives it only a brief mention:

> At noon, there came a tremor; cows
> Stopped chewing for a second . . .

He begins the second section of the poem with a quote that is full of hope and redemption. He tells us of the closeness of the men to their families as their wives see their husbands in a vision. The poet urges that this redemption and hope be shown to the women. He wishes them faith and that they would take heart in their love for their lost men. He hopes that the men will be seen by those they leave behind as having gone to a better place, as pure as they were when they left.

This poem is positive at the end where it shows the innocence of the men hasn't had a chance to be broken. Even though they have met a horrible fate and destiny the poet shows hope for their souls in the image of the 'eggs unbroken'.

.

Denise Levertov
What Were They Like?

This is a direct, angry, political poem about the Vietnam War. The poet sets up a question and answer session. Six questions are asked and then later they are answered. The tension is felt all through the poem. There is a boiling anger, yet the speaker in the poem is trying her best to be reserved and cautious.

The questions come first. They seem to be coming from an anthropologist who is trying to find information about a lost society. The questions seem to be harmless but when they are balanced by the answers their significance becomes obvious. The questions refer to innocuous items like 'lanterns of stone', 'opening of buds', 'laughter', 'ornament', poetry and 'speech and singing'. But when we hear the tenor of the responses we know these things are very important indeed.

In the first answer the speaker takes the metaphor of stone used in referring to their lanterns and uses it to refer to their hearts. In fact the thought of even asking about lanterns seems anathema to the speaker. She implies that it cannot matter about light when you have no heart.

Next she explains that without life or the beginnings of life there was no place for flowering beauty never mind celebrations of that. The third answer is perhaps the most terrifying and bleak, yet also the plainest.

Sir, laughter is bitter to the burned mouth.

It is obvious from the fourth answer that ornament is only an afterthought when you consider that they barely had bodies to put the ornament on.

In the fifth answer she explains that the victors often write history. There is nothing in these people's immediate history that they would want to celebrate. Even nature was destroyed for these people. They could not look in pools of water and see themselves any longer. Their language had been reduced to the language of the panicked;

When bombs smashed those mirrors there was time only to scream.

Again, the speaker tells us that singing can no longer be heard from these people who have been frightened into silence. She gives us the most beautiful image in the poem when she tells us that when they did sing 'their singing resembled / the flight of moths in moonlight'. This encapsulates the great, unified beauty that they were once capable of. She then reminds us of the fact that all that beauty is now irrelevant, for there is nothing left to see or hear.

This is a hauntingly powerful poem that tells the story of a forgotten people.

.

Liz Lochhead
Kidspoem/Bairnsang

THIS POEM WAS originally written to teach schoolchildren the difference between dialect (local forms of language) and the conventional English language.

The poem can be divided up into three sections. Section 1 (lines 1–12), in the distinctly Scottish dialect, recalls a child's first day at school. Section 2 (lines 13–24) translates the first 12 lines into understandable 'proper' English. The only change made to the text is that Section 2 is introduced in line 12 by saying that school was where she learned to forget her Scottish way of speaking. Section 3 (lines 25–37) repeats the start of the story all over again in the Scottish dialect proving that she hasn't forgotten it after all. But the final five lines bring about a bitter twist to the childish manner in which the rest of the poem is written.

> Oh saying it was one thing
> but when it came to writing it
> in black and white
> the way it had to be said
> was as if you were posh, grown-up, male,
>   English and dead.

These lines are a direct attack on the bland, homogenised, stuffy and lifeless English language often referred to as 'Proper English'. Liz Lochhead is very proud of her Scottish accent and way of speaking; she refuses to conform as that would mean losing her identity. She is unwilling to see her Scottishness as an obstacle to her aims as a writer. She once said that for a woman to excel in Scotland she had to have a very good relationship with her male side.

Lochhead rejects all the demands on her to conform to the preconceived notions of what a good poet should be. The message in this poem is direct and crystal clear. Lochhead's poetry is the poetry of the everyday person, no airs or graces, it appeals to the child in everyone, it rejects the traditional view of the English poet and most importantly it is alive. She considers that a poem is a voice and insists that it is spoken out loud.

·

Michael Longley
Wounds

THE POET IS describing two pictures from his father's memory. Immediately the reader can sense a bond of closeness between father and son as Longley feels confident to accurately describe something his father recounted to him. These were special memories and the poet tells us he has kept them secret until 'now'. 'Now' we find out later is the death of his father, which prompts him to write this poem.

The first scene is an image from the Somme during the First World War. We see soldiers from the Ulster Division going to their deaths screaming anti-Catholic rhetoric to the end. The poet's father admired the courage of these men but was also bewildered by their staunch religious bigotry so close to their own deaths. The exact exclamations are included in the poem in an attempt to bring to life the wild excitement felt by the young soldiers.

The second picture from his father's head is of the immediate aftermath of the battle. The padre walks through the carnage in an image that lacks dignity and any sense of respect. The padre doesn't bend to say a prayer or even pause to ask God 'Why?'. Instead he stylishly flicks a stick and resettles the men's kilts and says his prayers as he swaggers through the grotesque 'landscape of dead buttocks'. This image haunted Longley's father for the next fifty years. The intimacy between father and son is reiterated in the final line of verse 1: 'I touched his hand, his thin head I touched.' This is a beautiful image capturing a moment of love, tenderness and warmth. Longley's father did not die in the war but has never recovered from the horrors he witnessed, and has spent his life dying as a result – 'belated casualty'.

The images presented in verse 1 are powerful and moving. The war is not glorified, nor are the soldiers involved. Both images are from the same period of time yet they are vastly different. The first is full of bravado and daring, life and movement, and the second is one of solemnity and stillness. The only movement is the padre flicking kilts to cover bare buttocks in such a manner that he could be practicing his backhand in tennis.

Verse 2 is linked to verse 1 by the word 'Now'. The poet has kept these pictures private until now as he buries his father. 'Now' also awakens our awareness to the fact that the devastation of war cannot be consigned to the past. 'Now' is the present for Longley as he witnessed Northern Ireland being torn apart by conflict. At his father's funeral all the military regalia is present – badges, medals and his compass. The violent deaths of the soldiers at the Somme are remembered again in verse 2 as Longley's father is being buried beside three young soldiers. Like the soldiers at the Somme these boys were once full of 'Irish beer', indicating having a good time and enjoying life. We also see the link to the indignity of the kilt-wearing soldiers at the Somme as these young soldiers died with 'their flies undone'.

Longley catalogues the things he would like to bury with his father: cigarettes and a light, the Sacred Heart of Jesus – a religious icon in many Catholic homes – (Longley imagines the heart is paralysed as it watches the heavy

artillery in Northern Ireland pierce even the most treasured of locations, such as a nursery wall), the uniform of a bus conductor coldly shot in the head in front of his wife and family by a 'shivering boy' in Northern Ireland. Again Longley highlights the immaturity of youth in the face of death as the killer mutters 'Sorry Missus' to the bus conductor's wife.

These people were not prepared for war or death. They had not turned down the television or tidied away the supper dishes. Everyday life has been blighted by war and conflict. The battlefield is now the homeland, the streets, the nursery and even the once-secure home.

.

Michael Longley
Last Requests

THIS VERY SIMPLE poem speaks directly to the poet's father. It tells of two occasions when the poet's father faced death. In verse 1 he remembers a story his father told him of when he was buried alive on a battlefield. His 'batman' (assistant) left him to die and stole his watch and his cigarette case. His father did not die, instead his love of cigarettes ignited in him a will to live, and he so longed for 'a long remembered drag' that he pushed himself to the surface. This return to life prevented his cigarette case's engraved initials from becoming his epitaph.

Verse 2 tells of another confrontation with death, but this time his father succumbs, even though his desire for a cigarette is still strong. Longley stands aside watching his father make a gesture, waving his bony fingers to and fro. Longley is emotional as he knows his father is near to death, and he interprets the gesture as the blowing of a kiss. He is mistaken. There is no sign of bitterness here, only intense pathos and a hint of humour. Longley accepts that his father is actually making his last request – a cigarette, a Woodbine. We learn that his father has always smoked Woodbines (cigarettes synonymous with a soldier's last request as he lay dying on the battlefield).

After the war his father continued to smoke Woodbines and each one he consumed was a mark of respect to the men who died in warfare. Longley, the loving son, feels helpless and powerless. He denies his father his last request as he is dying not on the battleground but in an oxygen tent in hospital. We feel that Longley would do anything for his father, but unfortunately the one thing his father craves is the one thing he cannot give him. He feels distant and removed from his father; he cannot comfort his craving for a cigarette, and the offerings he brings, 'peppermints and grapes', are totally inadequate.

Michael Longley
An Amish Rug

THIS POEM IS very different to the other two Longley poems on the Leaving Certificate course. It is short and simple and deals mainly with his relationship with his wife. He has been away and has bought a rug from the Amish community well known for their dedication to a simple and austere way of life.

In verse 1 the poet encourages his wife to play a game of 'let's pretend'. He imagines they are part of the Amish community, and all they are used to is the simplicity of a one-roomed schoolhouse, the plainness and modesty of black clothes and underwear, the restraint of the only public display of marriage – a journey together to church, and the naturalness of having children and seeing them blend in with nature.

In verse 2 he makes the offering of the rug to his wife in an almost religious way. He compares its patchwork to a small farm. He imagines himself as a hired worker offering her some produce from the farm, something of value and importance. The rug, unlike the Amish people who made it, is colourful and ornamental. The colours are in stark contrast to the severe black and white images of verse 1. The threads used in this rug could also have been used in a more practical way in a number of farming chores.

Once the poet hands over the rug the power to do with it as she likes is passed on to his wife. He suggests two uses for it. Firstly, to continue the religious theme, they could hang it on the wall and it would resemble a stained glass window from a cathedral. Or they could lay it on the floor of their bedroom so that it becomes part of their everyday lives. It will resemble a flowerbed and grow with them and be a thing of beauty and fragrance for them every time they enter their bed. It will be a witness to their undressing, to their sleeping and their lovemaking.

The rug has moved the couple from the imagined scenario of verse 1 into the reality of their lives in verse 3, and in doing so the couple take with them the values of the Amish people which will enrich their lives. The rug is a symbol of what the Amish people represent and what the poet hopes for his own relationship – simplicity, sincerity, and naturalness with a bare splash of colour.

Derek Mahon
Grandfather

THIS SONNET PRESENTS a portrait of the poet's grandfather in old age. He used to work as a boilermaker, and later as a foreman in the Harland and Wolfe shipyard in Belfast. His work would have been intensive and tough at the time and would have required physicality. The grandfather is now retired, and Mahon writes about his life after he has no further use for his energy.

The first line is a curious one: 'They brought him in on a stretcher from the world'. There is a sense of a strange journey here. This is a man who has had to be forced to get where he ended up. His previous life is ended and he is at the beginning of a new one. However despite his reluctance he is 'wounded but humorous'.

His working life has given way to a simpler one. He is eager and ready to take on the world again now that he has been freed from the burdens of employment. This journey has brought him back to his childhood where he could play away to his heart's content. He is up at six in the morning, ready to take on the world 'with a block of wood / Or a box of nails'. He is clearly enjoying this journey of self-discovery. His enigma is clear in the second verse where he is hard to track down: 'Never there when you call'. He is only found 'after dark'.

The poet describes his grandfather as 'cute' which could refer to his child-like attitude or his shrewdness. When night-time comes he is careful to protect himself from the world. The final line of the poem tells us that the grandfather does not need to be pitied or patronised. He is living life as free and aware as ever. He is someone to be admired: 'Nothing escapes him; he escapes us all.'

Derek Mahon
After the *Titanic*

THIS POEM IS a lament. It is written in the voice of Bruce Ismay who was the manager of the White Star Line, owners of the *Titanic*. Ismay survived the *Titanic*'s sinking and was one of very few men who escaped alive. He was vilified later in his life as a coward. The *Titanic* itself was built in Belfast, where Derek Mahon is from, and was, as the name suggests, a colossus of a ship. On its maiden voyage to America it struck an iceberg and sank, leading to the death of 1,500 of its passengers and crew. The name is synonymous with disaster. This poem tells the story of what became of Ismay. It is presented in his own voice and is full of self-pity.

There is denial in the very first line: 'They said I got away in a boat' as if it were not true. There is also the accusing 'They'. Ismay sees himself as a victim. He gives out about being 'humbled' and having sunk 'as far that night as any / Hero'. The truth is that he didn't. He lived and many others died. He talks about the sinking of various things

> . . . in a pandemonium of
> Prams, pianos, sideboards, winches,
> Boilers bursting and shredded ragtime.

But he does not talk about people sinking to their deaths. It sounds as if he cares more about what happened to these material things than about all the people who died.

He brings us forward to his life in the present, and describes himself as a pathetic creature hiding in his big house, hiding from nature and the world. He maintains that he is doing his suffering now just like the people who died on the *Titanic*. He tells us that he is locked away as if he was in prison. He tells us of his drugged-out nightmares:

I drown again with all those dim
Lost faces I never understood, my poor
   soul
   Screams out in the starlight . . .

He ends the poem wishing to be treated like the rest of the dead. He wishes the people to allow his living soul to be pitied. The question is whether he deserves this: 'Include me in your lamentations.'

•

Derek Mahon
Antarctica

THIS POEM IS about Captain Laurence Oates. Oates was one of the explorers who travelled to Antarctica in 1911–12. Scott wanted to be the first person to reach the South Pole. Eventually when they reached their destination they discovered that they had been beaten by an expedition led by a Norwegian, Roald Admunsen. They had been beaten to the Pole by just three weeks. A catalogue of awful luck covered their return journey. The temperature plunged as low as −50 degrees. Another member of the team, Edgar Evans, died after a fall, having struggled on for two more weeks. They started to run out of food and their animals died.

Oates' feet became gangrenous. He asked the other surviving members to leave him behind and to save themselves. He was slowing them down. They refused to abandon him. Eventually he got up himself and walked out of the tent to his certain death. His last words were the ones quoted in this poem: 'I am just going outside and may be some time.'

Tragically, the rest of the explorers nearly made it to their base; they were only eleven miles away. A blizzard struck. Their bodies were not found for a further eight months. It would be easy to suggest that Oates's death was in vain, but Mahon suggests that it was not.

The poem itself is quite simple. It is very tightly structured with two chorus lines. The first: 'I am just going outside and may be some time' is the quote from Oates as he goes to die. The second: 'At the heart of the ridiculous, the sublime' is Mahon's comment on the act. Even though the statement is a ridiculous one for someone who is about to die, the poet, through his use of the word 'sublime', also sees it as a massively heroic act.

In the first verse he refers to the complicity of the others in this act. They are passive. He goes on to describe how Oates forces himself out to his death, 'Goading his ghost', and shows Oates looking back at the tent, going through the processes of his forthcoming death.

The fourth verse introduces the question of judgment of the act. Mahon is clear that this should not be seen as something weak or even 'some sort of crime'. He says that Oates can be seen as a catalyst for good, for not being selfish and for self-sacrifice. See how much Oates contrasts with the other man from his own times, Bruce Ismay in 'After the *Titanic*'.

The final verse repeats the two choruses together after first telling us that Oates should be admired for 'Quietly, knowing it is time to go.'

Roger McGough
Bearhugs

THIS LYRIC IS a portrait of the poet's two sons, who have grown up, and his relationship with them. It is a warm, loving picture that we get and is written in simple colloquial language.

From the start, the relationship is clear. The poet tells us about the hugs, but he points out that 'we hug each other'. The relationship is clearly two-way. The boys are growing up, but the poet has no regrets about this as you might expect him to have. He is proud of their growth into manhood. He does not condemn them for their smell of 'beer', 'tobacco' or 'women / Whose memory they seem reluctant to wash away'. His affection for them is still fatherly though, in the way that they are described when they were small – 'tiny'. He takes their visits as a sign of love.

When he examines them, he cannot see any resemblance to himself, but he can to his father and his uncle. When he was very young he looked up to these men who were fighting in the Second World War. He admired their confidence and self-assurance at the time and he sees the same traits in his sons now. Their confidence can be seen in the way they slouch back in their chairs, and he imagines them in the uniforms of their grandfather and grand-uncle.

The poet finishes the poem beautifully. He repeats much of the first verse with one crucial difference. He recognises the life, love and energy that he gets from his two sons.

Paula Meehan
Buying Winkles

IN THIS POEM, the poet presents an episode from her childhood that brought great joy to her. The action of the poem is very simple. The speaker in the poem goes to the corner of the street to buy some shellfish from an old lady. It is the detail that the poet brings to the proceedings that make this poem such a joyful recollection. We get a vivid sense of the time of the young girl's life, living in inner-city Dublin, and a sense of the innocence of the era.

The detail is given to us immediately. We are told the amount of money the child was given and what the mother would say. We get a feeling for her home and the social class of the girl with the 'ghosts / on the stairs where the bulb had blown'. We get the exact place, Gardiner Street on Dublin's north side. What we get most of all are the feelings of the girl as she takes on this task. She is delighted when she is sent out at night. She is happy if she can see the moon, but if it is raining she is still happy. Her outpouring of joy is plain to be seen as she would 'hold the tanner tight / and jump every crack in the pavement' and wave at everybody she passed.

She then describes the winkle seller, sitting outside the Rosebowl Bar. She is curious about the men in the pub; it seems like somewhere warm and exciting and exotic, with its 'hot interior' and 'light in golden mirrors'.

The ritual of talking to the old woman is to be enjoyed as well. There is wonderment at the methodology of opening and eating the winkles as if they were a rare delicacy. She savours 'The sweetest extra winkle / that brought the sea to me.' At the end of this experience, she feels like the carrier of the Olympic torch coming triumphantly home to glory.

This poem celebrates innocence; an

innocent child living in a more innocent time. It is nostalgic but gloriously so. It is a poem about how a child can revel in the simplest of pleasures.

·

Paula Meehan
My Father Perceived as a Vision of St Francis

THE WORLD IS slowly waking up, the milkman is delivering the milk, the bus is starting its first journey of the day and the poet is awoken by the sound of the neighbour's piebald pony. The sounds of the morning are wonderfully evocative – the horse's 'whinny' and the 'chink' of the bottles on the doorsteps.

The speaker is frightened as she is not in her usual surroundings; she has returned to her parent's house and is staying in the unfamiliar boxroom enclosed by her brother's belongings and secrets. We experience a sense of being surrounded and almost swamped in the alliteration of 'ties and sweaters and secrets'. Everyone else is asleep except for her father who is going through his morning routine of raking the ashes, plugging in the kettle and humming contentedly to himself. The silence of the rest of the family amplifies the sounds her father is making.

The first two verses are closely linked but verse 3 stands apart. It informs the reader that the seasons are moving out of autumn and into winter – just like the poet's father. She watches her father and sees him as she has never seen him before. He is aging, he is silver on top like the 'frost whitened' rooftops, and he is stooped and stiff. Verse 3 ends with two questions enticing the reader to read on and discover the answers.

Something extraordinary happens. Like St Francis of Assisi, who could communicate with the animals and attracted them to him all through his life, her father attracts birds from all around. The long and flowing sentence indicates the great volumes in which they come.

They came then: birds
of every size, shape, colour; they came
from the hedges and shrubs,
from eaves and garden sheds,
from the industrial estate, outlying fields,
from Dubber Cross they came
and the ditches of the North Road.

The scene is 'pandemonium'. But this scene is not the only similarity between the poet's father and St Francis. As the poet watches, the sun rises higher in the sky and her father appears saint-like, radiant and transformed – 'made whole, made young again'. While this is a fantastic and miraculous incident it is made real and believable, perfectly everyday, acceptable and comfortable, because it occurs, not in some exotic holy land, but in a 'Finglas garden'.

·

John Milton
When I Consider

IN THIS SONNET the poet meditates how half his life has been spent in darkness due to his blindness ('light deny'd'). He wonders if God will be angry with him for not making full use of his writing talent. He makes reference to the Parable of Talents in line 3. In this parable it is believed that God will punish ('is death to hide') those who do not make full use of the gifts (talents) he has bestowed upon them. Milton feels that his talent, writing, is now of little use to him as he can no longer see ('Lodg'd with me useless'). He is however still determined to serve God to the best of his ability and on Judgment Day he hopes to present to God a true and honest account of how he has made the most of his talent, and the condition of blindness in which he finds himself. He fears God may 'chide' him, and he questions whether or not God will expect his day's work to be equal to that of a fully sighted person. God is seen as an investor who has invested in Milton. Milton is deeply concerned about the repayment of dividends to God on Judgment Day.

In the octet the poet is full of anxiety and apprehension, but the tone changes dramatically in the sestet. In the sestet Milton receives a whispered reply from God, putting his mind at ease. God does not need the talents he has provided to be returned to him. If man bears the burden and makes the most of his situation he is serving God to the best of his ability. God is like a king; there are thousands of servants speeding over land and sea without rest doing his bidding. Milton concludes that one can be loyal to God by standing and waiting to openly receive his word and message. Not all of God's servants must be active 'doers'. Both active and passive service to God is cherished and valued.

John Montague
The Locket

IN THIS POEM Montague is mourning his mother, but he does not just mourn her death; he also mourns the relationship he never had with her. He does not feel bitterness towards her, after all he refers to her as 'a lady', but he informs us that she was a 'fertile ground for guilt and pain'. In italics comes the line '*The worst birth in the annals of Brooklyn*', a sentence obviously often spoken and recounted. That was how Montague's arrival into the world was remembered.

Verse 2 shows a childish acceptance that he wasn't all his mother had wished for; he was a boy and not the yearned-for girl, and the birth was a difficult one. For these two things he feels his mother could never forgive him.

Verse 2 finishes the story of his infancy, divulging the awful fact that his mother did not nurse or care for him as a new mother should. The maternal instincts were extinguished by her deeply felt sense of disappointment and pain. His father, portrayed as happy go lucky, could not provide for his family, and his mother sang a bitter but very real tune: '*when poverty comes through the door / love flies up the chimney*'. Montague was sent home to Ireland to be reared by his father's sisters, and his brothers went to live with his mother's family. 'Then you gave me away' is an honest childish accusation. He feels his mother would have forgotten him had he not made such a great effort to stay in touch. He 'courted' her like a suitor, teasing her and trying to entice her to tell him stories of her youth.

Verse 5 expresses pity and sympathy for the plight of his mother, 'lovely Molly'. Her life began full of hope and potential, 'the belle of your small town', but she ended wrapped in a 'cocoon of pain'. This is a powerful image of a pathetic woman trying to protect herself from the trials of life and the 'constant rain' punitively lashing her.

Life was hard for his mother, and verse 6 introduces the voice of Molly Montague. She speaks 'roughly' to her son, but the rough words are tinged with pain and sadness. The mother begs her son to leave her and stay away as she finds saying goodbye too heart-wrenchingly difficult. It is 'harsh logic' but understandable. She has accepted that she will always be alone and little snippets of love only tease her and show her what she will be missing in life.

The final verse introduces a note of resolution. The poet never knew how his mother really felt about him until she died. He received a 'mysterious blessing' in the form of the locket she always wore around her neck. Inside the oval locket was a picture of him as an infant in Brooklyn. He realises that she had not rejected him, she had cherished him and held him close in the locket if not in reality.

·

John Montague
Like dolmens round my childhood . . .

THE POET OPENS this poem with a direct introductory statement: 'Like dolmens round my childhood, the old people.' He feels that the presence of these old people during his childhood was as dominant and sturdy as the existence of dolmens on the landscape. The first five verses are flooded with the images of these dolmen-like members of his community. Jamie MacCrystal, kind and generous, died and had his cottage plundered; Maggie Owens was an animal lover who was renowned for her gossiping; the Nialls were a blind family; Mary Moore a hardworking farmer who lived in a decrepit gatehouse and fell asleep reading love stories; Billy Eagleson a Protestant who married a Catholic, deserted by both sectors and taunted by children.

These people relied on the doctor and the priest for care; they were outsiders in the community. The doctor and the priest trudged through snow and sun, through bad roads and laneways to look after these outcasts. These great figures from Montague's childhood have permanently haunted his dreams. On the one hand he is expressing sorrow at the hardships they endured during their lives, but on the other hand he accuses them of disturbing his dreams for years.

Looking at the poem as a whole, the message seems to be that these characters, in all their ordinariness, are as much a part of Irish history and folklore as what he was taught in school. They may not be the traditional figures but they represent Montague's past and history, and they have contributed greatly to the man that he has become. These sad and sometimes fearful 'Gaunt figures' have trespassed on his dreams, and can only rest in peace if he lets go of them. In a magical experience 'in a standing circle of stones' they become immortal as he allows them to become part of his past. They will never cease to be part of him and once he accepts this fact they pass 'Into that dark permanence of ancient forms'. They are now an integral part of his history and Ireland's history and should never be denied their status as such. Ireland's history consists of more than warriors and heroes, but it would be wrong to forget the poor and those neglected by society. Their place in history is just as valid as that of the 'Fomorian' demons of ancient Ireland.

·

John Montague
The Cage

THIS AUTOBIOGRAPHICAL POEM reveals a picture of the poet's father. The opening line is clear and direct. 'My father, the least happy / man I have ever known'. Although this appears to be a plain statement of fact one can't help but be moved by a son's declaration that his father was the unhappiest person he ever knew. A depressing picture unfolds as the poet describes his father's pasty paleness. He is an indoor worker, an underground worker, and this removes him even more from reality.

The hours and years spent working underground are lost and can never be replaced or re-lived. They were wasted years spent listening to the subway rumbling past and shaking the earth. The poet's choice of title now becomes obvious. This subway pay-booth is like a prison to the poet's father, depriving him of light, fresh air and the chance of a happy life.

Verse 2 reveals the father's release from the cage or 'grille'. He is a stereotypical Irishman – works hard and drinks harder. He drinks straight whiskey until he reaches the comfort of oblivion – a state of total forgetfulness. He feels at home in this intoxicated haze, but it does not bring complete ease and contentment as the poet tells us it is 'brute oblivion'.

The poet's father did not wallow in his drunkenness. 'Most mornings' the father picked himself up and donned an air of normality. Despite his hateful job, his extreme loneliness, his distance from his family and homeland, he marches proudly down the street and smiles at everyone in the good, all-white, Catholic neighbourhood 'belled by St Teresa's church'.

Verses 4 and 5 describe the father-son relationship when the father returns home to Garvaghy. Father and son assume their roles and walk together across the fields to see the beauty of nature on a summer's day in Ireland. It is as if the father had never left, but the reality is hovering in the background. He did leave and there is no smiling between father and son. The time has passed, the years have moved on mercilessly, and now that the father has returned home the time has come for the son to move on. It is just like the ancient Greek story of Odysseus, the great warrior who returns home after many years of battle, whose son Telemachus must leave. The father has returned in the hope of finding his lost years, and the son must leave to fulfil his life.

The final verse places the poet in a city – perhaps New York. Every time he enters a subway or an underground he is haunted by the ghost of his father – bald, scared and imprisoned in the small confines of a subway booth. This final verse is slow and drawn out. The poet uses alliteration and long vowel sounds to achieve this long-lasting image and the feeling of regret and disappointment for his unfulfilled father.

·

Edwin Morgan
Strawberries

THIS LOVE POEM does not have any punctuation, and that helps it to set in motion a beautiful reminiscence. The poet tells how the taste of strawberries brings him back to a particular moment. This moment was obviously very precious to him and as he recounts it, he wishes to return to it. The lack of punctuation adds a wistful, dream-like atmosphere to the story. There are also very strong 's' sounds scattered throughout the poem that add to a feeling of sensuality.

The memory is simple: the poet and his lover sit on a window eating strawberries on a humid afternoon. They face each other eating their strawberries, and even dipping the strawberries in sugar takes on a sensuality for them. When they cross their forks together it symbolises a coming together for the pair. They are completely at one with each other. As the poet kisses his lover he takes back the taste of strawberries from her mouth, and holds her with all the care given to an abandoned child.

He uses this memory to suggest that he would like to repeat that afternoon. To finish he recites an incantation that it should all happen again. He introduces images from nature to suggest the authenticity and naturalness of the scene.

This is a beautifully simple love poem.

•

Paul Muldoon
Anseo

'ANSEO' DESCRIBES HOW things happen in cycles and how the abused can often become the abuser.

The initial scene is set in a typical Irish primary school. The poet describes the roll-call system where everybody would answer 'anseo' as their name was called out. This word 'Was the first word of Irish I spoke' as was the case and possibly still is for many Irish school-children.

The poet remembers what would happen at the start of every class, when the teacher would call out the last name on the roll, which belonged to Joseph Mary Plunkett Ward. This name is significant for a number reasons. Joseph Mary Plunkett was one of the leaders of the Easter Rising in 1916. The 'Mary' part of

it is also significant in so far as it is a name usually associated with girls rather than boys, and certainly not with a military leader such as the 1916 leader, or the leader that this boy would become. Finally the name is also important because it gives the teacher a chance to make a pun on the boy's name. Every day he would ask the same question: 'And where's our little Ward-of-court?' There was a sense of expectancy around this question, the other students would look at each other to see their reaction to it. The teacher was obviously having fun at Ward's expense.

In the second verse we see the twisted nature of the teacher, as he would send Ward out to find his own stick to be beaten with. The teacher would refuse different options until he got the right one to beat him with. This is the sort of ritual that Ward was seeing and as we see later on he was learning from it as well. The poet gives us fine detail as he describes exactly the effort that Ward would go to in preparing his own tormentor. We can almost imagine Ward taking pride in his work or being given a lecture about it from the teacher. We can see the engraving almost like a commemoration on a gift:

> Its twist of red and yellow lacquers
> Sanded and polished,
> And altogether so delicately wrought
> That he had engraved his initials on it.

The poet then brings us further along in time. Joseph Mary Plunkett Ward is now doing what his part-namesake had also done. He is leading a secret IRA battalion and has obviously risen through the ranks. There are many contradictions in his life when we see that

> He was living in the *open*,
> In a *secret* camp

He is no longer the boy who is being bullied and victimised. Instead he is 'Making things happen'. He has become an important person in a vicious world. He has also learned from his old school teacher. He calls a roll just like in primary school. One feels the punishment for not answering the roll call this time could be much more severe than getting beaten by a hazel-wand.

He is now the one in the position of authority. He is able to put people in their place and tell them what to do. People have fear of him now.

Muldoon makes a simple point in a clever way and uses the simple Irish word 'Anseo' to illustrate it. He says that power must be used carefully. He also says that if not cared for properly the bullied can become the bully.

•

Richard Murphy
The Reading Lesson

'THE READING LESSON' is based on a dialogue between two people. The speaker in the poem is a reading teacher who is trying to help a fourteen-year-old traveller boy to read. The poem describes the boy's struggle to come to grips with the world of letters, the teacher's frustration at his lack of progress and the rest of society's reaction to their attempts. The poem uses images that are part of the boy's world to describe the struggle that goes on between them.

The boy either doesn't want to read or he is finding it so hard that he has almost given up. The first metaphor that is introduced by the poet to describe the situation is the dog hunting the hare. This gives the reader an image of a great wild chase. The teacher is

trying to tame and tie down the boy's wild nature and bring him to a passive trap. There is a sense here, understood by both the teacher and the boy, that if he is 'tamed' he may lose something in the trade-off between them. The hunt is brought to a finale when the teacher finally gets so frustrated that he challenges him with a stern question. The teacher may think he is being rhetorical but the boy takes him very literally and gives an equally stern reply:

'Don't you want to learn to read?'
'I'll be the same man whatever I do.'

The teacher compares this riposte to an animal that has been cornered who comes out with his teeth bared on his release.

The second verse continues with the nature imagery. The poet uses a mule, a goat and a snipe to describe the way the boy looks at the page. He explains that the atmosphere is tense and says that if there is

. . . A sharp word, and he'll mooch
Back to his piebald mare and bantam
    cock.

He finishes by explaining that his task is as difficult as catching mercury.

The third verse shows us that they have all but given up, and that the boy will not be using his fingers to follow words on a page but he will use them to go hawking scrap or even to go pick-pocketing. He says that the boy could easily revert to the stereotype that the chuckling neighbour ascribes to him. The neighbour says that the boy is untameable, that he will always have a yearning to escape and go back to being his natural, wild self as soon as he has the chance.

The final verse finishes with some images that are specific to travellers. He says that books are something that the boy feels will restrict him and stop him from making his own way. They are as restricted and separate from him as the idea of settling on a small farm to live for the rest of his life. He says that his life will be one of petty theft and poaching. He ends by comparing this book-learning to the wren. The wren became The King Of All Birds by being clever enough to sit on the back of an eagle, and therefore fly the highest in the sky. That is how inaccessible books are to the boy.

•

Howard Nemerov
Wolves in the Zoo

THIS POEM TRIES to tell us the truth behind the bad press that wolves have been given over time. The poet is on a visit to the zoo and muses over the fate of wolves in history and mythology. His first impression of them is interesting; they look odd or out of place, 'like big dogs badly drawn, drawn wrong'. The inscription beneath their cage is defiant, and tells the poet that there is no proof of any serious wrong-doing by any wolves.

He dismisses the stories of Romulus and Remus, and of Little Red Riding Hood. He says that she and her grandmother were the real bullies in the cautionary tale. He tells us that the two species of wolf are nearly extinct because of our attitude towards them. He points out that we have this attitude instilled in us from a very young age, and we have accepted and perpetuated the mythology until wolves have become enemies of humankind along with ghosts and monsters. They became animals worthy of killing by hunters even though they are only like 'big dogs badly drawn'. There is no logic for our fear of these animals besides our growing hatred, fostered by mythology.

Now, the few survivors of our fear have ended up in zoos along with other strange creatures we don't understand. This poem urges us to think twice before allowing myth to become fact.

•

Julie O'Callaghan
The Great Blasket Island

THIS IS A quirky lyric about nostalgia. It tells what looks like a typical story of returned emigrants who survey the changes in their island. It is in danger of being a sentimental story until the poet hits it with a sucker punch in the final two lines.

The poem begins by painting a portrait of six Blasket Islanders returning to the island after being away for twenty-one years. It is quite clear that they have forgotten why they went away in the first place. They see that the island has become more or less uninhabited, and they examine their old houses. The houses have been left completely decrepit. They think back to their good times only. Their negative memories 'scattered'. So they have forgotten

all the nagging and praying
and scolding and giggling
and crying and gossiping

They have become so charged with sentimentality that they have forgotten how to count now. One of the men tells of 'ten of us blown to the winds' when we are told at the start that there are only six of them! Their sense of exaggeration makes them think that Dublin is a place so far away that it takes twenty-one years to return from it! The idea of him as he 'blinks back the tears' becomes laughable. This is especially so when the poet tells him to 'Get over it!', and dismisses him in the final two lines:

Listen, mister, most of us cry sooner or
   later
   over a Great Blasket Island of our own.

•

Bernard O'Donoghue
Gunpowder

THIS POEM ALLOWS the poet to reflect on
his father and some of the contradictions in his
life. The father seems to have died a few
weeks previously and the poet finds his
father's jacket 'hung / Behind the door in the
room we called / His study'. We immediately
see the contradictions in the older man when
we see that the study is not a place for books
or letters, but rather for 'bikes and wellingtons'.
The son smells gunpowder from a jacket that
he is about to throw out. He quickly equates
the smell with

   Celebration – excitement – things like that,
   Not destruction.

He remembers the few times that his father
did use a gun and reminds himself that it was
never used in anger or violence. He couldn't
even bring himself to shoot a pheasant,
making the excuse that it might be a hen. Nor
could he bring himself to shoot a rat, firing a
warning shot to give the rodent time to run off.
   In the second verse he gives more
examples. A farmer had a wounded crow tied
to a stick, allowing it enough leeway to
struggle to free itself, but not to fly away. The
father obviously saw that as cruel and freed it.
He also put a rabbit from a dog's mouth back
in a warren, even though that warren was in
danger of causing a wall to collapse. The only

use for used cartridges that contained the
gunpowder was to support his fountain pen.
   This is a generous and moving portrait of a
peaceful man. By giving us these examples of
his passivity we get a picture of him very readily.

•

Sharon Olds
Looking at Them Asleep

THE SPEAKER IN this poem introduces us to
her children. She describes them to us as she
looks at them sleeping. She sees beyond their
sleeping faces and predicts what their
individual reactions would be if she woke them
up. The feeling of love in this poem is all-
consuming and overwhelming. The poet does
not name her children, but that does not
detract from the intense closeness she feels
towards them. Instead she refers to them as
'my girl' and 'the son'. In this poem we see an
outpouring of love for her children displayed in
two long sentences and two short ones.
   The poet feels compelled to communicate
her love for her children, and is passionate to
impart to the reader a picture of them in their
entirety. She does not describe them physically
but describes their individual traits and
characteristics.
   Firstly her daughter, deep in sleep, 'her
mouth slightly puffed'. The poet interprets this
look and sees that although her daughter has a
look of satisfaction she also has a hint of one
who 'hasn't had enough'. She is a contented
child, an achiever. She has a face 'like the face
of a snake who has swallowed a deer'. The poet
knows if she wakes her little girl she would
'smile and turn her face' towards her mother.
   Her son, although asleep and lying still, is
viewed as one full of life and activity. She

notices his position in the bed as one about to leap into action – 'climbing sharp stairs'. Everything about her son indicates movement and energy and bustling business. He is 'staring and glazed', 'breathing hard', 'his brow is crumpled', he is involved in a 'quest'. If his mother wakes him he will jump up and protest.

She is greatly moved and exclaims 'oh my Lord' when she considers just how well she knows her children. The poet's deep love for them is apparent throughout the poem. She watches them adoringly and deciphers their every move and characteristic.

Sharon Olds
The Present Moment

THIS THOUGHTFUL MEDITATION concerns issues of aging and how we perceive the aging process. A daughter sees her terminally ill father in hospital and tries to reconcile the image that she once had of her father as somebody who was physically and mentally strong with the frail figure who lies before her. Through the poem she gives a powerful description of what illness does to people, of how it can ravage the body and mind at the same time in a ruthless manner.

She combines the body and the mind at the start of the poem. She shows how the father has deteriorated in such a short time from being someone who was active to being just a passive entity on the edge of existence. The first instance comes when she sees him just lying on the hospital bed. He is now motionless, facing towards the wall. This is becoming the dominant image of him now, instead of the image that she had of him as he entered the hospital and he 'sat up and put on his reading glasses'. At that stage he was actively reading, taking things in, his eyes alive as the 'lights in the room multiplied in the lenses'.

She uses the image of food to show the changes he has gone through. He is now dependent on food that will pass through him for energy, not for taste. He eats 'dense, earthen food, like liver'; pure, tasteless fuel, not something more unusual and aesthetic, like pineapple with its exotic connotations.

She follows this by noticing the changes to his body over the years. He is none of the more appealing figures that he used to be. She goes in reverse chronological order through the phases of his life. She describes him as a portly man with a 'torso packed with extra matter'. As a young man he was a 'smooth-skinned, dark-haired boy'.

She admits to not knowing him when he was a baby, but she notes his dependence back then, when he would 'drink from a woman's / body'. Once again he is being fed. And his 'steady / gaze' now is again like when he was just born; sleep brings only relief to him now, just as it did then.

She finishes with a metaphor of a swimmer; only her father is swimming towards death and want as she might to help him, she is helpless. She can only look on while he continues in his struggle.

Sylvia Plath
Child

THIS VERY SPECIAL poem about Plath's love for her child is made all the more poignant in the knowledge that the poet committed suicide two weeks after writing it. The opening line stands alone in the poem. Not only is it the longest line presented on the page, but also it is full of love, joy and admiration for her child. The poet recognises that having a clear eye, unclouded by the difficulties associated with life, is an 'absolutely beautiful thing'. She wants to fill her child's sight with fantastic and interesting things that children love. She wants to present her child with colour and ducks and 'The zoo of the new'. The zoo is full of the unusual and the attention-grabbing. Children love seeing wild animals close up and this helps to broaden their imagination.

Everything new is meditated upon by the child. He is untouched by the outside world. He is like a little plant without signs of age or 'wrinkle'. He reflects all he sees and learns like a clear pool of water. The poet hopes that all he sees will be 'grand and classical'.

The final verse is dark and depressing. The poet is aware that she is not providing the things she had hoped for her child. He deserves the 'colour and ducks', 'The zoo of the new', but instead the child is being exposed to 'troublous / Wringing of hands' and a starless sky – a ceiling. There is no potential for adventure in the final verse, only desolation and depression. She should be offering beauty and adventure and potential to develop, but instead the final verse shows her and her child locked inside a cocoon of darkness and despair and there is no ray of hope. The poem ends in desolation.

There is no padding in this poem; it is direct in its hopes and aspirations and just as clear in its grimness and melancholy. She knows to what she should aspire to fulfil the child's development needs fully, but concludes knowing she cannot respond as she feels both helpless and hopeless; 'Wringing of hands, this dark / Ceiling without a star'. The reality is a sense of desolation and this completely overshadows the mother's great intentions.

•

Sylvia Plath
The Arrival of the Bee Box

SYLVIA PLATH'S FATHER, Otto, was a professor of biology at Boston University, and a devoted beekeeper. In 1962 Plath decided to follow in her father's footsteps and try beekeeping. She wrote a series of five poems about her experiences and this narrative is one of them. All five poems consisted of five-line verses and this poem is exceptional in that it ends with a single sentence, separate from the seven five-line verses.

The poem opens with the poet telling us this is of her own doing – she is in control – 'I ordered this'. The bee box has arrived. She describes it using internal rhyme: 'Square as a chair', and a humorous metaphor 'the coffin of a midget / Or a square baby'. We hear the constant buzz of the imprisoned bees in the onomatopoeic words 'din in it'. We are immediately faced with an image of something unusual and abnormal – a noisy coffin-like box fit for a midget or an oddly shaped baby.

Verse 1 displays the box as strange, but verse 2 highlights the threat involved. The box is locked for safety; it is dangerous. The poet has no choice but to endure it until morning. We sense that although she is scared, she is also drawn to the bee box. She is fascinated as she cannot see inside clearly. It is left to her imagination to build a picture of what is going on behind the 'little grid'. There is a sense of confinement and imprisonment in the two simple words 'no exit'.

Unable to contain her curiosity, the poet looks through the grid in verse 3. It is 'dark, dark', 'Black on black', resembling African slaves caged up. The atmosphere created is one of constant, furious movement; 'angrily clambering' and miniature hands desperately looking for an escape. No longer is the poet an outsider, she has become a player in the drama. She has been sucked in and feels great empathy for the bees: 'How can I let them out?'. She wants to help; she has forgotten her fear and fascination and now wants to become their liberator.

However, although verse 4 begins with empathy in the first line, the second line changes the poet's mood once again. 'It is the noise that appals me most of all.' She is distressed and dismayed and now compares the bees to a Roman mob – a force to be reckoned with. Individually the bees are acceptable, but as a large, disorderly mob they are to be feared. There is no way of reasoning with their 'unintelligible syllables'. Once again there is a hint of fear, and she is an outsider.

Verse 5 sees the poet examining her part in the scene. She listens to the foreign noise and knows that she is not like Caesar, a cold ruthless leader, but recognises that she is in control, she has choices. She can return the bees, she can starve them, she is their lord and master. They are 'maniacs' and she may do with them as she likes. Just as she says she is not a Caesar in verse 5, she shows her compassionate side in verse 6 as she wonders how hungry they are. She wonders if she released them and stood back, 'turned into a tree', would they forget her and go to feast on the fragrant laburnum and cherry blossoms. We see here that she would love to liberate the bees and watch as they greedily devour the beautiful pollen-rich flowers outside.

In verse 7 the poet is the alien in her 'moon suit'. Once the bees are freed, she is no longer part of their lives as she has nothing they need: 'I am no source of honey'. She would become unnecessary and irrelevant. She makes plans to set them free, to be their compassionate 'sweet God'. The last sentence, standing alone, promises freedom: the confinement will end, 'The box is only temporary'. The poet is the controlling power in the poem, and in exercising her power she will do the right thing and release her captives.

In this poem Plath deals with many issues – control, liberation and confinement, power and the choices available in life.

•

Adrienne Rich

Notes on the poems of Adrienne Rich have not been included for copyright reasons.

•

Christina Rossetti
Remember

THIS IS A sad poem that is often recited on sad occasions such as funerals. In a sense it is a prayer to a person who will be left behind by the one who will pass away. It is a very simple poem, yet very moving because of the strength of the emotion that it contains. It is a sonnet, and this form adds a great sense of balance and compactness to the poem.

The first quatrain is all one sentence (as are the second quatrain and the sestet). There is great sadness in the tone of the first line.

The length of the line adds to this sense of despair. The second line refers to 'the silent land'; this sense of unwillingness to use the words 'dead' or 'death' or 'heaven' directly makes the poem feel even more poignant. It makes one feel that there is a genuine fear of what is to come. She reminisces about happier times when there was a chance for comfort, or a chance to change her mind and come back. There is now no going back from where she is going:

> When you can no more hold me by the
>   hand,
> Nor I half turn to go, yet turning stay.

The second quatrain talks about the future that they could have had together, but will never share now. They can no longer plan together. The speaker in the poem asks her friend to remember her when these thoughts come into her friend's head.

The sestet marks a change. Whereas before the speaker was constantly beseeching her friend to remember her, now she leaves instructions about what to do if that person forgets. She says that there is no need to have regrets about this. She says that if remembering her brings sadness to her friend, then it would be better to forget her:

> Better by far you should forget and smile
> Than that you should remember and be
>   sad.

•

Siegfried Sassoon
On Passing the New Menin Gate

'WHO WILL REMEMBER, passing through this Gate, / The unheroic Dead who fed the guns?' asks Sassoon in the opening lines of this poem, immediately revealing a sense of disillusionment at the building of the new Menin Gate as a memorial to those who died in the First World War. This opening sentence is an attack on those who believed that building this gate could adequately commemorate the fallen. The poet also conveys a sense of absolute horror at the brutality and futility of war, while at the same time displaying a powerful fury at the weakness of the effort made to commemorate those who died. This gate is not, in the poet's opinion, a fitting monument to the soldiers who were little more than food for the enemy's guns.

The poet tells us that there was nothing heroic about dying in this war. Lines 2 and 3 communicate a feeling of futility at the soldiers' endeavours. These men never had a chance to live, they were 'conscripted' – obliged by law to fight, they were 'unvictorious' in that it was irrelevant whether or not the war was won or lost, as they were dead and could not celebrate the joy of victory. As quickly as they fell they were replaced. The new Menin Gate provides no compensation for the sacrifice made by these soldiers. These men endured the horrors of wartime, they 'struggled in the slime', and nothing, especially not this gate, could assuage the dreadfulness suffered. This tribute is an affront to the deceased, an insult – 'the world's worst wound.'

The gate assures that 'Their name liveth for ever', but Sassoon sees this as an impossibility, the dead are 'intolerably nameless names'. The poet concludes that the dead should not be condemned; if moved by insult, they might well rise from their graves and mock the memorial.

•

William Shakespeare
Fear No More the Heat o' the Sun

THIS IS A song taken from one of Shakespeare's final plays; 'Cymbeline'. It is set in a forest where Guiderius and Arviragus come upon the body of a young boy who appears to be dead. (The body is that of their sister, disguised and in a drugged state resembling death.) They lament the death but celebrate the person's release from an unpleasant world.

Guiderius begins by telling the corpse that it no longer has to fear or worry about the weather. The dead no longer need to fear the heat of the sun or the winter storms. Now that their worldly work ('task') is done, the dead can go 'home' and take payment ('wages') for their earthly work. 'Golden lads and girls' (the rich and privileged) will end life the same as chimney-sweepers, and succumb to death and become dust.

Arviragus continues the lament over the 'dead' body. Death to him is a release from strict rulers. For the dead there is no fear of 'frown' or 'stroke' from their superiors. There is no longer a need to care about food or clothing or everyday common needs. Arviragus mentions that the simple reed is the same as the great oak tree when you are dead. This links in with Aesop's tale that in a great storm, the simple, flexible reed stands an equal chance of survival as it bends in the wind, while the mighty oak is anchored by roots and unable to bend or flex in any direction.

Arviragus continues, telling his audience that royalty ('sceptre'), scholars ('learning') and even doctors ('physic') cannot withstand death. It visits everyone in every walk of life.

Each character now interjects with short simple sentences celebrating the release from fear and worry that comes with death. There is no need to fear lightning bursts, thunder-stones (meteorites) or criticism ('slander, censure rash'). Even 'all lovers' must eventually become dust. The repetition of the word 'dust' reminds us of a funeral sermon: 'Ashes to ashes, dust to dust'.

Once the person has died and is buried, Guiderius and Arviragus have further wishes as they hope the deceased may rest in peace. They hope that no 'exorciser', practitioner of witchcraft, ghost or anything 'ill' will disrupt the grave. The final rhyming couplet demands silence and respect for both the dead and the grave.

The abiding message of this song or poem is that death comes to us all – rich, poor, chimney-sweeper, doctor, monarch or lover. Death is inevitable and not to be feared. It is a release from fear and is therefore something to look forward to and welcome with open arms. Once you have entered death you have escaped from a world of danger, hurt, threats and negativity.

Percy Bysshe Shelley
Ozymandias

IN THIS POEM we meet an explorer who has travelled through ancient lands. The traveller tells of the sights encountered on his travels. In the middle of a desert he sees the remains of a statue: 'Two vast and trunkless legs of stone / Stand in the desert'. There is no remnant of the torso, all that remains are two huge legs. Beside the legs lies a head, half sunk into the sand. The head reveals the face of a tyrant. It displays a frown, a wrinkled lip and a look of hard, unfeeling authority. From examination of the statue the traveller deduces that the sculptor has succeeded in interpreting the pharaoh's personality and transferring it onto the statue.

On the base of the statue there is an inscription: 'My name is Ozymandias, king of kings: / Look on my works, ye Mighty, and despair!' This great Pharaoh issues a challenge to all other rulers to look at the greatness of his civilisation and acknowledge their inferiority. There is nothing else remaining of this once-great kingdom except miles and miles of sand.

This poem comments on power and the greatness of time – nothing can resist time. Humans, like Ozymandias, boast of their achievements and greatness but as time passes so too does their supremacy. Looking through the eyes of history those who were once powerful, reigning supreme, are now reduced to sand and dust. All empires will diminish with time; nature will conquer, time will pass and civilisations will be rendered powerless and inconsequential.

·

Dylan Thomas
The Hunchback in the Park

THIS POEM WAS written by Dylan Thomas as an ode to his hometown of Swansea's Cwmdonkin Park. It takes a single character – a loner, a hunchback – and portrays his life, or at least an average day in his life. It is a sad portrait of a lonely man who has been split from society and has become something else now. He has become something to be taunted or avoided. Thomas often wrote about himself being separated from normal society, and this poem could easily be interpreted as a metaphor for the poet's own life.

The hunchback is initially described as 'A solitary mister' being held up by nature. He becomes more of an animal-like creature or part of nature as the poem progresses, but we can initially see him 'Propped between trees and water'. He is there from the beginning of the day 'Until the Sunday sombre bell at dark'.

He is fed like the swans are: 'bread from a newspaper', and drinks like a dog 'from the chained cup'. The animal metaphor is continued when he is described as he 'Slept at night in a dog kennel'. He becomes closer to nature than to people:

> Like the park birds he came early
> Like the water he sat down

whereas the children tease him, waiting for a reaction or a chase from him.

He spends his day laughing to himself, reading scraps of paper and avoiding the park keeper in case he is thrown out of his temporary home. In the fifth and sixth verses we get a clear image of him as he sees the whole world pass him by; nurses and swans, boys playing, sailors. He wishes he could be seen as something that he is not. He wants to be regarded as straight-backed and as elegant as one of the women that he looks at but cannot talk to.

The last verse sees him alone and abandoned in the park, hiding from a society that never looks for him in his 'kennel in the dark'.

·

Edward Thomas
Adlestrop

THIS POEM IS a descriptive lyric. It contains a description of a moment in time. The poet describes when he was on a train journey and the train stopped momentarily. The poet brings together as many of the senses as he can to give us a vivid picture of this moment frozen in time. It is as if he is painting a multi-sensory picture of this moment.

He begins the poem in a conversational tone; maybe he is talking to himself or to others. He starts with an affirmation of having remembered the place, or at least the name. He hits the senses right away by mentioning the heat. He is specific in parts of the poem. He tells us when this happens. He tells us that it was unexpected. He tells us that this, after all, was an express train.

He appeals to the senses again in the second verse. This time he mentions what he hears: the hiss of the train and the sound of somebody clearing his throat. There is a sense of mystery then as no one is to be seen about. There is no reason given for the stop. He repeats that he did not see the town, only the name. But then he tells us of everything else that he sees and this brings total wonderment to his eyes and ears.

He goes on to describe the flowers and trees and the beautiful day, and it captures him totally for the moment that he is stopped there, and stays with him until the conversation that inspires this poem comes up.

The final verse celebrates the surrounding area. The sounds come back to him again as a blackbird conducts an orchestra of 'all the birds / Of Oxfordshire and Gloucestershire'.

This poem explores the idea of solitude and pensiveness. It is pastoral in its beautiful descriptions of one moment in time.

Henry Vaughan
Peace

IN 'PEACE' BY Henry Vaughan, the poet is addressing his own soul, telling of a great place far away where he can escape noise and danger and experience peace and smiles. This 'Countrie' (heaven) is guarded by a 'winged Centrie' and is ruled over by Jesus ('one born in a Manger'). He is not a ruthless ruler, instead he is a 'gracious friend'.

Vaughan implores his soul to wake up and take heed of the message. Jesus, Vaughan tells us, in an act of pure love, came to earth and died for his sake. Heaven, if he can gain entry, is a wondrous place where the flower of peace grows and will never wither. Vaughan pleads with his soul to abandon all his foolish endeavours and to concentrate on securing a path to the one true God.

All through this poem there is a sense of great calm, as the poet firmly believes the message he is delivering, that peace is to be found only in heaven. Earth is a place of noise and danger and 'foolish ranges'. There is a very definite rhyming pattern to this poem – every other line rhymes. There is a natural flow with no interruptions; even the exclamation in line 10 does not interrupt the writer's message.

•

Derek Walcott
To Norline

THIS POEM IS an elegy for a dead relationship. The poet writes to his ex-wife expressing regret for the ending of their association. Walcott is from the Caribbean and the beach that he mentions in the first line dominates the poem. This place obviously holds memories for him and was very important in their relationship.

He says that the beach will always be there and will do the same thing that it does every morning. It will always wake to the same red sky and the surf will always come up to the shore, unlike their relationship. He says that some other couple will take their place and go through all the rituals that they went through.

He says that other people will fall in love with each other and with the place they loved together. However, he ends with a brief caveat: he admits that it is very hard for him to move on from these beautiful memories and from this connection. He compares it to turning a page that he enjoys reading again and again. He does know that he must move on if he is to get to the end of his life's story.

·

Derek Walcott
Summer Elegies

THIS POEM IS called an elegy but it takes a while to see what the poet is mourning. The first seven of the nine verses appear to be a celebration of a tranquil time in the poet's life as he was falling in love on a beautiful, peaceful beach. It is only at the end that we see that the poet is mourning the loss of his own innocence, and the loss of the innocence in their relationship.

The poet is writing to a former lover in a playful way. The first line suggests light-heartedness as he muses over their time together. There is also an erotic tone very early on as the poet recalls taking off his lover's bikini top for the first time. He marvelled at this friend's breasts as he unpeeled the top

carefully and tenderly. He describes their swimming together and the way even nature marvelled at their lovemaking in the sea:

> We made one shape in water
> while in sea grapes a dove
> gurgled astonished 'Ooos' at
> the changing shapes of love.

He recalls eagerly the fact that they seemed to have as much time and as much of the island as they wanted to themselves. He regrets that time does, however, progress and they too had to move on. He introduces the image of the water reducing down to salt in the heat on their bodies, and the peeling skin after the sun, which has to be removed, so new skin can grow and so that they can move on with their lives. He concludes this part of the poem by saying that it was indeed a perfect, untroubled time with not even nature infringing on their pleasure.

He concludes with a qualification. He says that when Cynthia tempted him he gave in easily. He was changed as a result of it. He had lost his innocence.

·

Derek Walcott
The Young Wife

THIS POEM WAS written to a friend after the friend's wife had died of cancer. It is not about the wife but the friend, and attempts to instruct him in how to get on in the aftermath of the death. It tries to warn him of what will surely happen to him.

He tells his friend that he is expected to be dignified and direct. He should 'Make all your sorrow neat.' Try to keep things as she would have wanted them to stay. He says that the friend should not be afraid to write to the mourners, say what needs to be said. He talks about the different parts of the house, as this would have been where they spent most of their time together. He insists that his friend should take it all in again, to start noticing the place that they had made into a home together. At various times he mentions the pillows, the bed cover, the armchair, the curtains, the mirror, the wallpaper, the bedroom door, photographs, the telephone, the garden, the kitchen, cutlery and a chair. This was their kingdom and there are reminders of her everywhere.

When he mentions the mirror he warns the friend not to be afraid to look at himself. He should not consider himself a traitor for merely living on after she has gone. He is warned not to be afraid to cry. He says not to be afraid to see her everywhere around the place, to hear her voice on the telephone or to see her picture in a photograph.

He brings to mind their wedding vow (. . . till death do us part) which now has become a reality; even though he is the one still living it does not make it any easier.

> But the vow that was said
> in white lace has brought
> you now to the very edge
> of that promise . . .

He reminds his friend that nature, in the form of his hawthorn hedge re-flowering, moves on, and so must he. This is especially so when the family gather to eat. Despite the empty place-setting and the empty chair, the family will gather together to fill the space. Children, above all, adapt, and the friend should not be afraid or disappointed when he hears them laugh. More than anything else the friend should not think that love died when his wife did.

> She sits there smiling that cancer
> kills everything but Love.

•

Richard Wilbur
The Pardon

THIS IS A very sensuous narrative revealing a traumatic story with roots in the speaker's childhood, but manifesting itself in his adulthood. It appeals not just to the visual but also to the other senses, especially smell, sound and touch.

Wilbur tells the story from his childhood of finding his pet dog dead after five days. It is a suffocating, hot, 'thick' summer. The body is concealed by a 'clump of pine . . . and honeysuckle-vine'. The images here are demanding that the reader both see and feel the heat and lushness of the dog's final resting place.

Wilbur informs us that although he had really loved the dog this feeling left him once life left the dog: he did not love the dead dog. Now that the dog is dead he cannot go near to the body. He approaches but only close enough to smell the heavy smell of death mingled with the heavy, stifling, sickly sweetness of the honeysuckle. We can almost hear the humming of the flies in the words 'the flies' intolerable buzz'.

Wilbur forces us to feel the heat of that summer, see the body of the dead dog, hear the flies and smell the heavy odour of death. The ten-year-old has only gone close enough to satisfy childish curiosity before being frightened away. It is not, it seems, within a child's ability to deal with this death – this is 'out of range' to a ten-year-old boy. He finds it hard to forgive this scene, to come to terms with what he has seen and encountered whether 'sad or strange'. It is beyond his capabilities as he, as a child, is accustomed to fun and happiness. His father, he tells us, dealt with the situation, he 'took the spade / And buried him'. The speaker also tries to bury his feelings, but unfortunately it is not so simple for a child to rationalise such a grotesque event.

Wilbur wrote this poem immediately after the dog reappeared in a new incarnation. 'Last night', he tells us, the dog emerged in slow motion like an image from a horror movie. It takes the poet three lines to detail the dog's reappearance. First the grass slowly divided. The scene resembled the original, but there was the addition of some frightful elements. The grass glowed 'fierce' and 'mortal green'. It is alive, and the dog emerges awakening fearful thoughts he hoped he had buried years ago. 'I confess / I felt afraid again.' The dog continues to approach and is 'clothed in a hymn of flies'.

Once again we not only see the dog, we are also forced to hear the sounds surrounding it. Death is alive in this grisly dog's eyes and Wilbur is petrified. He cries out and calls the dog's name. He does not divulge the name to us but he does share the horror and terror. He begs for forgiveness from this repulsive 'tongueless head', and pleads for a pardon for not treating the dog's death with due respect and honour. As the ghostly figure haunts him in his adulthood he feels great remorse.

The final three lines tell us the lesson he feels he has learnt from the whole experience. He has learnt that it is never too late to make up for your shortcomings. This ghostly figure has demanded that the poet mourn the dead, and has shown that he cannot bury grief. Wilbur feels a sense of release now that he has faced his agony and grief. Although he has gone through a hellish ordeal he has benefited greatly by learning the coping skills needed to deal with death and mourn and grieve.

William Carlos Williams
The Red Wheelbarrow

Williams opens this poem by building a sense of great expectation and anticipation in just four words: 'so much depends / upon'. As the poem is visually presented in four separate pieces, we are forced to consider each section on its own merits. Williams is obviously excited and enchanted. What can have worked him up to this state? The reader is therefore surprised to read the next four words: 'a red wheel / barrow'.

The reader, who may have expected something of traditional significance or importance, is thrown off course to discover that the speaker feels so dependent upon a wheelbarrow. Williams develops this image in a simple, uncomplicated way. He constructs a very clear, vivid picture for the reader. The wheelbarrow is red and shining ('glazed') with rainwater. Even a shower of rain cannot diminish the poet's admiration for the wheelbarrow. If anything, the rain has enhanced his admiration.

The wheelbarrow, of obvious importance to the poet, stands out all the more as it stands beside white chickens. Its brightness is accentuated by its proximity to plain whiteness. No attempt is made by the poet to explain why the red wheelbarrow holds such pride of place in the poet's life or how it contributes so much to his existence. Williams himself has said 'I was touched by real things'. He sees the greatness in the ordinary and everyday. The short, simple lines reinforce the sense of great excitement. The poem is written in a conversational way. Williams writes just as he would speak.

William Wordsworth
Composed upon Westminster Bridge

THIS POEM IS, in structure, a Petrarchan sonnet divided into an octet and a sestet. However Wordsworth does not stick strictly to the Petrarchan idea of presenting the problem in the octet and resolving it in the sestet.

The sonnet opens with the poet challenging the reader to think of anywhere on earth 'more fair' than the scene he is describing. We are immediately filled with a sense of expectation. The poet then pursues this heightened sense of anticipation by telling the reader that only the 'dull' would fail to appreciate the impressive, stately grandeur of the scene. The poet uses a carefully constructed simile to describe the beauty of the city. The image is that of a beautiful garment worn by the city. In complete contradiction to this the poet then describes the city as 'silent, bare'. Wordsworth knows that this silence, calmness and simplicity can be cast off like a piece of clothing to reveal a hustling and bustling city later in the day. The city is dressed in silence, nothing is moving or making noise. Later when the city wakes up the beauty will disappear as the garment is removed.

Wordsworth is admiring the city at one particular time: early morning. He loves the 'smokeless air' and the sense of the boundless openness of the city before it fills up with people and activity.

In the sestet the poet declares that he has never felt a sense of calm so deeply, not even in the tranquillity of nature – 'valley, rock, or hill'. This is indeed high praise from Wordsworth who shunned city life in favour of the countryside. The serene, untroubled image is further enhanced by the river gliding along at its own pace, not driven to turn the mill wheel or carrying cargo up and down the busy trade channels of London. 'The river glideth at his own sweet will'. The sound patterns of these words evoke tranquillity and calmness. Wordsworth cries out 'Dear God!' in an exclamation uncharacteristic of the poem's tone. The view is overwhelming; Wordsworth cannot believe that even the bricks and mortar of the houses appear to be asleep.

The poem concludes with an unusual image: 'And all that mighty heart is lying still!' This image is disturbing as even when the body is in a deep slumber the heart continues to beat. The fact that Wordsworth sees the heart, the very life of the city, as 'lying still' could reflect his deeply felt belief that the man-made structures of urban sprawl are negative and dead, and only in nature and individuality can the soul flourish and triumph.

.

Judith Wright
Request to a Year

IN THIS POEM the poet is asking the coming year to grant her a wish. Her request is to be like her great-great-grandmother, who was a 'legendary devotee of the arts'. The poem develops as the poet reveals to the reader the extent of her great-great-grandmother's devotion to the arts. On one occasion her son was in a near-death situation, and knowing there was nothing she could do to help she continued sketching, only speeding up to capture the scene in a drawing.

Her great-great-grandmother had eight children and does not appear to have a great attachment to any of them. They are referred to as 'second son' and 'second daughter'. We learn that, although the great-great-grandmother had a love of art, she had very little time to enjoy her hobby because of her eight children. So, on this particular occasion in Switzerland, she seizes the opportunity to have some time to herself, and positions herself on a high rock far away from the children. She observes her family from this height and 'viewed' her son balancing on a small sheet of ice drifting towards a waterfall with an eighty-foot drop. There is no swift reaction from the poet's great-great-grandmother; it is her daughter who reacts to the situation. Although hindered by 'petticoats of the day' she holds out an alpenstock and 'luckily' saves her brother's life.

The poet's great-great-grandmother has watched the whole scene unfold from the distance of her high rock. She detaches herself completely and her 'artist's eye' takes over. She sees the scene not as a mother but as a painter, and quickly sketches the details.

The poet does not comment on her great-great-grandmother's unusual detachment from her family in the face of near-disaster, instead she coolly tells us that the sketch is still in existence as evidence that this really happened.

Finally in the rhyming couplet the poet directly addresses the incoming year. She implores that if the year has no gift planned for her perhaps it could reach into the past and capture from her great-great-grandmother the 'firmness of her hand'. The poet, on the one hand, idolises her great-great-grandmother's special talent of detaching herself and becoming an onlooker, but she also appears to be ridiculing her as an artist who does not react in any way to save her son from impending disaster. The maternal instincts were overwhelmed by the great-great-grandmother's artistic instincts, leaving us with a ridiculous scenario full of fun and humour. It is hard to believe that the poet expects the reader to take the whole 'Request to a Year' seriously.

W. B. Yeats
The Lake Isle of Innisfree

INNISFREE (Inisfraoich – Heather Island) is an island associated with local legends in Lough Gill, Co. Sligo. Yeats dreams of living alone there in his quest for contentment and wisdom. He is looking for paradise, and he does not perceive it to be a distant dream. He has built his dream on a reality; he has worked out all the details over time and with calculation and consideration has designed his own utopia.

Yeats wrote this poem while living in London in 1890. He dreams of rising and leaving, to go to Innisfree. He has simple plans of building a small cabin of traditional sticks and clay, of growing beans and of keeping honeybees. His main desire is to live alone in a clearing in the woods where the music of the buzzing bees fills the air. He is searching for inner peace; he wants to feel at one with nature and feel the tranquillity that comes like veils gently, slowly dropping. There is a dream-like quality to much of this poem – 'veils', 'glimmer' and 'purple glow' – as the poet imagines his escape to paradise.

Once again, in verse 2, the background music to this idyllic scene is the sound of nature – 'the cricket sings' and the swishing of 'linnet's wings'. The scene portrayed by the poet is a beautifully colourful one – a place to cast off the complications of urban life.

Verse 3 begins with Yeats reiterating his desire to 'arise and go'. Yeats is haunted by the allure of Innisfree both day and night as he hears the soft lake water softly flowing and lapping gently up against the shoreline, calling him home. This intense magnetism is felt deep in his 'heart's core'. He wishes to leave the impersonal city, the 'pavements grey' and live in harmony and peace in the rich tapestry of nature on Innisfree.

W. B. Yeats
The Wild Swans at Coole

THIS POEM OPENS setting a beautiful autumnal scene. Yeats is admiring the beauty of the Coole Park estate owned by his good friend and mentor Lady Augusta Gregory. The rhythm is slow and reflective as the October sun sets and another year is drawing to a close. Yeats is fifty-one years of age, and in the autumn of his life he is taking stock.

He sees fifty-nine swans on the brimming water. It is nineteen years since he first set eyes on the swans and he remembers that first vision. The image of the swans is one of greatness, strength, noise and activity. Line 14 interrupts this stream of thought as the poet admits his own state of mind. 'And now my heart is sore.' This is in complete contrast to the harmony and contentment surrounding him. In the nineteen years since Yeats first saw the swans everything has changed. Nineteen years ago he feels he was light-hearted and walked with a 'lighter' step. As he reflects he again turns his attentions to the swans and he envies them. After all these years they do not show signs of fatigue or wear and tear. The swans swim loyally side by side in a display of togetherness and companionship. They appear to have stood still in time, and Yeats craves this sense of eternal contentment.

There is, however, an uneven number of swans, and maybe the thought of one, alone, has triggered Yeats to consider his own romantic status. The first time Yeats saw the swans, nineteen years previously, he was recovering from the disappointment of a marriage-proposal rejection from his life-long love, Maud Gonne. Now looking at the swans he admires in them the qualities he most yearns for. To be 'unwearied', to be loved and enjoy companionship, and to feel a sense of freedom is all Yeats yearns for. Life has failed him but this does not detract from his admiration of the swans.

The poem ends pessimistically as Yeats thinks of the day he will discover the swans have all flown away and left him. They may move on and bring delight to others but he will remain feeling nostalgic desolation.

W. B. Yeats
An Irish Airman Foresees His Death

THIS POEM TELLS us about Major Robert Gregory, son of Yeats's great friend Lady Gregory from Coole Park, Co. Galway. Robert Gregory died in action in January 1918 as a member of the Royal Flying Corps. Yeats laments the death of his dear friend's son and portrays him as a brave and confident soldier who foresees his own death.

In this poem the speaker is the voice of Robert Gregory. He intuitively knows that he will meet his destiny among the clouds. He admits that he is not committed to the conflict of the war (the First World War) as he neither hates the enemy nor loves those he protects. He is from Kiltartan Cross, a place far removed from the battleground. He loves the local people there and it is irrelevant to them whether the war is won or lost; the outcome will not make them richer or poorer. Gregory further confesses that he joined the Royal Flying Corps not through any compulsion of law. What drove him towards the turmoil of war was a 'lonely impulse of delight', a mysterious calling which forced him to take stock of his life. It became clear to him that the past had been 'A waste of breath' and that the future held only the same. To enlist and die in the skies was the most attractive option when all was considered – 'In balance with this life, this death'.

Yeats admires Robert Gregory for his ability to calmly detach and succumb to a heroic impulse calling him to live for the moment and disregard the past and the future.

Approaching the unseen poem: some suggestions

1 *Read* through the poem once, then read it again slowly.
2 If you are still unsure about the meaning of the poem, *read the questions* set on it as they will often help you to work out the theme of the poem.
3 Read the poem *again*.
4 If the poem is punctuated, *break the poem into sentences* and read these sentences one at a time.
5 Try understanding *each part* of the poem first and then come back to the whole poem.
6 *Make notes* in the margins as you are doing this.
7 You must approach the *oral aspect* of the poem. Make sure you hear the rhythms and sounds of the poem in your head.
8 When *analysing* the *rhythm* of a particular poem, always consider the following elements:
   i) **Metre:** notice the regular pattern of stressed and unstressed syllables. Words more heavily stressed are usually central to the poem's meaning.
   ii) **Rhyme:** notice repetition of similar sounds in endings of words. Work out if the poem has a discernible rhyme scheme or not.
   iii) **Lines:** consider the use of end-stopped versus run-on lines. Look out for caesurae, which are breaks within lines.
   iv) **Punctuation:** consider how punctuation influences pausing, and thus the rhythm and effect of the poem.
   v) **Sound imagery:** consider use of sound techniques such as alliteration, assonance and onomatopoeia, all of which influence the rhythm of the poem.
9 Remember that *variation* in any of the above elements is usually meant to achieve a certain effect.
10 Try using the **SIFT** method, which involves analysing the **S**ense, **I**ntention, **F**eeling and **T**one of the poem.
11 In considering the **sense**, you should explain to yourself briefly what the poem is about.
12 Identify the poet's **intention** or purpose in writing the poem.
13 When you comment on the **feelings** that the poem evokes, you should refer to poetic language and techniques such as metaphors and images, use of sound effects and structural considerations.
14 Finally, you need to identify the **tone** of the poem which needs to be consistent with the poet's intentions.
15 Now start to answer the questions. The mark allocation for each question will give you an indication of the length of answer required. Take your time and think before you write, but if you change your mind about an answer, don't hesitate to cross out and rewrite. Examiners far prefer to see a correct, somewhat untidy answer than a beautifully neat, incorrect one.
16 Finally, read through the poem and the questions *again* followed by your answers to make sure there is nothing you have missed.

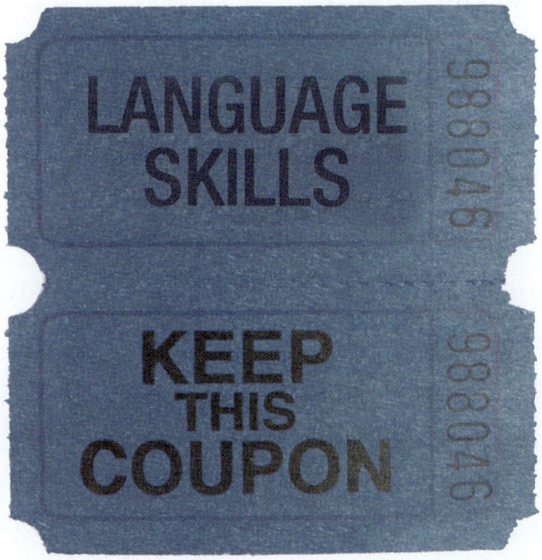
LANGUAGE
SKILLS
988046
KEEP
THIS
COUPON
988046

Paper 1 of the Leaving Certificate English exam tests your ability to:

1 **Comprehend** (understand)
2 **Compose** (write)

Section 1

- There are three texts. These can be newspaper reports, stories, letters, photographs or even advertisements.
- Each text is followed by Question A and Question B.
- Students must answer Question A (Comprehending) from one text and Question B (Composing) from either of the two remaining texts. **You must not answer Question A and Question B from the same text.**

Section 2

You are required to choose and write a composition from a list of ideas, titles and themes, some related to Section 1.

Criteria for assessment

The tasks set for candidates in both Paper 1 and Paper 2 will be assessed in accordance with the following criteria:

Clarity of purpose   30%
(Ability to display a clear and purposeful engagement with the set task)

Coherence of delivery   30%
(Ability to sustain the response in an appropriate manner over the entire question)

Efficiency of language use 30%
(Management and control of language to achieve clear communication)

Accuracy of mechanics   10%
(Correct spelling and grammar appropriate to the required or chosen register)

Approaching the exam paper

Timing: Paper 1
- You have *170 minutes* to answer Paper 1.

- Section 1 carries *100 marks.*
- Section 2 carries *100 marks.*

A suggested breakdown of your time:

15 minutes: *Read* through the full paper from start to finish. Decide which questions you intend to answer.

30 minutes: Section 1 – Question A: Comprehending

30 minutes: Section 1 – Question B: Composing

80 minutes: Section 2 – Composing

15 minutes: *Read* through all your answers from start to finish.

Writing Skills

We use language for many reasons and there are various types of language to suit different situations. It is important that students understand which type of language is appropriate to any given situation.

In preparation for Paper 1 the student must understand five types of language. It is important that students can *identify* and *write* in each of these modes.

1 Language of narration
2 Language of information
3 Language of persuasion
4 Language of argument
5 The aesthetic use of language

However in the examination over recent years students have been asked to write under a number of different headings:

1 Letter writing
2 Writing instructions
3 Speech writing
4 Describing an image or photograph
5 Diary writing
6 Creative writing
7 Summarising
8 Writing a newspaper article
9 Writing a review
10 Writing a personal opinion
11 Writing a commentary
12 Writing an interview

Guidelines for letter writing

Letter writing appears regularly in the exam paper especially as a Question B in Section 1, Paper 1.

While it is important to lay out your letter correctly the bulk of the marks will be allocated on the *body* of the letter.

There are two types of letters: informal and formal.

1 Informal letters
Informal letters are written to family and friends in a personal and chatty way.

Layout of an informal letter

4 Rue Mouffetard,
Paris 75006,
France.
— Your address

Casual greeting

27 July 2005 — Date

Hi Guys,

I made it! I am finally settled here in Paris. Nicole and her family seem really nice and I think I'll have a good time over the next few weeks on this exchange.

I'm not as lonely as I thought I'd be, probably because the family has planned something for us to do every day. What are we going to do with Nicole when she comes to Ireland?? We don't have an Eiffel Tower or an Arc de Triomphe to show her. Mum — get your thinking cap on quickly and plan some exciting things for us to do. We are going to EuroDisney on Tuesday and I can't wait. Remember the fun we had in Funderland in Dublin at Christmas? Well I imagine this is going to be even better.

The plan is that we stay here in Paris for the rest of this week and then go down to Nice on the coast to their family home for the next week — POSH!!! I hope to get a great tan and will do loads of shopping and find gorgeous presents for everyone. I'm sending you some photos Mrs Du Bois took of us on our sightseeing tour of the city.

— Relaxed conversational language

Missing you loads,
Love, Marie.
— Informal ending

2 Formal letters

In the exam you may be asked to write
- a letter of complaint
- a letter of enquiry / requesting information
- a letter of application
- a letter of invitation
- a letter to the editor of a newspaper

There is a very specific layout to be followed when writing a formal letter. Your letter should be *structured, organised* and *to the point.* The language should be *standard English.* The tone should be *businesslike* and *polite.* Avoid abbreviations and slang.

Layout of a formal letter

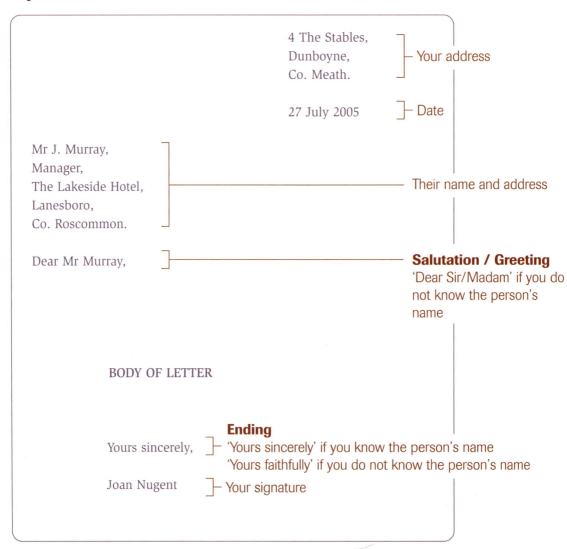

4 The Stables,
Dunboyne,
Co. Meath. ⎤ Your address

27 July 2005 — Date

Mr J. Murray,
Manager,
The Lakeside Hotel, ———— Their name and address
Lanesboro,
Co. Roscommon.

Dear Mr Murray, ———— **Salutation / Greeting**
'Dear Sir/Madam' if you do not know the person's name

BODY OF LETTER

Ending

Yours sincerely, ⎤ 'Yours sincerely' if you know the person's name
'Yours faithfully' if you do not know the person's name

Joan Nugent ⎤ Your signature

Sample letter of application

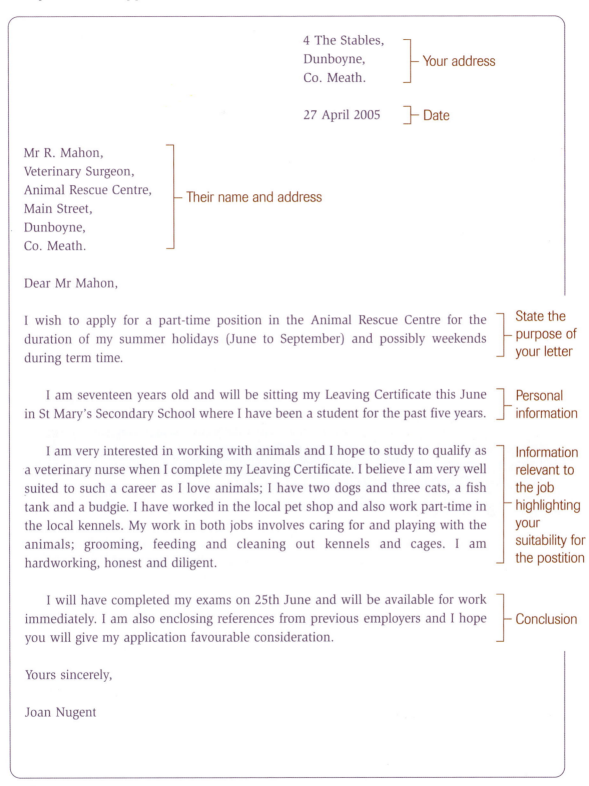

4 The Stables,
Dunboyne,
Co. Meath.

— Your address

27 April 2005   — Date

Mr R. Mahon,
Veterinary Surgeon,
Animal Rescue Centre,
Main Street,
Dunboyne,
Co. Meath.

— Their name and address

Dear Mr Mahon,

I wish to apply for a part-time position in the Animal Rescue Centre for the duration of my summer holidays (June to September) and possibly weekends during term time.

— State the purpose of your letter

I am seventeen years old and will be sitting my Leaving Certificate this June in St Mary's Secondary School where I have been a student for the past five years.

— Personal information

I am very interested in working with animals and I hope to study to qualify as a veterinary nurse when I complete my Leaving Certificate. I believe I am very well suited to such a career as I love animals; I have two dogs and three cats, a fish tank and a budgie. I have worked in the local pet shop and also work part-time in the local kennels. My work in both jobs involves caring for and playing with the animals; grooming, feeding and cleaning out kennels and cages. I am hardworking, honest and diligent.

— Information relevant to the job highlighting your suitability for the postition

I will have completed my exams on 25th June and will be available for work immediately. I am also enclosing references from previous employers and I hope you will give my application favourable consideration.

— Conclusion

Yours sincerely,

Joan Nugent

Sample letter of complaint

4 The Stables,
Dunboyne,
Co. Meath.

27 July 2005

The Manager,
'Nice Bites',
Main Street,
Navan,
Co. Meath.

Dear Sir / Madam,

I am writing in relation to an unsatisfactory meal I purchased in your café on Saturday last, 23 July 2005. State the purpose of your letter

I entered your café at 7 p.m. having read your menu displayed outside. I was however disappointed to be presented with a totally different menu once I was seated. A waiter informed me that the menu displayed outside was out of date and that your staff 'hadn't got around to changing it'.

Although disappointed I chose from the new menu and sat back waiting for my meal. A half hour passed and although the restaurant was not very busy I still had not been served. When I enquired about my order the waiter disappeared into the kitchen and was not seen again for the duration of my visit.

Finally at 7.45 p.m. my meal arrived. The burger was fine, but I had ordered a baked potato and side salad, and it came accompanied by chips and onion rings. I tried to catch the attention of the waiting staff to rectify this but gave up and ate only what I had ordered – the burger.

As I was paying I explained to the cashier, Ruth, that I was dissatisfied and did not want to pay for what I had neither ordered nor eaten. She was sympathetic but said that she could not charge for just the burger and that I had to pay for the full meal. I asked to speak to a manager but no one was available.

Outline the complaint

I am enclosing my receipt for €12.95 which I paid in full. I would be grateful if you could refund this amount to me in cash. I would also recommend that your waiting staff undergo more training on both dealing with customers and taking orders. I would also like to point out that the menu displayed outside your café still has not been changed and I suggest that this be done immediately to prevent more customers being disappointed before they even taste your food.

Conclusion and recommendations

Yours faithfully,

Joan Nugent

Sample letter to the editor

You may be required to write to the editor of a newspaper. People usually write to a newspaper to agree or disagree with an article or letter previously printed in the newspaper, or to highlight a topic about which they may feel strongly. The writer usually uses his/her own personal experiences as well as facts and figures to substantiate his/her viewpoint.

Sir,

I would like to add my support to your journalist Brendan Joyce who represented the views of young people living in cities and towns in his article 'Good for Something'. I am tired of the teenage-bashing that goes on every day in newspapers, on TV and in conversations in general. I would like to congratulate Brendan Joyce for his observations on young people and I recommend that adults stop and have a good think before they label all young people 'wasters'. My friends and I, all under eighteen, spent our summer holidays working and saving to support ourselves when we hopefully start college in September. We don't have time for drinking, wandering the streets in search of trouble or indeed lazing in front of the TV, as many adults tend to believe. We need more 'Reality Journalism' and less 'Reality TV'.

Yours etc.,

J.P.

Sligo.

Sir,

Last Thursday, August 4th, I booked by e-mail with Discount Air a return flight to Hamburg six weeks in advance of travel. The only fare available cost me €450 – and Discount Air calls itself a low-fare airline. Be warned.

Yours etc.,

P. Murray,

Dublin

Sir,

Having travelled on the Luas for the first time last Thursday, 20th July, I have to admit I was very impressed with our newest form of city travel.

There is no doubt but that this service will improve the lives of many thousands who live near the route and stops. It has enhanced life in Dublin in a most positive way and was well worth the months of disruptions.

I appeal to the Corporation and the planners to expand this service and improve the lives of many more who are prisoners in their cars as they chug along the clogged arteries of Dublin every morning and evening trying to get to and from work.

Mr Ahern recently announced that there could be no expansion due to lack of funds, yet the government can find money for state banquets and state jets. I implore the guardians of our state to get their priorities in order and spend our money wisely!

Yours etc.,

Mary Mc Murray,

Dublin 12

Guidelines for writing instructions

In the Leaving Certificate exam you may be asked to give simple yet detailed information on how to perform a task. You are required to give clear information without any personal opinions.

1 On a *rough work* page jot down all that the task requires. (Main steps to be taken, equipment needed, time scale etc.)
2 *Organise* these under headings.
3 Give a *brief* introduction.
4 Explain any technical details or *jargon*.
5 Use numbered, *step-by-step instructions*.
6 Use *simple, direct* language.
7 *Highlight any dangers* or downsides that the reader should be aware of.

How to set a solid fuel fire

Open fires are not as popular nowadays as they once were. The modern house is now usually equipped with a clean and efficient gas fire or oil-fired central heating. However a roaring open fire is not difficult to create.

You will need:
A fireplace designed to hold a solid fuel fire
Dry burning fuel – turf / coal / wood
Small thin pieces of wood / sticks
Firelighter
Old sheets of newspaper
Matches or lighter

Procedure:

1 Protect yourself and your surroundings by wearing an apron and rubber gloves.

2 Gently remove any ashes remaining in the grate and place in a metal fireproof bucket or box. Remember to be careful as there may be sparks and warm cinders from previous fires.

3 Place the firelighter in the centre of the grate.

4 Crumple up the sheets of newspaper into tight balls and place around the firelighter.

5 Arrange sticks in a criss-cross way over the newspaper.

6 Light the firelighter and allow the flames to grow.

7 Place a small amount of fuel loosely on top at first.

8 Once the fire is burning well add more fuel a little at a time. Avoid putting too much on at any one time as this will smother the flame and the fire will go out.

9 For safety always place a fireguard in front of the fire and keep children away from the fireplace.

Guidelines for writing a speech or debate

1 Decide on the *purpose* of your speech. Are you trying to convince, to persuade, to inform, to praise, to ask for help or support, or to entertain your audience? Whatever the reason for the speech you should start by making a clear and confident statement of your purpose.

2 *Brainstorm:* write down all the points, words, people and facts you know associated with your title.

3 *Prioritise:* put your most important points first and *support* your points with statistics and facts. It is also useful and interesting to include personal anecdotes to strengthen your argument.

4 When writing a speech or debate you must be aware of your *audience*. You should begin by addressing your audience. Regularly during your speech you should refer to them, appeal to them to agree with your points, and of course, in your conclusion, thank them for their support and attention.

5 Addressing your audience is not enough. You must adopt the appropriate *register*. Your language, tone and approach will differ depending on your audience. Imagine giving a speech on litter in your locality. Your speech to the County Council would be very different from your speech to the local primary school students.

6 Your *introduction* should capture the audience's attention. A good opening will allow the audience to know what to expect. *Challenge* the audience with a question, deliver a *quotation* from a respected source or *shock* the audience with an unexpected statistic.

7 If you are writing a debate *acknowledge* the opposition's arguments. Be aware of opinions that are contrary to yours and deal with them in a clear and logical way, using plenty of examples to support your view and dispute the opposing standpoints. Avoid emotional language and slang, and avoid offending the audience or indeed the opposition. Your presentation of the evidence should win the support of the listeners so there is no need to 'rant and rave'.

8 In *conclusion* you should sum up your main points making one final statement of purpose, appeal to the audience to support your point of view and thank them for their attention.

Guidelines for describing an image or picture

1 Start off with a *general* statement: 'This is a photograph / book cover / CD cover / poster . . .'

2 Mention the *shape* of the image and describe the border or frame if there is one.

3 You may choose to begin by describing the *background*. What do you see behind the main features of the photograph? Is it a country scene or an urban setting, is it inside a studio or out in the great outdoors?

4 Next describe the *foreground*. What is nearest the observer? Start with the centre and then describe what is to the right and the left. Point out what is the main focus of the image.

5 Discuss what you see in *detail*. Describe colours, shapes, expressions on faces, time of day or night, lighting, weather etc.

6 Where is the *camera* and *photographer*? Is this a wide-angle picture, a close-up or an aerial photo?

7 What is the *purpose* of the image? Is it part of an advertisement or an image to be used for promotional reasons, is it modern or an image from history, is it informative or is it aiming to arouse sympathy or anger or support?

Guidelines for writing a diary

1 A diary is a *personal account recording daily events*. The writer is telling about his/her own environment and experiences. The writer sometimes addresses the diary as if it were a close friend – 'Dear Diary'.

2 In the Leaving Certificate exam students may be asked to write *two to three diary entries* as part of Section 1, Question B, worth 50 marks; or a full composition structured as a diary, worth 100 marks in Section 2, Composing.

3 What is written in a diary is rarely intended to be read by anyone other than the author so the tone is very *open and honest*. The style can be revealing and reflective divulging personal feelings the writer may not tell anyone else. The language is chatty and conversational.

4 Remember that this is still a *narrative*. You still have a story to tell or a message to deliver.

5 Most diaries include a date, a salutation ('Dear Diary'), a description of something that has occurred that day and the writer's *feelings* on this incident.

Guidelines for creative writing

Writing a short story or narrative is not as simple as merely telling a story. The writer must engage the reader in the opening paragraphs and entice him/her to read on. Writing a good short story is a skill which does not come naturally to everyone. The following points are guidelines to assist the writer to develop his/her own style.

An original idea

When you choose a title from the list in Paper 1, Section 2: Composing, the idea for what you intend to write may be based on an essay you have already written or it may come 'out of the blue'. It might be something that has happened to you or someone you know, or it might be something you have read about or seen on television. Whatever the idea is it must inspire you; you must feel excited about it. If it is not of interest to you your audience will detect this and you will fail to capture their interest and attention. This central idea is your *theme*.

Characters

1 The characters in your story should be believable; the reader should feel that these are real people even though they may be fictional.

2 A short story usually revolves around one main character whose problem or dilemma is of interest to the reader.

3 Too many characters in a story means the reader cannot get to know any one very well and you, the writer, will not have an opportunity to develop them all fully.

4 You should show the story through the eyes of your central character. You may be that character (first person narrative) or you might tell the story as a narrator (third person narrative). The first person can be easier to write as you endeavour, through the use of 'I', 'me' and 'my', to express emotions naturally as if they were your own.

5 Avoid long descriptions of your characters, the general rule to follow is 'Show, don't tell'. A writer can bring the character to life by *showing* the reader what he/she is like rather than *telling*.

6 Paint the picture rather than describing it. For example to write 'He was a bully who intimidated everyone he met', is far less effective than showing the reader an occasion when the character uses menacing language to terrify others, allowing the reader to hear exactly what is said and draw their own conclusions.

7 Three elements the writer may use to make the characters real and believable are Name, Personality and Appearance.

Setting or background

1 It is very difficult to write about life on the moon if you have never experienced it. In the same way you should not attempt to describe life in New York or Dublin or the desert if you know little or nothing about that environment. It is wise to choose a setting you know; it doesn't even need to be somewhere real as long as you can picture it clearly in your mind.

2 Do not ignore lighting. Is it day or night? Daylight or dusk? Summer sunshine or a dull, grey, winter's evening? Describing the lighting evokes the atmosphere.

3 Allow your readers to hear the sounds, experience the smells, and notice the movements in an effort to help them envisage the scene.

A good opening

1 Start slowly.

2 Set the scene and outline the main problem in the first few paragraphs.

3 Do not tell all in the first paragraph.

4 Introduce your central character as soon as possible.

5 Interest and encourage your readers to read on. Grab their attention by presenting them with a situation which makes them have to read on to discover what the main character will do.

The story

To hold the readers' attention you must not try to take in too much. Keep the time span relatively short as you will not realistically fit in a full life story in 500–1000 words or in the time allowed.

Stick to the main storyline and avoid telling extra stories within the story. Only mention what is directly linked to your plot or information, which will help to develop the characters.

The ending

Your ending is a winding-up of the story. You do not need to have a happy 'they all lived happily ever after' ending, as this can be unrealistic. You can have your character learning a lesson in difficult circumstances but moving on through life with new hope. Experiment with different endings to your stories – the cliffhanger, the 'happily ever after', the stark reality. Avoid the 'it was all a dream' scenario as the reader is left feeling robbed and betrayed, and also avoid the ending where everyone dies or leaves having learnt nothing or taken anything from the experience.

Common mistakes in story writing

- Story line too ordinary
- Story line too far-fetched
- Nothing happens
- Too much 'padding' or descriptions
- Too many characters
- Not getting to know the characters in any depth
- Trying to cover too much
- No shape / no paragraphs / not divided into beginning, middle and end
- Time span too long
- Not enough dialogue
- Telling the reader instead of showing
- Flat ending – nothing is resolved
- Cheat ending – 'They all die' / 'It was all a dream'

Guidelines for summarising and paraphrasing

A written summary should always paraphrase first, rather than just repeating what was said. You must learn to paraphrase before you summarise.

1. PARAPHRASING

To paraphrase is to rewrite something using different words without changing the original meaning. This is what is usually meant by the phrase 'in your own words'. The paraphrase should be clearer and more easily understood than the original. It is usually similar in length to the original.

To paraphrase

1 Read the text carefully. Underline, or note, any important words.
2 Look at any difficult words, and try to find alternative words for them.
3 Try to find different ways of indicating time or place.
4 Rewrite each sentence. Try to simplify the sentence structure and the vocabulary without changing the meaning.
5 Revise what you have written, comparing it to the original. Your paraphrase should *clarify* the original.
6 Do not forget to include appropriate reference information at the end of your paraphrase, especially regarding facts.

2. SUMMARISING

A summary is much shorter than the original text. It should communicate the main idea of the text and the main supporting points, written in your own words, in a very brief form. The summary should give someone who has not read the original a clear and accurate overview of the text. A formal summary should also include the author, title, year of publication and source of the original.

Writing a summary requires a thorough understanding of the content of the text, and the ability to paraphrase.

To summarise

1 Record the author, title, year of publication and source of the text.
2 Skim the text. Note any sub-headings or try to divide the text into sections.
3 Read the text carefully. Use a dictionary if necessary, and be prepared to read very difficult texts more than once.
4 Pay special attention to the first and last paragraphs. Try to identify the main idea or argument.
5 Identify the topic sentence in each paragraph. This is frequently the first sentence in the paragraph.
6 Identify the main support for the topic sentence.
7 Write the topic sentence of your summary. Include the author's name, the title of the text, the year of publication and the author's main idea or argument.
8 Try to write one or two sentences for each paragraph. Include the main idea (usually a paraphrase of the topic sentence) and the main support for the topic sentence (also paraphrased).
9 Revise and rewrite.
10 Proofread and make corrections as required.

Guidelines for writing a newspaper article

The first thing prospective reporters must know is that newspaper articles are written differently depending on their format or purpose. Newspaper articles can be divided into three categories: news articles, feature stories, and columns.

HOW TO WRITE A NEWS ARTICLE
Pure news articles are the most structured type of newspaper article. A specific format must be followed in writing this type of article. *The purpose of this article is to convey the facts of an event to an interested reader.*

Guidelines for writing a news article

1 As with all newspaper articles, it should be set off with a headline. The headline should not be a summary of the article; instead it should serve the purpose of getting the reader's attention.
2 The story should start with a 'lead paragraph' which is the summary of the

story. Do not tease at the beginning or summarise at the end as you sometimes see on television news. Lay all your cards out on the table. The lead paragraph should include the *who, what, when, where, and why* of the story.

3 After the lead paragraph comes explanation and amplification, which deals with highlighting details. Use discretion in choosing which details to include. Some details may not be as important as others. Put them in order of importance from greatest to least. Don't feel the need to include everything you know, but do include everything you feel is important.

4 If the average reader will be confused, fill in the gaps with background information. When in doubt, give the information.

5 Do not use the first person. If you feel that it is absolutely necessary, think about writing a feature story or a column instead (see below).

6 *No bias.* Personal prejudices should not find their way into the article. Again, use of an opinion-editorial or column forum is recommended for personal opinions.

7 When possible, use quotes to flavour the article. However, don't use quotes for the sake of using quotes – make sure they are relevant. Also, make sure the quotes aren't a grammatical embarrassment – avoid run-ons especially.

HOW TO WRITE FEATURE STORIES

Features are interesting stories about people, places and events. They aren't as concerned with conveying basic facts as in conveying a mood, feeling, or theme. Unlike writing news articles, there are no hard and fast rules for composing features. Features are common in newspapers and even more common in magazines.

Guidelines for writing feature stories

1 Many feature stories are biographical sketches of individuals. Often interviews with public figures (athletes or entertainers) or compelling people (such as a homeless person) can make for interesting feature stories.

2 Unlike in a news article, the feature writer is allowed much creativity in the story's composition. The order of presentation is based solely on the criteria of what makes for the most interesting read.

3 Pretend you are telling a story. Draw on storytelling techniques from other media, such as movies, theatre, fiction, and music. This may include visualisation of the scene you are creating. Sounds, smells, and textures can even be a viable means of expression. *Paint a picture with words*.

4 Metaphors and comparisons are fair game in feature stories. Your impressions can be given.

5 Although personal insights are allowed in a feature, strive for objectivity. Tell both sides of the story. If you are featuring a homeless man include comments critical of the police for enforcing loitering violations, give a police spokesperson a chance to respond.

HOW TO WRITE A COLUMN

A column, or opinion-editorial (op-ed), is the most open-ended of newspaper articles. It is a chance to express your opinion. There are not many rules to writing this type of article. *The most important thing is to have all your facts correct.* Always keep in mind that it is difficult to persuade readers by offending or insulting them.

A final piece of advice

Become a vigorous reader of newspapers. Read pure news articles, features, and columns and note what makes them effective. Good writers are always good readers.

Guidelines for writing a review

BEFORE WRITING

What are you reviewing?

- Film
- Concert/event
- CD
- Video/DVD
- Book
- Restaurant
- Theatre
- Game
- Art exhibition

The medium that you are reviewing should directly affect how you approach it. In a review, detail is very important, so make sure that the peculiarities of the medium are shown; for example, with a DVD, are there special features on it? With a concert, what were the facilities like? What was the atmosphere like?

Who are you reviewing for?

What is your audience? Will they understand lingo like 'techno' or 'gig' etc.? Is your review written for a tabloid or broadsheet, or for a magazine or radio etc.?

Read plenty of reviews

The best writers are the best readers!

WRITING THE REVIEW

1 **Give a headline.** If the review is for a newspaper or magazine, keep the headline short and to the point.
2 **Name the material.** Identify what you are dealing with as early as possible, for example:
   '*Booked!* by Tom Humphries is a new collection of articles by the *Irish Times* journalist.'
   or
   'The Red Hot Chilli Peppers headlined another sell-out gig at Slane.'
   or

'*O* by Damien Rice has just been released to critical acclaim.'
   or
   'Mike Myers and Eddie Murphy are back for another whirlwind adventure in *Shrek 2*.'
3 **Summarise the story** but do not give away any twists or the ending.
4 **Give plenty of opinion.** Don't be afraid to be emotive. Let your feelings be known.
   'The best part of the book was when . . .'
   'My favourite character was . . .'
   'I felt let down by the performance of X in the role of Y.'
5 **Give detail of one part of the book etc.** Dedicate one paragraph to a detailed analysis of one element of the media or event you are reviewing.
6 **Give your verdict or final evaluation.** Would you recommend it to somebody else? Give a mark out of ten or a star rating.

Guidelines for writing a personal opinion piece

BEFORE WRITING

What are you asked to do?

This type of writing is often asked for in the exam papers. It usually asks you to write about your feelings on a certain topic or it can ask you about how a topic affects you and its importance in your life.

WRITING THE PIECE

1 **You do not have to tell the truth.** Use your imagination if you wish. The person marking the exam does not know who you are or anything about you and your opinions. Do not be afraid to make things up in order to make the writing more interesting. However, do not let your piece get too far-fetched. Keep it realistic.
2 **Don't be afraid of your feelings.** Do not be afraid to use emotive language. Tell

the reader clearly and directly what you feel on the topic.

3 **Vary your language when you are describing your feelings.** Get used to using a thesaurus and find as many words as you can to describe each of your basic emotions.

4 **Be exact,** for example:
'The very first time I felt that way was on the 17th of August, the day of my Leaving Certificate results.'
This allows the reader to identify with the events you describe and your feelings towards them.

5 **Introduce your topic directly and early.**

6 **Give good examples to back up your feelings.**

7 In your final paragraph, **summarise** by stringing all the points that you have made together to justify your position.

Guidelines for writing a commentary piece

BEFORE WRITING
You could be asked to write a commentary piece for radio or television. In this piece you will asked to describe a *period of action.* The most obvious types of commentaries are sports events, state funerals or nature programmes of the David Attenborough type. They will each need a different approach. It is important to pay clear attention to various radio and television commentaries.

WRITING THE PIECE
1 Remember that **you are the eyes of your audience.**

2 You must provide the details that they cannot see.

3 Provide details of colour and exact descriptions of clothing and movement.

4 Do not be afraid to use your opinions.

5 Keep your sentences short so you do not lose your audience.

6 Put enthusiasm into the tone of a sporting commentary.

7 Keep a funeral or nature commentary sombre and steady.

8 Remember to give details of names and scores as appropriate.

Guidelines for writing an interview or a question and answer piece

This format will be familiar to anybody who reads newspapers or magazines or those who listen to radio or watch television.

1 There are always at least two people involved; the interviewer and the interviewee.

2 Give an introduction to the interview, for example 'The Taoiseach has been in the news recently after the recent strike action taken by teachers. I met him in the Gresham Hotel to discuss his feelings on the issue.'

3 Structure your piece so that the interviewer's name comes first, then his/her question. Underneath this you can put the interviewee's name and his/her answers, for example:
Irish Times Taoiseach, what do you think . . .
Taoiseach I think . . .

4 The interviewee cannot be expected to give a good answer unless they are asked a good question.

5 Stick to relevant and interesting questions.

6 Be aware of the audience for the piece.

7 Do not ask questions that can be answered with a yes or no.

8 Do not give one-word answers. Do not be afraid to give too much information. Be afraid to give too little.

9 Do not be afraid to make the questions interesting and provocative. Be controversial if appropriate.

10 Do not be afraid to be humorous, but make sure you stick to the topic.

11 If you have a choice of interviewee, make sure it is somebody of interest to the audience that has been identified. For example if you are asked to write an interview with a rock star for a tabloid newspaper, ensure that it is somebody that the readers of a tabloid would know, not just an obscure person known only to you and your friends.

Questions based on exam papers
Section 1, Question B

Letters

1 Write a letter to your favourite pop star or celebrity inviting him or her to come to the launch of a charity to help the homeless. In your letter you should explain how you intend to raise money for the charity.
L.C. 2003

2 Write a letter to the owner of a hotel complaining about a bad experience.
L.C. 2001

3 Imagine you are a refugee in Ireland. Write a letter home telling your family how refugees are treated and how you feel about this. (100–150 words)
L.C. Sample

4 Imagine your friend has recently moved to Dublin to attend college. Write a letter to him or her enquiring about college life in Dublin.
L.C. Sample

5 'What is it about the *Titanic* that continues to grip our interest nearly 100 years after she sank on that "Night to Remember"?' Write a letter to David Robbins, author of a review of a new book on the *Titanic* giving your answer to the above question, which he asks in his review. (150–200 words)
L.C. Sample

6 Write a letter to the editor of a sports paper or magazine giving your views on boxing.
L.C. Sample

7 You are a student at a school for racing apprentices. Write a letter home to your parents describing your first week in the school.
L.C. Sample

Personal opinion

1 Write the answer you would give to the question 'What does entertainment mean to you?'
L.C. 2003

2 Write about the changes you would like to make to your room, or to your home, or to the area in which you live.
L.C. 2002

3 Imagine you were asked to give an interview during your final term in school. Write the answers you would give to Question 1: What positive memory will stay with you as you grow older? and Question 2: What hopes do you have for the world? Can you see yourself making any difference to the world, however small?
L.C. 2001

Newspaper articles

1 Computer games – do they have a good or a bad effect on young people? Write an article for a newspaper expressing your view on this question.
L.C. 2001

Review

1 Write a review of your favourite film or TV programme or radio programme.
L.C. 2003

Commentary / Speech / Debate

1 Imagine you are a radio or TV commentator for a sporting or non-sporting event. Write the commentary you would give on one important moment during that event.
L.C. 2002

Diary

1 Write two or three diary entries recording your own or your family's experiences during the first week of the changeover to the Euro.
L.C. 2002

2 Compose the diary entries that a girl, Phoebe, who has moved to Dublin, might write in her first month at college.
L.C. Sample

Sample paper 1: War

Section 1: Comprehending (100 marks)

WAR: TEXT 1

Birdsong

The German enemy has rescued Stephen Wraysford, a British captain during the First World War, after an explosion buries him underground for many days.

They helped Stephen to the bottom of the rope and gave him water. They lifted him up, and Levi walked with his arm round him to the end of the tunnel while Lamm and Kroger went back into the darkness to bring out the body of Jack Firebrace.

Levi guided Stephen's slow steps up the incline towards the light. They had to cover their eyes against the powerful rays of the sun. Eventually they came up into the air of the German trench. Levi helped Stephen over the step.

Stephen breathed deeply again and again. He looked at the blue and distant sky, feathered with irregular clouds. He sat down on the firestep and held his head in his hands.

They could hear the sound of birds. The trench was empty. Levi climbed on to the parapet and raised a pair of binoculars. The British trench was deserted. He looked behind the German lines, but could see nothing in front of the horizon, five miles distant. The dam had broken, the German army had been swept away.

He came down into the trench and sat next to Stephen. Neither man spoke. Each listened to the heavenly quietness.

Stephen eventually turned his face up to Levi. 'Is it over?' he said in English.

'Yes,' said Levi, also in English. 'It is finished.'

Stephen looked down to the floor of the German trench. He could not grasp what had happened. Four years that had lasted so long it seemed that time had stopped. All the men he had seen killed, their bodies, their wounds. Michael Weir. His pale face emerging from his burrow underground. Byrne like a headless crow. The tens of thousands who had gone down with him that summer morning.

He did not know what to do. He did not know how to reclaim his life.

He felt his lower lip begin to tremble and the hot tears filling his eyes. He laid his head against Levi's chest and sobbed.

They brought up Jack's body and, when the men had rested, they dug a grave for him and Joseph Levi. They made it a joint grave, because the war was over. Stephen said a prayer for Jack, and Levi for his brother. They picked flowers and threw them on the grave. All four of them were weeping.

Then Lamm went looking in the dugouts and came back with water and tins of food. They ate in the open air. Then they went back into the dugout and slept.

The next day Stephen said he would have to rejoin his battalion. He shook hands with Kroger and Lamm, and then with Levi. Of all the flesh he had seen and touched, it was this doctor's hand that had signalled his deliverance.

Levi would not let him go. He made him promise to write when he was back in England. He took the buckle from his belt and gave it to him as a souvenir. *Gott mit uns.* Stephen gave him the knife with the single blade. They embraced again and clung on to each other.

Then Stephen climbed the ladder, over the top, into no man's land. No hurricane of bullets met him, no tearing metal kiss.

He felt the dry, turned earth beneath his boots as he picked his way back towards the

British lines. A lark was singing in the unharmed air above him. His body and mind were tired beyond speech and beyond repair, but nothing could check the low exultation of his soul.
FROM *BIRDSONG* BY SEBASTIAN FAULKS

N.B. Candidates may NOT answer Question A and Question B on the same text.
Questions A and B carry 50 marks each.

Question A
(i)   Describe the reception Stephen receives from the Germans upon his rescue. (10)
(ii) What are Stephen's feelings when he hears that the war is over? (20)
(iii) Describe, using evidence from the passage, what life was like in the trenches during the First World War. (20)

Question B
Write out the script of a news reporter for television reporting on the end of a war. (50)

WAR: TEXT 2
When the killing finally stopped
On 2 November 1944, more than three years after the first gassing experiments at Auschwitz, an order arrived from Heinrich Himmler: "I forbid any further annihilation of Jews." On his orders, all but one of the crematoria were dismantled, the burning-pits covered up and planted with grass, and the gas pipes and other equipment shipped to concentration camps in Germany. The single remaining crematorium was for the disposal of those who died natural deaths and for gassing about two hundred surviving members of the Sonderkommando.

The final solution was formally over. Although tens of thousands of Jews and others would go on dying of neglect and brutality, the systematic killing had ended. Why Himmler made this decision is not certain. One possible reason was that the Reich was desperate for labour, even Jewish workers. Evidence suggests, however, that Himmler foresaw the disaster that awaited the Third Reich and was desperately trying to save his own skin by compiling a record of what he might have termed "leniency". Indeed, his order to stop the killing contained a further, ingratiating directive instructing that "proper care be given to the weak and the sick".

Less than three months later, on 17 January 1945, the last roll call was conducted at Auschwitz. The Germans counted 67,012 prisoners at the main camp and the satellite camps. This amounted to less than half the peak population of 155,000 tabulated during the previous August. Many had already been sent westwards to camps in Germany, and more had died. Now, with the artillery of the approaching Red Army thundering on the horizon, the Germans ordered the evacuation of all but about 6,000 inmates who were too infirm to make the trip by train or on foot.

The 58,000 or so evacuees struggled westwards in agony. Even those who were put aboard trains suffered privation. Many thousands died of starvation or exposure in the unheated wagons. Many had to march all the way to Germany in freezing cold. Staggering along in rags, barefoot or on wooden clogs, sustained only by a starvation diet, thousands fell by the wayside and were shot by their SS guards. One march lasted for more than 16 weeks and claimed the lives of all but 280 of the 3,000 who began it.

Those left behind at Auschwitz suffered too. Without food, water, or heat, sick and despairing, they died by the hundreds each day. The SS guards disappeared bit by bit until finally the inmates had the camp to themselves. On 27 January 1945, the Russians arrived. It was a "beautiful, sunny winter's day," a survivor wrote in his diary. "At about 3.00 p.m., we heard a noise in the direction of the main gate. We hurried to the scene. It was a Soviet forward patrol – Russian soldiers in white caps! There was a mad rush to shake them by the hand and shout our gratitude. We were liberated!"

By that time, about 2,800 people remained alive at Auschwitz. The soldiers fed the survivors, tended to the sick, and buried the dead. Thousands upon thousands had died before these at Auschwitz, but this mass burial was the "first dignified funeral" ever held there, an inmate observed.

FROM *THE THIRD REICH AT WAR* EDITED BY MICHAEL VERANOV

Question A

(i)   From your reading of the above passage why did Himmler issue an order forbidding 'any further annihilation of Jews'? (20)

(ii) What is your understanding of the term, used in the second paragraph 'the final solution'?

(iii) What happened to prisoners who were fit enough to be evacuated from Auschwitz as the Russian 'Red' army approached? (10)

(iv) What happened to the 6000 prisoners who were too ill to be evacuated? (10)

Question B

Imagine you are a newspaper reporter who has been sent to report on the discovery of a death camp in the aftermath of the Second World War. Write the headline you would use and a short and informative article. 100–150 words (50)

WAR: TEXT 3

Here are some images relating to war. Look at them and then answer the questions.

Question A

(i)   In your opinion do these images represent an exciting or a frightening view of war? (15)

(ii) Choose the image that best captures what war is really about. Explain your choice. (20)

(iii) Write a description of the image you have chosen in (ii) above. (15)

Question B

Imagine you have been awarded the Victoria Cross Medal for Bravery. Write the letter you receive from the authorities informing you of your award. (50)

Sample paper 2: Memories

Section 1: Comprehending (100 marks)

MEMORIES: TEXT 1

Delusions

When I was nine, I started turning into John Wayne. At first it wasn't that obvious – just a hint of a swagger and a US marshal badge pinned to my chest during every waking moment. Which made bathtime pretty painful.

But the more John Wayne movies I saw, the more he took over my life. I started insisting people call me The Duke. Or Marion. I spent hours mastering the lasso. By the time I was 10, I could corral any guinea pig that'd stay still for more than two minutes – three if the rope still had washing on it. I started chewing tobacco, and when I couldn't get tobacco, I'd lick ashtrays.

I'll never forget swaggering out of *How the West Was Won* with Wayne's distinctive rolling gait and wondering if he walked like that because he too had a plastic holster that stuck to his leg and made his shorts ride up. I asked the usherette about this in his distinctive drawl. She didn't understand, probably because my front three teeth were missing so it was more of a drool. I didn't care. I went to the nearest rocky outcrop and threw myself with a fearless cry on to a passing Comanchero. Luckily for me, bikies were quite tolerant in those days.

The most exciting hours of my adolescence were the ones I spent watching *The War Wagon, Hellfighters, True Grit* and *A Midsummer Night's Dream*. (That last one was a mistake. When I read in the review about the Duke wearing tights, I rushed straight out and bought a ticket.)

I'm not sure now what finally broke the spell. News that Wayne had started to wear a girdle, perhaps, and Mum's refusal to lend me one. Or perhaps it was the lousy service I got in my local Vietnamese restaurant once I took to wearing that green beret.

Whatever it was, one day I realised I was no longer John Wayne. I couldn't be, because I was Dustin Hoffman. I'd just seen *The Graduate* and, in two hours, my life had changed. Here at last was a hero without a hair on his chest. Even more exciting, the close-ups showed that, like me, he didn't even have follicles in that area.

I was captivated. A hero I could emulate, even in rooms with mirrors. Plus, I mused as I left the cinema with Dustin's distinctive anaemic slouch, a hero who shared my bad posture and love of high-pitched singing. (The moment I first heard Simon and Garfunkel I knew they'd had plastic holsters.)

I emulated Dustin in every way I could. I spent days in deep introspection. It wasn't hard because I already knew the required facial expression. It was the one John Wayne used when he looked down and saw he had an arrow in his leg.

The years passed and I waited for another screen hero to occupy my psyche. It didn't happen. I did drive a car that displayed the number 007 for a few months, but only because the trip meter was broken. I did say 'I'll be back' a few times at one stage, but only because I was negotiating which part of the school fete donkey I'd be.

Screen heroes have come and gone, and I've remained strangely unaffected. Until recently. I didn't even notice what was happening at first. I thought the hair loss was just the result of genetics and wearing a cowboy hat too young. I thought my swelling midriff was just the result of too many calories. (Nobody told me that when you chew tobacco you're not meant to swallow it.)

Okay, I have been watching a lot of TV lately, but only because they've been showing so many John Wayne and Dustin Hoffman movies. And I have developed a big appetite for bacon, cheese slices, doughnuts and ribs, but not always in the same meal.

So you can imagine how surprised I was at dinner the other night when, just after I mistakenly ate a cheese slice with the wrapper on and said 'Doh', the kids gave a loud wail. 'Oh no,' they cried, 'Dad's turning into Homer Simpson.' I was indignant. Bitterly so. In my mind I formulated a carefully structured argument listing my many intellectual, artistic, humanist and cultural qualities. As dessert arrived I opened my mouth and let them have it.

'Mmmmm,' I said, 'chocolate chip.'

FROM *SELF-HELPLESS* BY MORRIS GLEITZMAN

N.B. Candidates may NOT answer Question A and Question B on the same text.
Questions A and B carry 50 marks each.

Question A

(i) 'But the more John Wayne movies I saw, the more he took over my life.' In what ways did John Wayne take over the author's childhood? (20)

(ii) Apart from John Wayne what other screen heroes did the writer copy and how did he imitate them? (15)

(iii) In what way is the writer becoming more and more like Homer Simpson? Is he happy with the transformation? (15)

Question B

Write the answer you would give to the question: Where would you like to be in five years' time? (50)

MEMORIES: TEXT 2

Rich teas

A lunch is being held in honour of a French writer who is in Dublin to organise a writers' festival. The conversation turns inevitably to food and, as often happens with a large group around a table, the general conversation breaks down into sub-plots of chat. After a while, the visiting writer notices the animation of your neighbours at the table and wants to know what is the reason for all this excitement. He seems puzzled when you tell him – biscuits.

But he need not have been so surprised. Marcel Proust unlocks his past not with a rare steak or a slice of pâté de foie gras but with a small teacake, a madeleine. Sweet dreams are our key to memory. The naming of biscuits was for the Irish guests at the table a guided tour through childhood – the sugared crumbs, a trail of recollection. Marietta was there at the beginning of the path. The round coin of austerity with its suggestion of poorly heated parish halls and convent parlours and prudent excess. Or else the dismembered Marietta biscuits reduced to the scale of the doll's world, sustaining Sindy or Barbie through those endless afternoon teas of the winter months, miniature dramas played out with droplets of milk in scratched red plastic cups and the occasional scolding from the director when Barbie fouled her twin set with great boulders of biscuit. Butter redeemed Marietta's puritan plainness. Spread on two biscuits that were then put together, the butter that oozed through pinpricks on the surface like inquisitive earthworms carried with it the promise of luxury and a faint intimation of decadence.

Digestive biscuits in their gritty wholesomeness were associated like all things that are good for you with the sickroom. In the same category as coarser breakfast cereals, they suggested disciplined recovery from mumps or the measles or a bad flu. Hot lemon drinks and the tentative crumbling of the plain digestive biscuit broke up the sick-day routine of endlessly reread *Treasure* and *Tiger and Jag* comics from the last school garden *fête* – where it always rained despite the promise of Gallic summer in fête. Chocolate on digestive biscuits was always confusing, like a category confusion in logic, so that these biscuits were consumed with something like lingering guilt, as if you were found stuffing yourself with Belgian chocolates on a health farm.

Rich Tea and Morning Coffee. The decorous abandon of late morning, the fountain trickle of talk radio and the house huge with the silence of the children gone to school or a day snatched from work, yawning with possibility. The biscuits that adorn the dark tables of meetings never seem to have the same effect, as if the suggestion of leisure is scotched by the seriousness of purpose, the tea going cold and the biscuits, more worry beads than sweetmeats, dismembered by fidgety fingers. Afternoon Tea Assorted. The panic of want as the unexpected arrival of a neighbour or a relative (*Just thought I'd say hello, Margaret*) means turmoil in the kitchen. The only biscuits left are four Lincolns, soft with age, and shards of cream cracker. Behind the welcoming smiles are urgent, whispered commands to go to Donnelly's and buy a packet of biscuits. While your bike carries you to the shop, your mother is back at the house talking to the neighbour-relative as if she was an accomplice in a robbery, distracting the police officer's attention with bogus requests for directions to go to Blackhall Place or Constitution Hill. As the tray arrives with the tea and the biscuits are spread in a bountiful landslide on the plate (not too large, of course, otherwise the biscuits thin into insignificance), the complimentary guest (*How big you are now! What class are you in?*) secretly appraises the offering. Excessive plainness in the biscuit is a subtle affront, the Marietta snub. Chocolate fingers or Bourbons suggest a social ambitiousness that needs to be watched. Away from the grand manoeuvres of the Good Room, there is, however, the campfire of gossip in the warm kitchen where biscuits are dunked and time dissolves in the Great Plains of a weekday afternoon and the doilys stay in the sideboard.

With Empire came the lure of the exotic. Kimberley, Mikado, Coconut Creams. A late Victorian map of plenty, handlebar moustaches and steamships plotting passages for the cargo of raw materials and spices from the four corners of the earth. But our minds soon tired of the *Look and Learn* immensity of overseas possessions and began to focus in on the one abiding passion of childhood – demolition. The trick was to use your front teeth like a barber's razor, removing the two white banks of coconut, leaving the thin stream of strawberry in the middle, resting on its biscuit base. A similar gopher-like application was used to remove the coconut mound in another biscuit from its base: the cleaner the cut, the keener the triumph. Chocolate Snack biscuits were other contenders for the demolition derby. Here, the aim was to remove chocolate in a series of quick, decisive bites until only the biscuit was left, pale, slightly moist, the cream fragment of bone exposed by the energetic dig. The pleasure was in removing whole sides of chocolate in one carefully aimed nip. If only a piece came away, or the top section had to be scraped off, there was a vague sense of irritation, an irritation that returns in adult life when taking off wallpaper, obstinate islands of ancient paste interrupting the triumphant march of the paper stripper. Chocolate mallows involved more delicate surgery. Here, the fine chocolate membrane had to be removed from the sticky dome underneath while leaving the dome intact. Only when the marshmallow lay exposed, vividly white, could the next operation begin: the severing of the marshmallow from its base. As the sweet oyster dissolved in your mouth, the final act was to eat the base itself, moist now and striated with the ploughed ridges of teeth marks. FROM *TIME TRACKS* BY MICHAEL CRONIN

N.B. Candidates may NOT answer Question A and Question B on the same text.
Questions A and B carry 50 marks each.

Question A

(i) Why are biscuits so important to the writer? (10)

(ii) Of what do Marietta and Digestive biscuits remind the writer? (10)

(iii) Which of the biscuits did the writer most enjoy eating? Explain your answer. (10)

(iv) What comparisons does the writer draw between childhood and adulthood in this piece of writing? (20)

Question B

In the above piece of writing the writer gives a detailed account of how he ate a Chocolate Mallow. Write detailed instructions on how to do one of the following:

(i) Make a cup of tea.

(ii) Peel an orange.

(iii) Set the video recorder to record a film from TV.

MEMORIES: TEXT 3

Here are some images looking back in time. Look at them and then answer the questions.

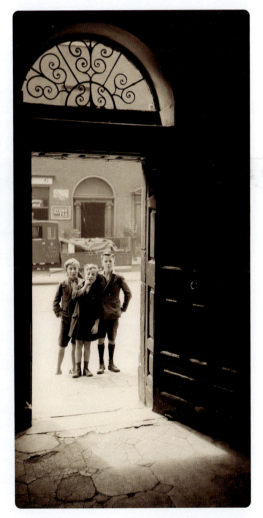

Question A

(i) Select one of the images and explain what it reveals about the mood of the characters or the scene. (15)

(ii) Write a caption for each of the images. (20)

(iii) Which of the images do you like best and why? (15)

Question B

Write the dialogue / conversation that you imagine takes place in any one of the images. (50)

Sample paper 3: Music

Section 1: Comprehending (100 marks)

MUSIC: TEXT 1

Ride On

True you ride the finest horse
I have ever seen
Standing sixteen-one or two
With eyes wild and green
And you ride the horse so well
Hands light to the touch
And I could never go with you
No matter how I wanted to

Chorus
Ride on, see ya
I could never go with you
No matter how I wanted to

And when you ride into the night
Without a trace behind
Run the claw along my gut
One last time
I'll turn to face an empty space
Where you used to lie
And smile for the spark that
Lights the night
Through a teardrop in my eye

Chorus
Ride on, see ya
I could never go with you
No matter how I wanted to
No matter how I wanted to

People often ask me about this song but, purely and simply, it is a song of parting. The parting of lovers, the parting of emigrants from their homeland and friends, the parting when illness or accident takes the life of a loved one. I have been asked to sing this song at many funeral services and, somehow, it always feels right.

Christy Moore recorded this song on his *Ride On* album in 1984 and it was my first hit. I will always be grateful to him for giving me the start with what would have been then regarded as a most unlikely song-writing voice. Christy obviously recognised 'Ride On' as a song of parting when, on its release, he dedicated it to the memory of the great Luke Kelly.

I am often asked about the line 'Run the claw along my gut one last time' (in the same way as I'm asked about the line 'I am the geek with the alchemist's stone', from my song 'The Bright Blue Rose'). These dramatic lines jolt the listener into a deeper engagement, or at least this was my intention in employing such devices. That is not to say that they were not a natural part of the flow of expression but, while most writers would edit them out, I feel that a song, like life, depends on the decisions one makes and these decisions were not taken lightly. Some people may think that I just throw paint at the canvas, but there is exactitude and detail in the placing of every word and phrase until I am satisfied that the lyric is absolutely watertight. It has always bothered me that the previously mentioned line from 'Ride On' has often been changed to 'Run *your* claw along my gut one last time', which clearly denotes an intention to cause pain, when the pain I envisioned is simply the pain of living life. The pain of parting and separation that no life can escape. Life is hard, Ride on.
FROM 'RIDE ON' IN *RIDE ON* BY JIMMY MCCARTHY

N.B. Candidates may NOT answer Question A and Question B on the same text.
Questions A and B carry 50 marks each.

Question A

(i) Why is Jimmy McCarthy grateful to Christy Moore? (15)

(ii) What does Jimmy McCarthy say about the line 'Run the claw along my gut one last time'? (15)

(iii) Do you think that Jimmy McCarthy takes his songwriting seriously? Give examples to back up your argument. (20)

Question B

Write a short article for a magazine on the importance of music in your life.

MUSIC: TEXT 2

Music

To claim that you can stroll into a back street Irish pub, or a pub way out in the wilds, and stumble on spontaneous sessions of wonderful music, sounds like a myth. On the whole, it isn't. You can come across champion performers almost anywhere. One reason for this is that almost every Irish musician is hyped as a champion.

Traditional Irish music lives on partly because it takes easily to being blended with more up-to-date stuff. The Irish music scene has produced some wonderfully creative combinations of traditional music with rock, punk, classical, cajun, native American and the like. One of the most alluring sounds in the country, apart from 'I'm paying for the drinks', is that of a woman singing unaccompanied in the native language. In this 'sean-nos' (old-style) form of song, the voice is used more as an impersonal instrument than as an expression of individual personality. You let the tradition sing through you rather than aim for originality, and keep personal emotion to the minimum. Irish musicians dislike flashy self-presentation, and some fiddlers have been known to play with their backs to the audience. Even if Irish musicians have an audience, they sometimes tend to behave as though they're not there.

A lot of Irish music comes to us only from the oral tradition, collected and written down by scholars who roamed the countryside in search of tuneful old codgers. One such expert asked an old woman where she had found a particular song, to be told that she had heard it sung by a blind harper from a village over the mountain. And where had he got it from? inquired the expert. From his old uncle, she replied, who had been a roving tinker. And where had he got it from? He got it from the radio.

In fact, there's a serious point behind the joke. A lot of what people regard as traditional Irish songs aren't traditional at all, and some of them aren't even Irish in origin. The words of 'Danny Boy' weren't written by an Irish composer. Genuine Irish singers and musicians wouldn't be found dead performing the sentimental drivel which some visitors think of as typically Irish.

Another story is told in Ireland of three fiddlers at a musical festival. The first stepped up wearing an expensive black suit and carrying a Stradivarius violin in a richly ornamented case made of Florentine leather. He took the violin out with exquisitely manicured fingers, placed it under his chin with a flourish, and drew the bow across it. And by God he was useless.

Then up stepped a second fiddler, a bit of a Flash Harry in a sequined suit and spotted bow tie, carrying a well-polished, moderately expensive fiddle. He placed it under his chin, swept back his oiled locks, bared his teeth to the audience in a glittering smile and began to play. And by God he was useless.

A third fiddler then shuffled to the front: a bent, wheezing little fellow in a beer-stained jacket with matchstick-thin legs and his behind hanging out of his trousers. He had no violin case, just a battered old instrument he had played since he was a lad. By this time the audience had lost patience and was barely listening. But the little old man fixed the fiddle under his grizzled chin with a shaking hand, and began slowly, tenderly, to play.

And by God he was useless too.
FROM *THE TRUTH ABOUT THE IRISH* BY TERRY EAGLETON

Question A

(i)   Do you think that the writer likes traditional Irish Music? Why do you think this? (15)
(ii) What does the writer say about originality in paragraph 2? Does he see this as a good or a bad thing? (15)
(iii) What does the writer say about appearances in traditional music? (20)

Question B

Imagine you are an American tourist and have gone to see your first traditional music session. Write a letter home explaining what it felt like. (50)

MUSIC: TEXT 3

Question A

(i)   Choose the image of Irish music that you think is the one that most young people would relate to. Describe that image. (15)
(ii) Which type of music pictured below or overpage appeals most to you? Explain your choice. (15)
(iii) Write a short note on the typical audience for each type of music. (20)

Question B

Write a review of your favourite song, album or concert for your school magazine. (50)

Sample paper 4: Sport

Section 1: Comprehending (100 marks)

SPORT: TEXT 1

All aboard for the chicks with sticks revolution

Camogie, despite itself perhaps, has undergone a huge change. In those estates which teem with kids, GAA clubs and soccer clubs have always thrived, while sport for girls has always been something of an afterthought, if even that. Now, perhaps because of a change in the safety of the environment and a change in the expectation levels of girls and their parents, camogie has been in there competing for customers. Girls still play basketball and soccer and Gaelic football, but more and more of them walk around with hurleys in their hands.

Some clubs just can't get enough coaches for their mini leagues. It's intriguing and thrilling to watch. Girls are as different from boys in team situations as cats are from dogs. A dog will fetch sticks without thinking about it. A dog will pull a sled through snow without question. Just happy to be there. That's boys, the incessant tail-waggers of the sporting world. Girls have to see the point of everything.

'You're going to run out there, jab-pick the ball and solo back and handpass,' says the coach.

'Yeah? Why?' comes the answer.

But they love it. Their play is an extension of their personality, their intensity, and the will to win is sometimes frightening.

And camogie was there all along? . . . I asked three twelve-year-olds this week what they were going to be when they got older.

One surgeon (Clare), two professional hurlers (Fionnuala and Carol).

Camogie has problems, though. It's a competitive world out there and the game has more skills to be learned than any other you can think of. Takes time. Needs money. Requires patience. Gaelic football has gobbled up the imagination of much of its natural constituency. Soccer too. Fixture lists are often chaotic, with not enough games being played in summer, while minor grade is at under-16 so the sport haemorrhages good kids too early. And the game needs, not to be gender specific about it, a make-over, not to make it look like something it isn't, but for its image to begin to reflect what it has become.

Next year is the centenary of the association, and camogie is looking to put as much life into its image as it has into its game. To that end, the association has formed a committee, the average age of which is twenty-seven and which will be electrifying the sport's image over the next year or so.

This isn't unusual. Sports market themselves all the time for the better.

It's a world full of sharks out there, and the tragedy of camogie is that it has suffered for too long from its image of being something for big girls with fat ankles to do between Macra dances. It has no face, no stars, no real impact on those who don't play it or know it.

How radical are they going to be? Well, try 'Chicks with Sticks!' as a slogan. The working group (I repeat, average age twenty-seven, not a Macra dance between them) will be moving at last towards a stronger GAA/camogie alliance, with all the benefits that would bring. That alliance on a national level will change both the GAA and camogie forever.

Tests have shown that, once you've tried a GAA club with a thriving and vibrant camogie section, you'll never go back to the old 'men stewing in their own bitterness' model. The GAA club at its best is part of the community, not a men's retreat house.

Having a camogie section means the club represents the community better and opens itself up to new perspectives and new ways of thinking. We have a strange way of thinking about sport in this country. Largely, we view it the wrong way around. A Sonia O'Sullivan happens despite ourselves, really. Then we start rewarding elite athletes to make up for our earlier negligence. We don't target girls for sporting development and we don't reward them. We don't cover enough girls' sports on Monday mornings. Oddly, we don't view women as a market for sport.

It's shocking that, despite the huge impact camogie has on ordinary, day-to-day life in Ireland, the senior inter-county leagues and championships in the sport are still available for sponsorship, and no one has taken those competitions by the neck, tagged their name to them and committed the rest of their spend to telling the stories and revealing the person-alities.

Girls don't stand up laneways and throw rubber balls against walls anymore. You hardly ever see them skipping. They are housebound and baby-sat by the Gameboy and the TV. But, let loose, the chicks with sticks get to play on teams and grow and express themselves strenuously.

Girls have discovered camogie for themselves. They are waiting now for the rest of the world to discover them.

Life begins at 100.
FROM *BOOKED!* BY TOM HUMPHRIES

Question A

(i)   What does the author say about the differences between boys and girls when it comes to sport? Do you agree with him? (10)

(ii)   What does the author say about the way in which sportspeople have been treated in Ireland? (10)

(iii) How does camogie intend to move forward? Do you think it will work? (10)

(iv)   What does the author say about women's input into GAA clubs? (20)

Question B

Imagine you are a reporter for a sports magazine. You have been asked to write an interview with a famous sportswoman. Write six questions and the answers you would expect to get. (50)

SPORT: TEXT 2

There's only one red army

Back to Rovers. The first we knew that my father had a new woman in his life was when he arrived to pick Eoghan up at Connolly Station to bring him to a match and the woman was with him. She is still with him. It's a few years ago. The incident hurt my mother very much. We were playing Bray Wanderers that day and drew 1–1 with a late goal from a Scottish guy called Barry Cliff. Harry crossed the ball to him, Fago had put Harry away down the wing.

It hurt my mother because following Rovers had been part of what we were as a family. My father's introduction of his new woman into this private space showed that he was determined to confront us with her. He wasn't going to go away and live his life elsewhere. He would continue to follow Rovers and he would subsume it into his new life.

My mother coped with it as people learn to cope with what is.

My father was back at the games. It seemed ridiculous to ever have expected he would be able to keep away from The Showgrounds. None of us talked much to him then. But we managed to discover a language which could re-admit him to our lives. The language of Sligo Rovers. The problem of what you say to a father who has deserted you was solved. When you met him, you had ninety minutes of the Sunday gone by to discuss and ninety minutes of the Sunday coming to anticipate. Under that shelter you could talk.

My father even calls to the house sometimes on his way to home matches. Himself and my mother exchange a few words and when the conversation understandably palls, they can always be rescued.
- Is Ian Gilzean fit enough?
- Was Johnny Kenny better a couple of seasons ago?
- Why did we let Gavin Dykes go?
- Do you remember Pat McCluskey, Gabriel Ojo, Johnny Brooks, Kevin Fallon, David Pugh?

And when they begin to remember together players from the past who they saw together in The Showgrounds before I was born, I realise that there is no judgement I can make on these two people who have known each other for so much longer than I know either of them.

My father's partner comes to the games. I don't think she has much of a choice. Herself and my mother often sit in the same pubs after the game. They don't like each other. But they each recognise that this is how things have turned out and they can't stop the other person having a drink wherever they want to. It's messy but at back it's decent, like a lot of the new difficult real Ireland.

The family from the 1975 photo is still in The Showgrounds, except it has been dispersed throughout the ground. Myself, Eoghan and

Colm in The Shed, My mother and Maura in the main stand, my father in the stand facing them. Our lives have changed in ways we could not have imagined then, but there is a constant fortnightly ninety minutes which has remained the same.

FROM *THERE'S ONLY ONE RED ARMY* BY EAMON SWEENEY

N.B. Candidates may NOT answer Question A and Question B on the same text. Questions A and B carry 50 marks each.

Question A
(i)   What part does soccer play in the family's life? (10)
(ii) How has sport helped to heal problems in the author's family? (15)
(iii) What does the writer mean by the line: 'My mother coped with it as people learn to cope with what is.'? (10)
(iv) How does the family treat the father's partner? Discuss this. (15)

Question B
Imagine you are a supporter of a team which is not doing well. Write your diary entries for the last three matches of the season. (50)

SPORT: TEXT 3

Question A

(i) What do the images suggest to you about the effort that goes into sport? (10)

(ii) Which image is your favourite? Describe the image. Explain your choice. (20)

(iii) In your opinion what makes a great sportsperson? Give an example and reasons for your choice. (20)

Question B

Imagine you are a radio commentator. Write your radio commentary for the most important moment during a match or a sporting event. (50)

Important words and terms for the study of English

Alliteration	When two or more words starting with the same letter or sound are placed consecutively, e.g. 'Not a cute card or a kissogram'.
Ambiguity	When words have one or more meanings and this meaning is not made clear. In poetry this can often be intentional.
Anthology	A collection of literature by various writers.
Assonance	Internal rhyme, especially the repetition of vowel sounds in words close to each other. e.g. 'of clay and wattles made'.
Ballad	A poem or song that tells a story.
Caricature	An exaggerated portrait.
Cliché	A phrase that has been over-repeated, e.g. 'It rained cats and dogs'.
Climax	The point of greatest intensity in the work.
Closure	The way a poem ends.
Compare	Examine similarities between two things.
Conceit	When an interesting and unlikely connection is made between two seemingly very different things, e.g. in 'The Flea' by John Donne.
Contrast	Point out differences between two things.
Couplet	Two consecutive lines which have the same metre and rhythm, e.g. 'Pour away the ocean and sweep up the wood. For nothing now can ever come to any good.'
Define	Give a clear and exact meaning.
Describe	Give a detailed account.
Dialect	A local variation of a language, see 'Kidspoem/Bairnsang' by Liz Lochhead.
Dramatic monologue	A poem written in a specific situation where a character is speaking directly to somebody else, e.g. in 'For Heidi with Blue Hair' by Fleur Adcock.
Elegy	A poem which mourns the dead, e.g. 'Funeral Blues' by W. H. Auden.

Epigram	A short witty poem often written with simple rhyme.
Epigraph	A relevant quotation at the start of a poem or a book.
Epiphany	A moment of revelation.
Euphemism	Substitution of milder words for ones that may have been more crude or blunt.
Evaluate	Analyse the arguments that have been put forward.
Fable	A legendary story with a moral.
Free verse	A poem without rhyme.
Hyperbole	Use of exaggeration in poetry, e.g. 'Ride ten thousand days and nights'.
Illustrate	Make clear; explain with examples.
Image	A picture in words.
Irony	a) When something is said in such a way that the opposite of the true meaning is meant.
	b) When somebody says something that has deeper meaning for what is about to happen to them. This is often obvious to the reader but not to the speaker (dramatic irony).
Lyric	A short personal poem, often with musical qualities.
Metaphor	When a comparison is made without using 'like' or 'as', e.g. 'And time itself's a feather / Touching them gently'.
Mood	The feeling a reader gets from a poem.
Myth	A traditional story that has ancient religious or supernatural ideas or a widespread but false idea.
Octet	An eight-line verse. In a Petrarchan sonnet it is the first eight lines.
Ode	A poem that is written in celebration.
Onomatopoeia	Words whose sounds accentuate their meaning by sounding like what is being described, e.g. 'slap', 'clip-clop'.
Outline	Describe without detail.
Oxymoron	A figure of speech where seemingly opposite ideas are brought together.
Paradox	A statement that at first appears inconsistent but is really true.
Parody	A close but mocking imitation of a well-known work.
Pathetic fallacy	This occurs when human feeling is given to nature, e.g. 'The winter evening settles down'.
Pathos	Evoking pity.
Persona	When the poet uses a voice in the poem that is not his own, e.g. the voice of Bruce Ismay in 'After the Titanic' by Derek Mahon.

Personification	When a poet gives voice to non-human characters, e.g. in 'The Ladybird's Story' by Elizabeth Jennings.
Poetic licence	Permission given to writers that allows them to tamper with true facts.
Prose	Ordinary language written without metre or rhythm.
Pun	Wordplay where words may have the same sound but different meanings.
Quatrain	Four-line verse.
Repetition	Repeating sounds, words, lines or verses for poetic effect.
Rhetorical question	A question where the answer is already known.
Rhyme	Identical or close similarity of sounds in the final syllables of two or more words.
Rhyming scheme	The pattern of rhyme in a poem.
Rhythm	How sounds or words move within a poem. The critic Neil Astley has called it the 'essence of poetry'.
Run-on-line	Also known as enjambment, this occurs when a sentence or phrase continues past the end of one line and into the next.
Sarcasm	Bitterly ironic statement.
Satire	Act of attacking a silly or evil act by using mockery.
Sentimentality	Presentation of a feeling in an over-the-top way.
Sestet	A six-line verse or the final six lines in a sonnet.
Simile	A comparison using the words 'like' or 'as', e.g. 'Silence between them like a thread to hold / And not wind in.'
Sonnet	A fourteen-line poem.
Stanza	Verse.
Subject matter	The details that a poet writes about in order to express his theme.
Symbol	Word or image which represents something other than itself.
Syntax	The arrangement of words in a sentence.
Tercet	Three-line verse.
Theme	The main idea in a poem.
Tone	The attitude of the poet as conveyed through his poem.
Trace	Explain stage by stage.
Verse	A subsection of a poem.
Voice	The person speaking in the poem, not necessarily the poet, see Persona.

Past Examination Questions
(Ordinary Level)

Poems also prescribed for
Higher Level

W.B. Yeats

An Irish Airman Foresees His Death (page 164)

1. (a) What, in your view, is the attitude of the airman to the war in which he is fighting? (10)
   (b) Write out the line or phrase from the poem that best shows his attitude. Give a reason for your choice. (10)
   (c) Write a short paragraph in which you outline your feelings towards the airman. Support your view by quotation from the poem. (10)

2. Answer **ONE** of the following: [Each part carries 20 marks]
   (i) 'I balanced all, brought all to mind' What are the kinds of things the airman is referring to in this line from the poem?

   OR

   (ii) Imagine the airman has to give a short speech to his fellow pilots as they prepare for battle. Write out the text of the speech he might give.

   OR

   (iii) Suggest a different title for the above poem. Give reasons for your answer, supporting them by quotation from the poem.

(Ordinary Level 2002)

The Lake Isle of Innisfree (page 160)

1. (a) How in the first two stanzas of the above poem does the poet help us to imagine the kind of place Innisfree is? (10)
   (b) In your opinion what qualities of the place are most important to the poet, W.B. Yeats? Support your answer by reference to the text of the poem. (10)

2. This poem by Yeats is very popular among readers of poetry. From the following list of reasons why it is so popular, choose the one that is closest to your own view and explain your choice. Support your answer by illustration from the text.
   – *The descriptions of the place are very appealing*
   – *The poem contains many beautiful sounds*
   – *The main idea in the poem is attractive to people* (10)

3. Answer **ONE** of the following: [Each part carries 20 marks]
   (i) 'While I stand on the roadway, or on the pavements grey, I hear it in the deep heart's core.' What do you understand these last two lines of the poem to mean?

   OR

   (ii) Write a paragraph outlining the reasons why you like or dislike the poems by W.B. Yeats on your course.

   OR

   (iii) Would Innisfree appeal to you as a place to live? Support your answer by reference to the poem.

(Ordinary Level 2003)

Philip Larkin

The Explosion (page 74)

1. (a) What impression of the miners do you get from reading the opening four stanzas of the above poem? Support your view by reference to the text. (10)
   (b) Stanza five ('At noon, there came a tremor…') describes the moment of the explosion. What effect does the poet achieve by describing the event in the manner in which he does? Give a reason in support of your view. (10)

2. Why, in your opinion, does Larkin end the poem with the image of the 'eggs unbroken'? Support your answer by reference to the poem. (10)

3. Answer **ONE** of the following: [Each part carries 20 marks]
   (i) Compare *The Explosion* with any other poem by Philip Larkin that you have studied as part of your course.

OR

(ii) What, in your opinion, can we learn about Philip Larkin himself (the things he values or considers important) from reading this poem? Support your view by brief reference to the poem.

OR

(iii) Imagine that the wife of one of the men killed in the explosion were to write an article describing the event for her local newspaper. Write out a paragraph that you think she might include in her article.

(Ordinary Level 2002)

Sylvia Plath

The Arrival of the Bee Box (page 124)

1. (a) What impression of the poet, Sylvia Plath, do you get from reading this poem? (10)
   (b) What words or phrases from the poem especially help to create that impression for you? (10)

2. The following list of phrases suggest some of the poet's attitudes to the bee box:
   – She is fascinated by it
   – She is annoyed by it
   – She feels she has great power over it
   Choose the phrase from the above list that is closest to your own reading of the poem. Explain your choice, supporting your view by reference to the words of the poem. (10)

3. Answer **ONE** of the following: [Each part carries 20 marks]
   (i) Imagine you were asked to select music to accompany a public reading of this poem. Describe the kind of music you would choose and explain your choice clearly.

OR

   (ii) 'The box is only temporary.'
   What do you understand the last line of the poem to mean?

OR

   (iii) Write a paragraph in which you outline the similarities and/or differences between *The Arrival of the Bee Box* and the other poem on your course by Sylvia Plath, *Child*.

(Ordinary Level 2003)

Derek Mahon

After the Titanic (page 88)

1. (a) What effect did the sinking of the *Titanic* have on Bruce Ismay, the speaker in this poem? (10)
   (b) Do you sympathise with him after reading this poem? Give a reason. (10)
   (c) What details in the poem make you sympathise with him, or not sympathise with him? (10)

2. Answer **ONE** of the following: [Each part carries 20 marks]
   (i) 'This poem gives you a vivid picture of the disaster.'
   Would you agree? Support your answer with reference to the poem.

OR

   (ii) 'Letter from a ghost'
   Imagine you are one of the people who drowned on the *Titanic*. Write a letter to Bruce Ismay telling him about your memories of that night. Use details from the poem in your letter.

OR

   (iii) In this poem Mahon speaks *as if he is* Bruce Ismay. How well do you think he gets into Bruce Ismay's mind? Give reasons for your answer.

(Ordinary Level 2004)

Eavan Boland

This Moment (page 22)

1. (a) Why in your opinion does the poet call the poem, 'This Moment'? (10)
   (b) Write out two images from the poem that best help you to picture the neighbourhood at dusk. Give a reason for your choice in each case. (10)
   (c) Taken as a whole, does this poem give you a comforting or a threatening feeling about the neighbourhood? Explain your answer. (10)

2. Answer **ONE** of the following (i) or (ii) or (iii). [Each part carries 20 marks]
   (i) Imagine you were asked to make a short film based on the poem, 'This Moment'. Describe the sort of atmosphere you would

try to create and say how you would use
music, sound effects and images to create it.

OR

(ii) 'Stars rise.
Moths flutter
Apples sweeten in the dark.'
Do you think these lines provide a good
ending to the poem? Give reasons for your
opinion.

OR

(iii) Write a short letter to Eavan Boland in
which you tell her what her poems on your
course mean to you.

(Ordinary Level 2001)

Alternative Poems
(Ordinary Level)

WH. Auden
Funeral Blues (page 8)

1. (a) How did this poem make you feel? (10)
   (b) Do you think that the poet really loves the
   one who has died? Explain your answer.
   (10)
   (c) Do you like the way the poet expresses
   sadness at the death of his friend? Give a
   reason. (10)

2. Answer **ONE** of the following: [Each part
   carries 20 marks]
   (i) Imagine that the poet wanted to choose a
   line or two from the poem to be written on
   his lover's tombstone. Which line or lines
   would you advise him to choose? Write the
   lines and give reasons for your choice.

   OR

   (ii) Imagine you wanted to perform this poem to
   music with a group of musical friends. How
   would you perform it so that people would
   remember the experience?

   OR

   (iii) What things did you learn about the poet
   W.H. Auden from reading the poem? Refer
   to the poem in your answer.

(Ordinary Level 2003)

Richard Wilbur
The Pardon (page 153)

1. (a) What impression of the young boy do you
   get from reading the first three stanzas of
   this poem? (5)
   (b) What words or phrases from the poem best
   convey that impression to you? (10)
   (c) Choose two phrases from the poem that, in
   your view, describe the dead dog most
   powerfully. Write each phrase down and
   comment on why you have chosen it. (10)
   (d) In an overall way, how does this poem
   make you feel? Give one reason for your
   answer. (5)

2. Answer **ONE** of the following (i) or (ii) or (iii).
[Each part carries 20 marks]
(i) How, in your opinion, does the father's reaction to the death of the dog compare with that of the young boy's? Support your view by reference to the poem.

OR

(ii) 'Well, I was ten and very much afraid.'
Write a short letter to the poet, Richard Wilbur, in which you show how this poem reminds you of a childhood experience of your own.

OR

(iii) Why, in your view, did Richard Wilbur choose the title 'The Pardon' for this poem? Illustrate your answer by reference to the poem.

(Ordinary Level 2001)

Fleur Adcock
For Heidi with Blue Hair (page 2)
1. (a) What impression of Heidi do you get from the above poem? (5)
   (b) Where does the language used by the poet especially create that impression for you? (10)

2. (a) From the following list, choose the phrase that is closest to your own reading of the poem:
   – *a funny and clever poem*
   – *an important poem about people's rights*
   – *a sad poem*
   Explain your choice, supporting your view by reference to the words of the poem. (10)
   (b) 'The battle was already won.'
   What do you understand the last line of the poem to mean? (5)

3. Answer **ONE** of the following (i) or (ii) of (iii).
[Each part carries 20 marks.]
   (i) 'It would have been unfair to mention your mother's death, but that shimmered behind the arguments,'
   How do these lines from the fifth stanza affect your attitude to Heidi and what she had done? Give reasons for your answer.

OR

(ii) Does Heidi remind you of anyone you know in real life? Write a short paragraph that shows how that person is most like Heidi.
[N.B. You should not give the person's real name.]

OR

(iii) What impression of Heidi's father emerges from the poem? Support your answer by reference to the text.

(Ordinary Level 2001)

Carol Ann Duffy
Valentine (page 32)
1. (a) 'I am trying to be truthful.'
   In your opinion, what is the speaker of the poem trying to tell her lover about her feelings? (10)
   (b) Write down one line or phrase from the poem that tells you most about the kind of relationship the lovers have. Say why you think it is an important line. (10)
   (c) How do you imagine a lover would feel if he or she received this poem on St Valentine's Day? Explain your answer. (10)

2. Answer **ONE** of the following: [Each part carries 20 marks]
   (i) In what way is this poem different from the normal poems or rhymes that lovers send to each other on Valentine's Day?

OR

(ii) In your opinion, what reply might the lover write to this Valentine? You may, if you wish, write your reply in verse.

OR

(iii) 'Lethal.
Its scent will cling to your fingers, cling to your knife.'
Do you think that this is a good ending to the poem? Explain your view.

(Ordinary Level 2003)

Simon Armitage
It Ain't What You Do, It's What It Does To You (page 6)
1. (a) What kind of life does the poet say he has *not* lived? (10)

(b) What do the things he *has* done tell you about him? Refer to the poem in your response. (10)

(c) Do you think he creates a feeling of stillness in the following lines?
'But I
skimmed flat stones across Black Moss on
  a day
so still I could hear each set of ripples
as they crossed. I felt each stone's inertia
spend itself against the water; then sink'.
Give a reason for your answer. (10)

2. Answer **ONE** of the following: [Each part carries 20 marks]
   (i) Armitage thinks that titles are very important. Do you think he has chosen a good title for this poem? Refer to the poem in your response.

   OR

   (ii) Someone asks you to suggest a poem to be included in a collection for young people. You recommend this one. Explain why.

   OR

   (iii) 'That feeling, I mean.'
   What kind of feeling do you think Armitage is describing in the last stanza? Do you think he describes it well? Explain your view.

(Ordinary Level 2004)

Acknowledgments

The author and publisher are grateful to the following for permission to reproduce copyrighted material:

'For Heidi with Blue Hair' by Fleur Adcock, *Poems 1960–2000* (Bloodaxe Books, 2000);

'Phenomenal Woman' by Maya Angelou reproduced from *The Complete Collected Poems* by Maya Angelou, by permission of Virago Books, a division of Time Warner Book Group UK;

'It Ain't What You Do, It's What It Does to You' by Simon Armitage, *Zoom!* (Bloodaxe Books, 1989);

'Funeral Blues' (Twelve Songs IX) by W. H. Auden from *Collected Shorter Poems 1927–1957* published by Faber and Faber Ltd reproduced by kind permission of Faber and Faber Ltd;

'The Voice' by Patricia Beer from *Collected Poems* (1990) reproduced by kind permission of Patricia Beer;

'The Fish' and 'Filling Station' from *The Complete Poems: 1927–1979* by Elizabeth Bishop. Copyright © 1979, 1983 by Alice Helen Methfessel. Reprinted by permission of Farrar, Straus and Giroux, LLC;

'Child of Our Time' and 'This Moment' by Eavan Boland from *Collected Poems* (1995) reproduced by kind permission of Carcanet Press Limited;

'Naming My Daughter' by Rosita Boland reproduced by kind permission of the author;

'Midwife' and 'Jasmine' by Paddy Bushe reproduced by kind permission of Paddy Bushe and Dedalus Press;

'Valentine' is taken from *Mean Time* by Carol Ann Duffy published by Anvil Press Poetry in 1993;

'Going Home to Mayo, Winter, 1949' by Paul Durcan reproduced by kind permission of Paul Durcan;

'Preludes' and 'Aunt Helen' by T.S. Eliot from *Collected Shorter Poems 1909–62* published by Faber and Faber Ltd reproduced by kind permission of Faber and Faber Ltd;

'Taking My Son to School' by Eamonn Grennan reproduced by kind permission of the author and The Gallery Press, Loughcrew, Oldcastle, County Meath, Ireland. From *Wildly for Days* (1983);

'May' by Kerry Hardie reproduced by kind permission of the author and The Gallery Press, Loughcrew, Oldcastle, County Meath, Ireland. From *A Furious Place* (1996);

'Postscript' by Seamus Heaney from *The Spirit Level* published by Faber and Faber Ltd reproduced by kind permission of Faber and Faber Ltd;

'One Flesh' and 'The Ladybird's Story' by Elizabeth Jennings from *Collected Poems* published by Carcanet Press Limited reproduced by kind permission of the author and publisher;

The three poems by Patrick Kavanagh are reprinted by kind permission of the Trustees of the Estate of the late Katherine B. Kavanagh, through the Jonathan Williams Literary Agency;

'Night Drive' by Brendan Kennelly, *Familiar Strangers: New & Selected Poems 1960–2004* (Bloodaxe Books, 2004);

'At Grass' by Philip Larkin is reprinted from *The Less Deceived* by permission of The Marvell Press, England and Australia;

'An Arundel Tomb' and 'The Explosion' by Philip Larkin from *Collected Poems* published by Faber and Faber Ltd reproduced by kind permission of Faber and Faber Ltd;

'What Were They Like?' by Denise Levertov reproduced by permission of Pollinger Limited and the proprietor;

'Kidspoem/Bairnsang' by Liz Lochhead reproduced by kind permission of Birlinn Limited;

'Wounds', 'Last Requests' and 'An Amish Rug' by Michael Longley reproduced by kind permission of Michael Longley;

'Grandfather', 'After the Titanic' and 'Antarctica' by Derek Mahon reproduced by kind permission of the author and The Gallery Press, Loughcrew, Oldcastle, County Meath, Ireland. From *Collected Poems* (1999);

'Bearhugs' by Roger McGough from *Defying Gravity* (Copyright © Roger McGough 1991, 1992) is reproduced by kind permission of PFD (*www.pfd.co.uk*) on behalf of Roger McGough;

'Buying Winkles' by Paula Meehan reproduced by kind permission of the author and The Gallery Press, Loughcrew, Oldcastle, County Meath, Ireland. From *The Man who was Marked by Winter* (1991);

'My Father Perceived as a Vision of St Francis' by Paula Meehan reproduced by kind permission of the author and The Gallery Press, Loughcrew, Oldcastle, County Meath, Ireland. From *Pillow Talk* (1994);

'The Locket' 'Like dolmens round my childhood...' and 'The Cage' by John Montague reproduced by kind permission of the author and The Gallery Press, Loughcrew, Oldcastle, County Meath, Ireland. From *Collected Poems* (1995);

'Strawberries' by Edwin Morgan from *Collected Poems* (1990) reproduced by kind permission of Carcanet Press;

'Anseo' by Paul Muldoon from *Why Brownlee Left* published by Faber and Faber Ltd reproduced by kind permission of Faber and Faber Ltd;

'The Reading Lesson' by Richard Murphy reproduced by kind permission of the author and The Gallery Press, Loughcrew, Oldcastle, County Meath, Ireland. From *Collected Poems* (2000);

'Wolves in the Zoo' by Howard Nemerov reproduced by kind permission of Mrs Margaret Nemerov;

'The Great Blasket Island' by Julie O'Callaghan, *What's What* (Bloodaxe Books, 1991);

'Gunpowder' from *Gunpowder* by Bernard O'Donaghue published by Chatto & Windus. Used by permission of the Random House Group Limited;

'Looking At Them Asleep' and 'The Present Moment' from *The Unswept Room* by Sharon Olds published by Jonathan Cape. Used by permission of the Random House Group Limited;

'Child' and 'The Arrival of the Bee Box' by Sylvia Plath from *Collected Poems* published by Faber and Faber Ltd reproduced by kind permission of Faber and Faber Ltd;

'Aunt Jennifer's Tigers'. Copyright © 2002, 1951 by Adrienne Rich, 'Power'. Copyright © 2002 by Adrienne Rich. Copyright © 1978 by W. W. Norton & Company, Inc., 'Storm Warnings'. Copyright © 2002, 1951 by Adrienne Rich, from *The Fact of a Doorframe: Selected Poems 1950–2001* by Adrienne Rich. Used by permission of the author and W. W. Norton & Company, Inc.;

'On Passing the New Menin Gate' Copyright Siegfried Sassoon by kind permission of George Sassoon;

'The Hunchback in the Park' by Dylan Thomas from *Collected Poems* published by Dent reproduced by kind permission of the author and publisher;

'To Norline', 'Summer Elegies' and 'The Young Wife' by Derek Walcott from *Collected Poems* published by Faber and Faber Ltd reproduced by kind permission of Faber and Faber Ltd;

'The Pardon' from *Ceremony and Other Poems*, copyright 1950 and renewed 1978 by Richard Wilbur, reprinted by permission of Harcourt, Inc;

'The Red Wheelbarrow' by William Carlos Williams from *Collected Poems* reproduced by kind permission of Carcanet Press Limited;

'Request to a Year' by Judith Wright from *Collected Poems* (1994) reproduced by kind permission of Carcanet Press Limited;

'The Lake Isle of Ininsfree', 'The Wild Swans at Coole' and 'An Irish Airman Foresees His Death' by W. B. Yeats are reproduced by kind permission of A P Watt Ltd on behalf of Michael B Yeats;

Extract from *Birdsong* by Sebastian Faulks published by Hutchinson. Used by permission of The Random House Group Limited;

Self-Helpless by Maurice Gleitzman published by Penguin Books Australia Ltd reproduced by kind permission of Penguin Group (Australia);

Extract from *Time Tracks* edited by Michael Cronin reproduced by kind permission of New Island;

Lyrics of 'Ride On' by Jimmy McCarthy (Universal Music Publishing) reproduced by kind permission of Jimmy McCarthy (Universal Music Publishing);

Extract from *Ride On* by Jimmy McCarthy reproduced by kind permission of Townhouse;

Extract from *The Truth About the Irish* by Terry Eagleton reproduced by kind permission of New Island;

Extract from *Booked!* by Tom Humphries reproduced by kind permission of *The Irish Times*;

Extract from *There's Only One Red Army* by Eamon Sweeney reproduced by kind permission of New Island;

The author and publisher have made every effort to trace all copyright holders, but if any has been inadvertently overlooked we would be pleased to make the necessary arrangements at the first opportunity.

18502064